PERSPECTIVES ON COGNITION AND ACTION IN SPORT

PERSPECTIVES ON COGNITION AND ACTION IN SPORT

DUARTE ARAÚJO, HUBERT RIPOLL
AND
MARKUS RAAB
EDITORS

Nova Science Publishers, Inc.
New York

For permission to use material from this book please contact us:
Telephone 631-231-7269; Fax 631-231-8175
Web Site: http://www.novapublishers.com

NOTICE TO THE READER

The Publisher has taken reasonable care in the preparation of this book, but makes no expressed or implied warranty of any kind and assumes no responsibility for any errors or omissions. No liability is assumed for incidental or consequential damages in connection with or arising out of information contained in this book. The Publisher shall not be liable for any special, consequential, or exemplary damages resulting, in whole or in part, from the readers' use of, or reliance upon, this material. Any parts of this book based on government reports are so indicated and copyright is claimed for those parts to the extent applicable to compilations of such works.

Independent verification should be sought for any data, advice or recommendations contained in this book. In addition, no responsibility is assumed by the publisher for any injury and/or damage to persons or property arising from any methods, products, instructions, ideas or otherwise contained in this publication.

This publication is designed to provide accurate and authoritative information with regard to the subject matter covered herein. It is sold with the clear understanding that the Publisher is not engaged in rendering legal or any other professional services. If legal or any other expert assistance is required, the services of a competent person should be sought. FROM A DECLARATION OF PARTICIPANTS JOINTLY ADOPTED BY A COMMITTEE OF THE AMERICAN BAR ASSOCIATION AND A COMMITTEE OF PUBLISHERS.

LIBRARY OF CONGRESS CATALOGING-IN-PUBLICATION DATA

Perspectives on cognition and action in sport / editors, Duarte Araujo, Hubert Ripoll , Markus Raab.
    p. cm.
  Includes index.
  ISBN 978-1-60692-390-0 (hardcover)
  1. Sports--Psychological aspects. 2. Cognition. I. Araújo, Duarte II. Ripoll, Hubert. III. Raab, Markus.
  GV706.4.P463 2009
  796.01--dc22
                                                                        2008053068

Published by Nova Science Publishers, Inc. ✦ *New York*

CONTENTS

PREFACE

There has been considerable debate on sport psychology about the status and the function of cognition and action in sport (Bar-Eli and Raab, 2006; Ripoll, 1991; Schack and Tenenbaum, 2004a, 2004b; Straub and Williams, 1984). This debate is very relevant since it will improve both theory and practice of sport psychology and human movement science.

After all these discussions, more than the conclusion that "we agree that we disagree" (Summers, 1998), there was a refinement of the different positions, and there were several attempts to integrate apparently contrasting perspectives.

A main goal of this edited book is to put the links between cognition, perception and action into the discussion both oriented towards theory and practice, and thus, cast a new look on cognition and action in sport.

The book gathers recent work on cognition, decision-making, action, and perception in sport that goes beyond the current dominant perspective (e.g., information processing). On the other hand, this does not mean that the book will strictly oppose this perspective. It rather aims to add different perspectives to a holistic understanding of cognition and action in sport.

Thus, the book provides a balanced and representative overview of what we currently know about cognition and action in sport. The authors have been requested to provide overviews of their theoretical approach and their own research. They are experts in their field and gain their reputation from outstanding publications in high quality journals. They are urged to write in a way that is easily understandable even for those who are not trained in academic psychology. They are also urged to make references to each other's work.

The idea for this book appeared when the editors were organizing three symposia for the Congress of the International Federation of Sport Psychology (FEPSAC), that was held in Halkidiki, Greece, in September 2007. These symposia reflect the three sections of this book. Section I discusses the organization of action attending to its dynamics and complexity. It shows how multiple levels of complexity are involved in performance and learning. Section II discusses not only what is knowledge, but also how it is used by athletes during performance. Section III presents different perspectives about judgment and decision-making as well as applications to training.

We could not finish without acknowledging the important contribution of the colleagues that invisibly shaped these "Perspectives of cognition and action in sport": Michael Bar-Eli, Chris Button, Evelyne Cauzinille-Marmèche, Didier Delignierès, Damian Farrow, Yeou Teh Liu, Daniel Memmert, Hermann Müller, Jörn Köppen, Gert-Jan Pepping, Philipp Philippen, Alexander Pizzera, Henning Plessner, Ian Renshaw, Thierry Ripoll, and Jean-Jacques

Temprado. We would also like to thank all the authors of the papers in this book for sharing their valuable insights.

This book is directed towards a post graduated reader, at a masters level. In addition researchers and students in the field of sport science, prevention and rehabilitation, exercise psychology, robotics, human factors and related domains will find the content of this book a source of up-to-date knowledge on perception, cognition and action.

Duarte Araújo
Technical University of Lisbon, Portugal

Hubert Ripoll
Aix-Marseille Universities, France

Markus Raab
German Sport University Cologne, Germany

REFERENCES

Bar-Eli, M., and Raab, M. (Eds) (2006). Judgment and decision making in sport and exercise. *Psychology of Sport and Exercise, 7*(8).

Ripoll, H. (Ed) (1991). Information processing and decision-making in sport. *International Journal of Sport Psychology, 22.*

Schack, T., and Tenenbaum, G. (Eds) (2004a). The construction of action: New perspectives in movement sciences (part 1). *International Journal of Sport Psychology* 2.

Schack, T., and Tenenbaum, G. (Eds) (2004b). The construction of action: New perspectives in movement sciences - part 2: Representation and planning. *International Journal of Sport Psychology* 2.

Straub, W.F., and Williams, J.M. (Eds.) (1984). *Cognitive sport psychology.* Lansing, NY: Sport Science Associates.

Summers, J.J. (1998). Has ecological psychology delivered what it promised? In J. Piek (Ed.), *Motor control and skill: a multidisciplinary perspective* (pp. 385-402). Champaign: IL: Human Kinetics.

LIST OF CONTRIBUTORS

D. ARAÚJO
Faculty of Human Kinetics, Technical University of Lisbon, Portugal

M. BAR-ELI
Ben-Gurion University of the Negev, Beer Sheva, Israel
Zinman College of Physical Education and Sport Sciences, Wingate Institute, Israel

R. BRAND
Institute of Sport Science, University of Potsdam, Germany

J. Y. CHOW
Physical Education & Sports Science, National Institute of Education, Nanyang Technological University, Singapore

R. CORDOVIL
Faculty of Human Kinetics, Technical University of Lisbon, Portugal
Lusófona University of Humanities and Technologies, Portugal

K. DAVIDS
School of Human Movement Studies, Australia Queensland University of Technology, Australia

O. FERNANDES
University of Évora, Portugal

L. GOUVEIA
Faculty of Pharmacy, University of Lisbon, Portugal

R. HRISTOVSKI
Faculty of Physical Culture, University of St. Cyril and Methodius, Republic of Macedonia

J. G. JOHNSON
Department of Psychology, Miami University, USA

J. KÖPPEN
Institute of Psychology, German Sport University, Germany

W. M. LAND
Florida State University, USA

E. LAURENT
Laboratory of Psychology, University of Franche Comté, France

M. MICHELBRINK
University of Mainz, Germany

J. MILHO
Lusófona University of Humanities and Technologies, Portugal

J. S. NORTH
Sheffield Hallam University, England

P. PASSOS
Faculty of Human Kinetics, Technical University of Lisbon, Portugal
Lusófona University of Humanities and Technologies, Portugal

H. PLESSNER
Institute of Psychology, University of Leipzig, Germany

M. RAAB
Institute of Psychology, German Sport University, Germany

J. RIBEIRO
Faculty of Human Kinetics, Technical University of Lisbon, Portugal

H. RIPOLL
Information and System Science Laboratory & Sport Sciences Faculty, Aix-Marseille
Universities, France

G. SAVELSBERGH
Research Institute MOVE, Faculty of Human Movement Sciences, VU University
Amsterdam, The Netherlands

W. I. SCHÖLLHORN
University of Mainz, Germany

G. SCHWEIZER
Institute of Sport Science, University of Potsdam, Germany

S. SERPA
Faculty of Human Kinetics, Technical University of Lisbon, Portugal

G. TENENBAUM
Florida State University, USA

J. VAN DER KAMP
Research Institute MOVE, Faculty of Human Movement Sciences, VU University Amsterdam, The Netherlands

B. VEREIJKEN
Human Movement Science Programme, Norwegian University of Science and Technology, Norway

J. VICKERS
Faculty of Kinesiology, University of Calgary, Canada

D. WELMINSIKI
University of Münster, Germany

M. WILLIAMS
Liverpool John Moores University, England

Section 1. Complex Systems Approach to Situated Action in Sport

In: Perspectives on Cognition and Action in Sport
Editors: D. Araújo, H. Ripoll and M. Raab

ISBN: 978-1-60692-390-0
© 2009 Nova Science Publishers, Inc.

Chapter 1

THE ORGANIZATION OF ACTION IN COMPLEX NEUROBIOLOGICAL SYSTEMS

Keith Davids
Queensland University of Technology, Australia

ABSTRACT

This chapter elucidates key ideas behind neurocomputational and ecological dynamics perspectives for understanding the organisation of action in complex neurobiological systems. The need to study the close link between neurobiological systems and their environments (particularly their sensory and movement subsystems and the surrounding energy sources) is advocated. It is proposed how degeneracy in complex neurobiological systems provides the basis for functional variability in organisation of action. In such systems processes of cognition and action facilitate the specific interactions of each performer with particular task and environmental constraints.

INTRODUCTION

Skilled cognition and action in complex performance contexts is easily recognised, even by non-specialists. As elucidated by Vereijken in this book (Chapter 6), skilled cognition and action supports behavior in a variety of complex performance contexts exemplified by the sophisticated dexterity of a rhythmic gymnast, a deft side-step from an attacking player in a team game or the speed and precision with which a surfer catches a wave in rough ocean waters. Skilled actions emerge from a complex combination of past experience, physical training and innate abilities expressed through coordination and control of human movement. In all performance contexts adaptation to changing task constraints is a key index of the organisation of high skilled behavior. This chapter provides an overview of major theoretical approaches for studying the organisation of multiarticular actions, particularly focusing on neurocomputational and ecological dynamics theories. The aim is to elucidate the different philosophical rationales and emphases of each approach for readers.

NEUROCOMPUTATIONAL MODELLING
OF CONTROL OF COMPLEX ACTIONS

Some previous studies of movement behavior have preferred closed systems analyses, predicated on a reductionist scientific method and based on a determinate world view (Glimcher, 2005). These theoretical approaches tended to emphasise the construction of mental models or representations to regulate cognition and action (Maule, Hockey and Bdzola, 2000). They explain movement organisation through the development of extensive and highly differentiated knowledge structures mapped into memory circuits to expedite functional performance (e.g., Anderson's ACT* theory, 1983; Hodgkinson, Maule, and Bown, 2004). Many early investigations of movement behavior were biased away from the study of complex actions such as dynamic multi-articular coordination patterns because of the belief that experimental rigor could be better maintained in the laboratory, compared to studying performance of natural tasks in more dynamic performance environments. In line with this philosophical approach, many early theories contemplated electronic and mechanical storage devices to model how information might be stored and represented in the CNS. These devices served as metaphors for processes of cognition and action and demonstrated the influential role of physics on the development of psychological theories of movement behavior. To exemplify, Keele (1968) adopted the computer program as a functional analogy of how the brain produces consistent and reliable movement outputs. The basic assumption of the neurocomputational analogy was that the brain functioned like a biological computer to process information and produce behavioural outputs.

Many recent theories of neurocomputational control have tended to utilise a more integrative modelling approach founded on evidence from the cognitive and behavioral neurosciences (e.g., Kawato, 1999). For example, Willingham's (1998) control-based learning theory (COBALT) proposed that the brain creates different types of representations so that information for perception and action can be symbolically represented and stored. According to COBALT, motor learning results in the acquisition of different types of representations in the brain. It proposed how learners created mental models of the world, including categories based on environmental features, intentions, and spatial or temporal patterns of muscle activation at different levels of the CNS. For instance, organisation of an action like a tennis serve was hypothesised to be regulated by an egocentric representation (perceptions from the individual's viewpoint) of the "knowledge of a sequence of locations to which one should respond" (Willingham, 1998, p. 574). This sort of approach was also advocated by Arbib, Érdi, and Szentágothai (1998) who proposed that perception, decision making and action was mediated by schema as hypothetical mechanisms that intervened between the neural structure and movement system dynamics.

As well as modelling coding mechanisms that mediate movement dynamics and nervous system structure, neurocomputational researchers have also been concerned with identifying regions of the brain that are responsible for controlling movement. For example, Muellbacher and colleagues (2002) suggested that the primary motor cortex is the site of consolidation or stabilization of movement representations, particularly in the early stages of learning a new motor skill. Another common approach has been to consider how the brain uses its networked, parallel processing capabilities to cope with multiple information streams (e.g., through neural mechanisms such as cortical cell assemblies and neural net modelling; Bullock and Grossberg, 1989; Wickens, Hyland, and Anson, 1994). This approach was recently instantiated by the work of Pesaran et al. (2008) who compared activity in the long range circuitry between the frontal and parietal cortex supporting free choice and prescribed decision-making activity during the planning of reaching movements.

A significant challenge for neurocomputational models has been to explain how cognition and perceptual processes regulate complex multi-articular actions in dynamic environments, since imputing traditional cortical input-elaboration-output schemes as instantiating perception, cognition and action processes has been criticised as misleading (e.g., Logothetis, 2008). A particular issue for neurocomputational theories concerns the communication between levels of representations, such as spatiotemporal representations of the environment and representations of movement patterns. This level of modelling is needed to understand how the activity of perceptual systems and action systems are integrated within biological nervous systems. One line of research has attempted to examine how the neural code is transformed from egocentric representations of time and spatial locations into the CNS coding of specific muscle forces used to produce a movement pattern (e.g., Flash and Sejnowski, 2001). In early work, researchers hypothesized that interneurons (perhaps at the level of the spinal cord) acted as code translators for communicating between egocentric representations of the world and the specific muscles used to achieve movement goals.

Recent trends in neurocomputational modelling have also been influenced by research on the engineering design of 'biologically inspired' robots (i.e., robots that act more like typical neurobiological systems, including insects, animals, and humans). This generation of robotic design is tackling the problem of engineering machines that can undertake multi-articular actions, adapt their behaviors to complex environments and terrains, and even cooperate in teams during complex activities like exploration for minerals during mining (e.g., Mataríc, 1998). Some work in artificial intelligence has been aimed at providing insights into how the CNS controls movements in humans, drawing inspiration from theories of how neurobiological systems interact with complex environments. Traditional models of robotic design, based on the principles of 'sense, model, plan, and act', are being complemented by behavior-based control approaches that have the explicit goal of engineering machines to operate in unpredictable and challenging environments, such as during space exploration or RoboCup soccer competitions (Mataríc, 1998). Alternative design principles, including situated robotics, draw inspiration from research on how neurobiological systems search for and pick up information to support sophisticated interactions with their environments (e.g., DiPaolo, 2002; Paine and Tani, 2005). As noted later in this chapter, these principles are consonant with an ecological dynamics perspective on cognition and action.

More recent modelling in artificial intelligence has addressed how movement representations support the co-adaptation of the individual and environment during motor learning (e.g., Davidson and Wolpert, 2003; Wolpert, Ghahramani, and Flanagan, 2001). This approach attempts to understand how cognition is mediated by the physical constraints of the human body. In this type of computational modelling, anticipating the outcomes of an action underpins planning and organization of goal-directed movement (see also Johnson, Chapter 14). The traditional problem of communication between sensory representations and motor systems is resolved by requiring two types of representations: forward and inverse models (Kawato, 1999). Forward modelling refers to the mapping of motor commands to the related sensory consequences of a movement. Within the brain, this representation is used to predict the sensory consequences of planned movements. For example, when planning to serve a tennis ball above the head, expected sensory consequences might include information about reaching upwards, leaning and overbalancing that would require adaptation of postural muscles, knee flexion and a stepping adjustment to successfully contact the ball. Inverse modelling refers to transforming anticipated sensory consequences into the motor commands needed to achieve them. Skilled cognition and action involves the acquisition of forward and inverse representations for varying tasks and environments. In forward models, one learns to use perceptual feedback to regulate movements, whereas under task constraints which are too rapid for this information to be available, inverse models provide performers with a feed-forward control mechanism. The acquisition of forward models enables adaptation to rapidly changing environments and prevents an overreliance on immediate sensory information to regulate movements (Wolpert et al., 2001). As long as environments remain stable and planned actions do not require significant adaptation, feed-forward control mechanisms allow performers to use 'what-if' mental simulations in a kind of pre-planned reactive adaptation to predicted changes in the environment.

To summarise, traditional investigations of limited-degree-freedom actions have provided models for understanding how control systems might operate during goal-directed activity. But they have shed fewer insights on understanding how the multitude of biomechanical degrees of freedom might be (re)organized in performing multi-articular actions in dynamic environments involving multi-agent interactions in sport (Davids, Button, Araújo, Renshaw and Hristovski, 2006). More recently, studies of self-organisation processes in biological systems (see Camazine et al., 2001) have provided fresh insights for understanding the organisation of multiple degrees of freedom in complex, neurobiological systems. Understanding the regulation of multi-articular actions in neurobiological systems has been influenced by advances in ecological psychology (Gibson, 1979) and nonlinear dynamics (e.g., Jirsa and Kelso, 2004). As noted next, from an ecological dynamics perspective, neurobiological systems rely less on sensorimotor representations and their transformations as mechanisms for organising complex actions. Rather the frame of analysis in ecological dynamics involves identifying how information continuously constrains the dynamical patterns formed between components of complex neurobiological systems during action.

ECOLOGICAL DYNAMICS AND THE ORGANISATION OF MULTI-ARTICULAR ACTIONS

Ecological dynamics is concerned with the regulation of cognition and action in neurobiological systems characterized as dynamic pattern-forming entities. They exemplify complex systems whose component parts show tendencies to continuously form rich, interdependent connections during goal-directed behavior. It seeks to capture how these spontaneous coordination tendencies provide neurobiological systems with stability and the flexibility needed to function in and adapt to complex, ever-changing environments (Kelso, 1995; Turvey, 1990). In ecological dynamics, the investigation of multi-articular actions has provided important insights into the role of degeneracy, a hallmark of complex neurobiological systems. Degeneracy subserves the capacity of neurobiological systems to achieve the same functional outcomes in varying situations, with structurally different components of the musculo-skeletal sub-system (Edelman and Gally, 2001; Hong and

Newell, 2006). Degenerate neurobiological systems demonstrate the flexibility and adaptability to organise actions to fit continuously evolving task constraints so that performance goals can be attained (Edelman and Gally, 2001). Degeneracy differs from the characteristic of system redundancy, more common to engineering systems, in which additional components can perform identical functions to provide back-up against system failure (see Newell et al., 2005). Neurobiological systems differ from engineering systems in which spare components can be designed into system structure. While some theories, such as optimal control (e.g., Braun and Wolpert, 2007), use the term 'redundancy' to explain how the motor system responds to perturbations by finding different movement solutions to achieve the same task goal, the use of the term degeneracy is more appropriate than redundancy in examining coordination in neurobiological systems (Newell et al., 2005). Flexibility and adaptability of cognition and action in the organisation of complex actions by neurobiological systems can be facilitated by degeneracy (Davids, Bennett and Newell, 2006).

In ecological dynamics, the movement models used to gain theoretical insights into neurobiological processes of coordination and control are being provided by a rich range of multi-articular actions, many of which are popular in sports and physical activities (e.g., Araújo et al., 2005; Davids, et al., 2002). Such actions and activities include playground swinging (Post et al., 2003), pole-balancing (DeGuzman, 2004), hula-hooping (Balasubramaniam and Turvey, 2004), sit ups (Cordo and Gurfinkel, 2004), kicking a football (Chow et al., 2008), javelin and discus throwing (Schöllhorn, 2003), basketball shooting (Button et al., 2003), sailing (Araújo et al., 2005), volleyball serving (Handford, 2002), long jumping run-ups (Montagne et al., 2000), basketball ball bouncing (Broderick, Pavis and Newell, 2000) and golf driving (Knight, 2004).

Ecological dynamics is predicated on key concepts of nonlinear dynamics and has also been influenced by key ideas from several scientific subdisciplines including ecological psychology, chaos theory, the sciences of complexity, nonlinear theormodynamics, and synergetics (for comprehensive reviews, see Kauffman, 1993; Haken, 1996; Warren, 2006). The concept of emergence of form under constraints in complex systems has been imported into human movement science from theoretical physics and physical biology where scientists have long been interested in how living systems assemble, sustain and disassemble the large-scale (or macroscopic) patterns between the huge number of system components (e.g., see Kugler, 1986; Kugler and Turvey, 1987). Complex systems are able to exploit the constraints that surround them in order to allow functional patterns of behavior to emerge in specific contexts.

Complex systems in nature are often 'open' systems that are sensitive to many factors or constraints acting on the system. Achieving and maintaining stability of action could be a problem for open, complex systems such as degenerate neurobiological systems because of the potential for interaction between the environment and the system. Physical processes of self-organization support biological systems in using environmental energy to sustain functional periods of action stability (e.g., Prigogine and Stengers, 1984). Surrounding energy flows constitute a source of information shaping the patterns of cognitions and actions that emerge during task performance. Self-organization of neurobiological systems into different states of order occurs when the many micro components interact and begin to influence each other's behavior. These micro level dynamics typically lead to no large-scale changes in system behavior, merely a lot of underlying fluctuation, which mildly perturbs system stability (Camazine et al., 2001). However, key events, for example, critical changes in values of energy arrays surrounding the system (e.g., optical or acoustic energy sources gained from approaching objects), can alter the whole system structure leading to macroscopic level changes and reorganization into a different state.

Self-organization in complex neurobiological systems is not a random or completely 'blind' process in which any pattern can result; rather it is partly determined and somewhat predictable. Typically, complex, dynamical systems only adopt very few states of organization, and a neurobiological system only inhabits certain parts of the landscape of all possibilities that it could hypothetically adopt (Kauffmann, 1993). The type of order that emerges is dependent on initial conditions (existing environmental conditions) and the constraints that shape a system's behavior. A key issue for understanding the behavior of complex neurobiological systems concerns how large-scale coordination patterns occur between the huge number of small-scale degrees of freedom or component parts. The multiple degrees of freedom of a complex system can often show unexpected organizational structure and coherence in the long term, because they are conditionally-coupled (Van Geert, 1994). That is, each separate degree of freedom does not function in a completely independent way from other degrees of freedom in the system. As the chapter by Passos et al. proposes, behavior that is conditionally-coupled occurs because the state of a system micro-component at one time remains dependent on previous states of the system (see Passos, Araújo, Davids, Gouveia, Milho and Serpa, Chapter 3).

Understanding how each individual employs and constrains the large number of relevant motor system degrees of freedom, concurrently, during tasks like soccer kicking, exemplifies Bernstein's (1967) *degrees of freedom* problem. Bernstein's (1967) definition of acquiring movement coordination captures the fundamental problem in ecological dynamics. The acquisition of coordination is viewed as "...the process of mastering redundant degrees of freedom of the moving organ, in other words its conversion to a controllable system" (p. 127).

Complex open systems are dynamical in that they have variable amounts of energy moving between their components at any given moment (von Bertalanffy, 1950). The internal energy within the system (e.g., as a result of limb movements) interacts with the available forces in the environment (e.g., reactive forces, gravity, friction, air resistance). Complex living systems have on-board sources of energy (e.g., stored in muscle) that allow them to be self-sustaining and adaptive, and, with experience and development, they can exploit environmental energy flows acting as a form of information to guide the system (Kugler and Turvey, 1987). According to Bernstein (1967), the organisation of action is not just the result of muscular force production alone. A comprehensive theory of the organisation of action needs to consider how motor system degrees of freedom are coordinated as a consequence of muscular force production, as well as the forces generated by motions of body segments (inertial forces) and as a result of contact with important surfaces and objects in the environment (reactive forces) (see Kugler et al., 1982).

As noted earlier, constraints surround complex systems and reduce the number of configurations that are available to it as it interacts with the environment (see also Clark, 1995; Kugler, 1986; Newell, 1986). There are many different types of constraints influencing the behaviour of complex systems, categorised in various ways in different theoretical models. In ecological dynamics, Warren (1990) attempted to capture the link between perception and action systems by dividing constraints into *informational* and *physical* categories. James Gibson (1979) argued that biological organisms, including humans, are surrounded by great banks of energy flows or arrays, that can act as information sources (e.g., optical, acoustic, proprioceptive) to support movement behavior, including decision making, planning and organization, during goal-directed activity. As noted in the chapter by Savelsbergh and Van der Kamp in this book (Savelsbergh, and Van der Kamp, Chapter 2), informational constraints, such as haptic, optic, proprioceptive and acoustic sources of information are important, because they can tune the organisation of complex actions and enhance a neurobiological system's capacity to adapt to the environment. For example, informational constraints can be used to continuously guide the actions of a tennis player on court. An important attribute of skilled performance in tennis is that actions are precisely and ongoingly adapted to dynamic environments. As circumstances change, skilled players can vary the nature of their coordination to achieve the same task goal in slightly different ways. A skilled tennis player returning a topspin serve, for instance, can adapt movements throughout the shot to cope with changing demands imposed by the 'kick' of the ball, which will vary on different court surfaces. An important implication of these ideas is that the study of cognition and action should take place in realistic environments, because coordination between parts of a movement system needs an "...environment of forces for its proper expression." (Turvey et al., 1982, p. 239).

In neurobiological systems, the organisation of actions is predicated on coordination processes, defined as the way in which movement system components are assembled and brought together into proper relation with each other during goal-directed activity (Turvey, 1990). An ecological interpretation of coordination refers to the correct configuration and sequencing of appropriate joints and muscles in the body as an individual attempts to achieve specific movement goals. The organisation of such a huge number of micro-components of the human body might seem daunting, but neurobiological systems can exploit inherent self-organisation processes to achieve specific movement goals. For example, in the task of one handed catching, even a simple movement of reaching and grasping an object with the hand and arm could require the catcher to regulate 7 degrees of freedom (dof) of the arm, involving flexion-extension, medial-lateral movement and rotation of joints (3 at the shoulder, 1 at the elbow and 3 at the wrist). Even more dof need to be regulated in more complex multi-articular actions such as kicking a ball in soccer or the triple jump in ice-skating.

Bernstein (1967) proposed the formation of specific functional muscle-joint linkages or synergies as a method of managing the large number of degrees of freedom to be controlled in the human movement system. He suggested that such functional groupings compress the physical components of the movement system and specify how the relevant dof for an action become mutually dependent. Synergies between motor system components help to make it more manageable for learners when they discover and assemble strongly coupled limb relations to cope with the huge number of movement system degrees of freedom (Mitra, Amazeen and Turvey, 1998).

Synergies or coordinative structures are functional, being designed to achieve a specific purpose or activity, such as when groups of muscles are temporarily assembled into coherent units to achieve specific task goals, such as hitting a ball or performing a T-balance. Synergies capture the immediate functional relationship between a performer and a specific performance context since they are assembled to achieve a particular action goal (i.e. relationship) within an environment (Withagen and Michaels, 2005). To achieve a particular functional relationship with the environment, such as intercepting a projectile or maintaining a balanced posture with the ground, multiple means are available to performers due to the inherent degeneracy of neurobiological perceptual and action systems (Edelman and Gally, 2001; Withagen and Michaels, 2005). Neurobiological degeneracy provides a sound platform for the soft assembly of a synergy in response to the functional demands on an athlete.

Good quality perceptual information is necessary in assembling coordinative structures, because the details of their specific form or organization are not completely pre-determined and emerge under the constraints of each performance situation. The assembly of synergies is a dynamical process that is dependent on relevant sources of perceptual information related to key properties of the performer (e.g., haptic information from muscles and joints) and the environment (e.g., vision of a target or surface). They emerge from the rigidly fixed configurations that learners use early on to manage the multitude of motor system dof and become dynamic and flexible as learners use information to tune their functional organisation. Since, generally, personal and task constraints do not change dramatically between movement repetitions, synergies retain a relative permanence, typically requiring some refinement between specific performances.

CONCLUSION

This chapter discussed current approaches to understanding cognition and action in complex neurobiological systems. It highlighted how recent theories of neurocomputational control of cognition and action were based on integrated modelling of brain, behavior and dynamic environments, with the advent of approaches like ecological robotics to capture how systems can harness variability to adapt actions. It also emphasized how advances in ecological dynamics, combined with a constraints-led perspective, provides the foundation for a theory of the organisation of complex actions. Ecological dynamics provides a valuable theoretical impetus for considering perception, decision making and action because it adopts a systems perspective in viewing neurobiological systems as examples of a degenerate system composed of many interacting subsystems. This has led to many recent attempts to study complex task vehicles, avoiding reductionist approaches, in research on human movement. The ideas in this chapter suggested that observing the nature of changes during performance might reveal insights into how inherent system variability can be used for adapting and refining complex multi-articular actions.

REFERENCES

Anderson, J. R. (1983). *The architecture of cognition*. Cambridge, MA: Harvard University Press.

Araújo, D., Davids, K., and Serpa, S. (2005). An ecological approach to expertise effects in decision-making in a simulated sailing regatta. *Psychology of Sport and Exercise. 6*, 671-692.

Arbib, M.A., Érdi, P., and Szentágothai, J. (1998). *Neural Organization: Structure, function and dynamics*. Cambridge, MA: MIT Press.

Balasubramaniam, R., and Turvey, M.T. (2004). Coordination modes in the multisegmental dynamics of hula hooping. *Biological Cybernetics, 90,* 176-190.

Bernstein, N. (1967). *The co-ordination and regulation of movements*. Oxford: Pergamon Press.

Braun, D.A., and Wolpert, D.M. (2007). Optimal control: When redundancy matters. *Current Biology, 17*(22), R973-R975.

Broderick, M.P., Pavis, B., and Newell, K.M. (2000). Assessment of the adiabatic transformability hypothesis in a ball-bouncing task. *Biological Cybernetics, 82*, 433-442.

Bullock, D., and Grossberg, S. (1989). VITE and FLETE: Neural modules for trajectory formation and postural control. In W. Hershberger (Ed.), *Volitional action* (pp. 253-297). Amsterdam: North-Holland.

Button, C., McLeod, M., Sanders, R., and Coleman, S. (2003). Examining movement variability in the basketball free-throw action at different skill levels. *Research Quarterly for Exercise and Sport, 74*, 257-269.

Camazine, S., Deneubourg, J.-L., Franks, N.R., Sneyd, J., Theraulaz, G., and Bonabeau, E. (2001). *Self-organization in biological systems*. Princeton, N.J.: Princeton University Press.

Chow, J.-Y., Davids, K., Button, C., and Koh, M. (2008). Coordination changes in a discrete multi-articular action as a function of practice. *Acta Psychologica, 127*, 163-176.

Clark, J.E. (1995). On becoming skillful: Patterns and constraints. *Research Quarterly for Exercise and Sport, 66*, 173-183.

Cordo, P.J., and Gurfinkel, V.S. (2004). Motor coordination can be fully understood only by studying complex movements. *Progress in Brain Research, 143*, 29-38.

Davids, K., Bennett, S., and Newell, K.M. (2006). *Movement system variability*. Champaign, IL: Human Kinetics.

Davids, K., Button, C., Araújo, D., Renshaw, I., and Hristovski, R. (2006). Movement models from sports provide representative task constraints for studying adaptive behavior in human movement systems. *Adaptive Behavior, 14*, 73-94.

Davids, K., Savelsbergh, G.J.P., Bennett, S.J., and Van der Kamp, J. (2002). *Interceptive Actions in Sport: Information and Movement*. Routledge: London.

Davidson, D.L.W., and Wolpert, D.M. (2003). Motor learning and prediction in a variable environment. *Current Opinion in Neurobiology, 13*(2), 232-237.

DeGuzman, G.C. (2004). Using visual information in functional stabilization: Pole balancing example. In V.K. Jirsa and J.A.S. Kelso (Eds.), *Coordination Dynamics: Issues and Trends* (pp. 91-101). N.Y.: Springer-Verlag.

DiPaolo, E. (2002). Spike-timing dependent plasticity for evolved robots. *Adaptive Behavior, 10*, 243-263.

Edelman, G.M., and Gally, J. (2001). Degeneracy and complexity in biological systems. *Proceedings of the National Academy of Sciences, 98*, 13763-13768.

Flash, T., and Sejnowski, T.J. (2001). Computational approaches to motor control. *Current Opinion in Neurobiology, 11*, 655-662.

Gibson, J.J. (1979). *The ecological approach to visual perception*. Hillsdale, New Jersey: Lawrence Erlbaum Associates.

Glimcher, P.W. (2005). Indeterminacy of brain and behavior. *Annual Review of Psychology, 56*, 25-56.

Haken, H. (1996). *Principles of Brain Functioning*. Berlin: Springer.

Handford, C. (2002). Strategy and practice for acquiring timing in discrete, self-paced interceptive actions. In K. Davids, G.J.P. Savelsbergh, S.J. Bennett and J. Van Der Kamp

(Eds.), *Interceptive Actions in Sport* (pp. 288-300). London: Routledge, Taylor and Francis.

Hodgkinson, G.P., Maule, A.J., and Bown, N.J. (2004) Charting the mind of the strategic decision maker: A comparative analysis of two methodological alternatives involving causal mapping. *Organizational Research Methods, 7*, 3-21.

Hong, S.L., and Newell, K.M. (2006). Practice effects on local and global dynamics of the ski- simulator task. *Experimental Brain Research, 169*, 350-360.

Jirsa, V.K., and Kelso, J.A.S. (2004). *Coordination Dynamics: Issues and Trends.* N.Y.: Springer-Verlag.

Kauffman, S. (1993). *The Origins of Order. Self-organization and selection in evolution.* NY: Oxford University Press.

Kawato, M. (1999). Internal models for motor control and trajectory planning. *Current Opinion in Neurobiology, 9*, 718-727.

Keele, S.W. (1968). Movement control in skilled motor performance. *Psychological Bulletin, 70, 387-403.*

Kelso, J.A.S. (1995). *Dynamic patterns: The self-organisation of brain and behaviour.* Cambridge, MA: MIT Press.

Knight, C.A. (2004). Neuromotor issues in the learning and control of golf skill. *Research Quarterly for Exercise and Sport, 75, 9-15.*

Kugler, P.N. (1986). A morphological perspective on the origin and evolution of movement patterns. In W. Wade and H.T.A. Whiting (Eds.), *Motor development in children: Aspects of coordination and control* (pp. 459-525). Dordrecht, Netherlands: Martinus Nijhoff.

Kugler, P.N. and Turvey, M.T. (1987). *Information, natural law and the self-assembly of rhythmical movement.* Hillsdale, N.J.: Erlbaum.

Kugler, P.N., Kelso, J.A.S., and Turvey, M.T. (1982). On the control and coordination of naturally developing systems. In J.A.S. Kelso and J.E. Clark (Eds.), *The development of movement coordination and control* (pp. 5-78). New York: Wiley.

Logothetis, N.K. (2008). What we can do and what we cannot do with fMRI. *Nature, 453*, 869-878.

Mataríc, M. (1998). Behavior-based robotics as a tool for synthesis of artificial behavior and analysis of natural behavior. *Trends in Cognitive Sciences, 2*, 82-87.

Maule, A., Hockey, G. R. J., and Bdzola L. (2000). Effects of time pressure on decision making under uncertainty: changes in affective state and information processing strategy. *Acta Psychologica, 104*, 283 - 301.

Mitra, S., Amazeen, P. G., and Turvey, M. T. (1998). Intermediate motor learning as decreasing active (dynamical) degrees of freedom. *Human Movement Science, 17*, 17-65.

Montagne, G., Cornus, S., Glize, D., Quaine, F., and Laurent, M. (2000). A perception-action coupling type of control in long jumping. *Journal of Motor Behavior, 32*, 37-43.

Muellbacher, W., Ziemann, U., Wissel, J., Dang, N., Kofler, M., Facchini, S., et al. (2002). Early consolidation in human motor cortex. *Nature, 415*, 640-643.

Newell, K.M. (1986). Constraints on the development of coordination. In M.G. Wade and H.T.A.Whiting (Eds.), *Motor development in children: Aspects of coordination and control* (pp. 341-360). Dordrecht, Netherlands: Martinus Nijhoff.

Newell, K.M., Liu,Y.-T., and Mayer-Kress, G. (2005). Learning in the Brain-Computer Interface: Insights about Degrees of Freedom and Degeneracy from a Landscape Model of Motor Learning. *International Quarterly of Cognitive Science, 6*, 37 - 47.

Paine, R.W., and Tani, J. (2005). How hierarchical control self-organizes in artificial adaptive systems. *Adaptive Behavior, 13*, 211-225.

Pesaran, B., Nelson, M.J., and Anderson, R.A. (2008). Free choice activates a decision circuit between frontal and parietal cortex. *Nature*. (in press).

Post, A.A., Peper, C.E., and Beek, P.J. (2003). Effects of visual information and task constraints on intersegmental coordination in playground swinging. *Journal of Motor Behavior, 35*, 64-78.

Prigogine, I., and Stengers, I. (1984). *Order out of chaos*. New York: Bantam Books.

Schöllhorn, W. I. (2003). Coordination dynamics and its consequences on sports. *International Journal of Computer Science in Sport, 2*, 40-46.

Turvey, M.T. (1990). Coordination. *American Psychologist, 45*, 938-953.

Turvey, M.T., Fitch, H., and Tuller, B. (1982). The Bernstein perspective: I. The problem of degrees of freedom and context-conditioned variability. In J.A.S. Kelso (Ed.), *Human Motor Behavior: An Introduction*. (pp. 253-281). Hillsdale, NJ: LEA.

Van Geert , P. (1994). *Dynamic systems of development: Change between complexity and chaos*. New York: Harvester.

Von Bertalanffy, L. (1950). The theory of open systems in physics and biology. *Science, 111*, 23-29.

Warren, W. (2006). The dynamics of perception and action. *Psychological Review, 113*, 358-389.

Warren, W.H. (1990). The Perception-Action Coupling. In H. Bloch and B. I. Bertenthal (Eds.), *Sensory-Motor Organizations and Development in Infancy and Early Childhood* (pp. 23-37). Dordecht: Kluwer Academic Publishers.

Wickens, J., Hyland, B., and Anson, G. (1994). Cortical cell assemblies: A possible mechanism for motor programs. *Journal of Motor Behavior, 26*(2), 66-82.

Willingham, D.B. (1998). A neuropsychological theory of motor skill learning. *Psychological Review, 105*, 558-584.

Withagen, R., and Michaels, C.F. (2005). On ecological conceptualizations of perceptual systems and action systems. *Theory and Psychology, 15*, 603-620.

Wolpert, D.M., Ghahramani, Z., and Flanagan, J.R. (2001). Perspectives and problems in motor learning. *Trends in Cognitive Sciences, 5*, 487-494.

In: Perspectives on Cognition and Action in Sport
Editors: D. Araújo, H. Ripoll and M. Raab

ISBN: 978-1-60692-390-0
© 2009 Nova Science Publishers, Inc.

Chapter 2

CATCHING TWO VISUAL SYSTEMS AT ONCE: VENTRAL AND DORSAL SYSTEM CONTRIBUTIONS IN THE VISUAL REGULATION OF HUMAN MOVEMENT

Geert Savelsbergh[1,2,3] and John van der Kamp[1,4]

[1] Faculty of Human Movement Sciences
VU University Amsterdam, The Netherlands
[2] Research Institute for Biomedical Research into Human
Movement and Health Faculty of Science and Engineering,
Manchester Metropolitan University, United Kingdom
[3] Academy for Physical Education, University
of Professional Education, The Netherlands
[4] Institute of Human Performance,
University of Hong Kong, Hong Kong

ABSTRACT

The aim of the chapter is to examine how studies into interceptive actions like catching, provide evidence for the two-visual system model. This model advocates two dissociated visual streams with separate functions: a dorsal stream that picks up the visual information for the online control of movements and a ventral stream that contributes to the detection of visual information in order to obtain knowledge of the world. The chapter ends with the possible consequences for sport practice when the two-visual system model is endorsed; especially the concept of anticipation is discussed.

INTRODUCTION: CATCHING UP

Over the past few decades, the study of human movement has matured into a science of its own. Moreover, the study of human movement with special attention to the visual regulation in interceptive action has become one the core areas of research in sports sciences. Why interceptive actions? Because, over the years, it has become a major testing ground for examining basic theoretical concepts and questions. Questions that have been posed are: *'how much* visual information is needed for successful interceptive actions', 'what is the *minimum amount* of information needed to control interceptive actions', '*what* visual (and/or proprioceptive) sources of information are used to control interceptive action?', and '*how* are these information sources used to control interceptive actions?' A second reason to study interceptive action is its applied value. Interceptive actions are crucial skills in many different ball sports, like baseball, cricket, tennis, badminton, squash, handball and football, but are also part of many athletic events such as jumping over hurdles or positioning the feet at the take-off board in the long jump.

Especially, one–handed catching has been an attractive task to study for many sport scientists. The history of research on one-handed catching neatly shows the different theoretical perspectives that have been in vogue in the study of human movement for the last three to four decades (for different theoretical paradigms see chapters of Passos, Araujo, Davids, Gouveia, Milho and Serpa, Chapter 3; Schöllhorn, Michelbrink, Welminsiki, and Davids, Chapter 5; Vereijken, Chapter 5). Pioneering was the work of Whiting and Sharp (1974; Sharp and Whiting, 1974), who framed their work within the information-processing approach that dominated psychology at that time. In their studies, they manipulated the vision of the ball trajectory and found that viewing the ball too early or too late in its trajectory led to decreases in catching performance. Although it is true that information about ball flight trajectory is necessary for successful catching performance, it became clear from Whiting and Sharp's work that it is unnecessary to view the entire trajectory. This speaks to the issue of the minimum amount of information needed to successfully perform a task, a topic that figured prominently within the information-processing approach of the nineteen-seventies.

From the early nineteen-nineties onward, catching served as vehicle to examine and provide evidence for the perception-action approach (Gibson, 1979; Turvey, 1990). A paradigmatic example is the 'deflating ball' study by Savelsbergh and Whiting (Savelsbergh et al., 1991, 1993). They examined the involvement of the expanding optical patterns generated by an approaching ball in the control of one-handed catching. In theory, these optical expansion patterns contain accurate predictive temporal information about time remaining before the approaching ball will make contact with the observer/actor. David Lee's (1976) study demonstrated mathematically that the inverse of the relative rate of expansion of the optical angle generated by an approaching object in the optic array specifies the remaining time-to-contact of the approaching object with the point of observation. Lee called this optical variable 'tau'. One hypothesis is that a catcher, who controls the onset of the action at a particular threshold value of tau, would initiate their (catching) action at a constant time before contact, independent of object velocity. Savelsbergh and co-workers required their participants to catch a luminous ball attached to a pendulum in a totally dark room (i.e., only expansion information was available). Both balls with constant diameter and shrinking or deflating balls were used. In contrast to the constant balls, the expansion pattern generated by the deflating balls specifies a longer time-to-contact. Savelsbergh et al. (1991) found that the moment of maximal closing velocity of the fingers occurred later for the deflating ball and thus, provided qualitative evidence for the use of tau in closing the hand. Savelsbergh et al. concluded that, 'the findings [...] are consistent with subjects' use of relative expansion information on which to base their catching movements' (Savelsbergh et al., 1991, p. 321)[1]. These findings support the perception-action coupling paradigm.

A relatively recent theoretical framework relevant to the study of interceptive actions is the two-visual system model put forward by Milner and Goodale (1995). Milner and Goodale proposed a division between vision for perception and vision for action processes (Goodale and Milner, 1992, 2004; Milner and Goodale, 1995). They argued that two separate, neuro-anatomically and functionally different visual systems exist, referred to as the dorsal and ventral systems. The dorsal system is involved in the visual control of movement execution. For instance, it controls the spatio-temporal characteristics of the arm movements (i.e. the kinematics) such that a ball will be intercepted at the right place at the right time. The ventral system is involved in the perception of objects, events and places. An observer, for example, may recognize a ball as a tennis ball or basketball based on its size or colour. Moreover, the ventral system can also obtain knowledge about what the environment offers for action. It may gather information for tactical game decisions. For instance, whether to throw the ball toward a team mate at the first base or, alternatively to the team mate at home plate. In other words, the ventral system contributes to the perception of what action is appropriate in a given situation (Milner and Goodale, 2008; Van Doorn, van der Kamp, and Savelsbergh, 2007; Van der Kamp, Rivas, van Doorn and Savelsbergh, 2008). It is not surprising, therefore, that in recent years many researchers have alluded to the idea that the two-visual system model is directly relevant for the study of sport, especially for the understanding of interceptive actions in fast ball sports (e.g., Van der Kamp et al., 2008). Systematic research in this area, however, has yet to be reported.

In this chapter, we examine how studies into interceptive actions such as catching, may provide further evidence for the two-visual system model, and secondly, what the possible consequences for sport practice would be when endorsing the two-visual system model. But, first we will describe the two-visual system model in somewhat more detail.

CATCHING THE TWO-VISUAL SYSTEM MODEL

The collaboration between Milner and Goodale resulted in the idea that two dissociated visual streams with separate functions can be discerned in the cerebral cortex (Goodale and Milner, 1992, 2004; Milner and Goodale, 1995; figure 1). The dorsal stream, projecting from the primary visual cortex to the posterior parietal cortex, supports the pick up visual information for the online control of movements. In other words, it contributes to *vision for action* processes. The ventral stream, on the other hand, contributes to *vision for perception* processes and projects from the primary visual cortex to the inferotemporal cortex. This stream supports the detection of visual information to obtain knowledge of the world. In contrast to the dorsal stream, the ventral stream has only indirect connections with the premotor cortex, such as, for instance, the projections to the ventral prefrontal cortex, which are thought to support memory and decision-making processes (Rossetti and Pisella, 2002).

---

[1] The results of the deflating ball experiments also indicated that the effect of dilation is much more pronounced in the monocular condition than in the binocular condition, suggesting that binocular information is involved as well (Savelsbergh, 1995: Caljouw, van der Kamp & Savelsbergh, 2004).

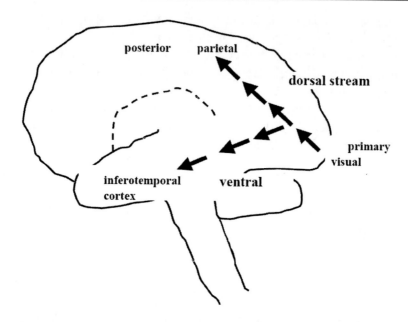

Figure 1. Schematic representation of the two visual streams in the human cortex of one of the author's brain (adapted from Van der Kamp et al., 2008).

These vision for action and vision for perception processes can be differentiated on the basis of the spatial and temporal scales at which they operate. Take for instance a moving object. The ventral system would be involved in obtaining knowledge about the properties of moving objects, such as their colour, location or speed relative to other objects. Recognition of objects or their properties thus demands information that is independent of an observer's momentary viewpoint. Vision for perception processes therefore are presumed to rely on world-centred or allocentric information that specifies the location, motion, and size of an object in relation to other objects. Further, the information should be available over longer periods of time; it is long-lived (Rossetti and Pisella, 2002). By contrast, the dorsal system functions to detect visual information in order to adjust movement to the spatio-temporal characteristics of the moving object. It therefore is tuned to metrically precise information about the location, speed, and orientation of an object relative to the actor: vision for action processes are thought to rely on body-centred or egocentric sources of information. Furthermore, in order to achieve adequate movement control information must be used immediately or 'on the fly' (i.e., on-line control). Information is short-lived, because when it is more than a fraction of a second old it is of little use (Goodale and Westwood, 2004). In other words, the vision for action processes operate relatively fast and the information it detects is quickly lost.

There are many kinds of experimental evidence that provide support for the two-visual system model. We discuss two. The most prominent is the study of patients with brain damage to either the dorsal or ventral stream. Famous is the case of patient DF, who has a lesion in the ventral stream areas. When presented with a slot (like in a post box) in various orientations, patient DF is unable to match the orientation of her hand with the orientation of the slot; damage to the ventral stream clearly disturbed vision for perception processes. However, when she is requested to actually post a letter through the slot, she is capable of orienting the letter in line with the various orientations of the slot, underlining that movement control requires an intact dorsal stream and does not entirely rely on the ventral stream (Goodale and Milner, 2004 for an overview).

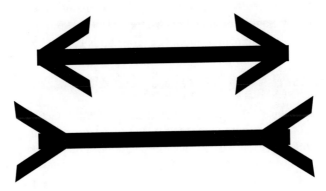

Figure 2. The Müller-Lyer Illusion. Even though one sees the shaft of the bottom configuration to be larger than the one in the top figuration, the maximal hand aperture when grasping the shafts does not differ.

A second source of evidence is a growing number of studies that examine visual illusion in participants without brain damage. In the Müller-Lyer illusion, for instance, perception of the length of a line or shaft is influenced by the direction of the tails at the end-points of the shaft (figure 2). The shaft is perceived as longer with the tails pointing outward, but shorter when the tails are pointing inward. In contrast, grip scaling to pick up the shaft remains relatively unaffected by the illusion (e.g., Otto-de Haart, Carey, and Milner, 1998; Van Doorn et al., 2007). This dissociation between visual perception and movement control is commonly attributed to the ventral and dorsal systems' differential reliance on allocentric versus egocentric information; because the dorsal system is dedicated to detecting egocentric information, the illusion does not bias grasping.

In the next session, we explore how studies on one-handed catching provide further evidence for the two-visual system model.

CATCHING EVIDENCE

In a by now classic study that used high speed film recordings, Alderson, Sully, and Sully (1974) revealed the spatial and temporal requirements that have to be met to successfully catch a ball with one hand. Three different phases in the performance of the catch were discerned. Firstly, the hand has to be moved to the region where the interception will take place (i.e., the gross spatial orientation phase). This is followed by more precise spatial adjustments of the hand such that the ball makes contact with the hand in the metacarpal region (i.e., the fine orientation phase). Finally, the grasp has to be initiated and completed within a restricted time-window, depending on the speed of the approaching ball, thus requiring precise timing (i.e., the grasp and hold phase). In the remainder of this section, we will discuss two of our previous catching studies that examined the final grasp and hold phase.

To time the grasping phase in catching, the catcher needs information about the time it takes before the ball reaches the interception point or hand (if the hand is located at the interception point). As we explained above, the time-to-contact of a ball heading for the catcher is specified by the inverse of the relative rate of expansion generated by the approaching ball (i.e., tau). Evidence for the use of the expansion pattern was provided in the 'deflating ball' studies by Savelsbergh and co-workers (1991, 1993; Caljouw et al., 2004). To reiterate, in these studies, participants caught luminous balls of different diameter attached to a pendulum in a totally dark room. Two balls were of constant size (i.e., 5.5 and 7.5 cm), the third ball decreased in size during flight from 7.5 to 5.5 cm. In comparison to the constant balls, the deflating ball specifies a longer time-to-contact.

In the final grasp phase of catching action, participants closed their hand later when catching the deflated ball. But there is more to it. When we consider the hand aperture during the last 200 ms of the catch (figure 3), we see accurate adjustments are made. The hand aperture is neatly adjusted to the different ball diameter that is to the large and small ball, but most important, the hand aperture is adjusted to the changing size of the deflating ball during this 'ball' approach. Presumably, these adjustments in hand aperture reflect the very accurate and fast workings of the dorsal vision for action processes. In addition, after completing the experiment the participants were asked to make a visual judgement about the size of the balls without making an attempt to catch it. Table 1 reports the findings. Although they could discriminate the large and small constant sized balls, they were not aware of the deflating ball and guessed it to be either small or large. On the one hand, participants made a 'wrong' perceptual judgement; while on the other hand they were capable of accurately adjusting hand aperture to the changing ball size.

Table 1. Judgments of Individual Participants on the Type of Balls Used in the 'Deflating Ball' Study (Savelsbergh et al., 1991)

	Type of ball		
	Large (constant size)	Small (constant size)	Deflating (changing size)
Participant 1	Large	Small	Small
Participant 2	Large	Small	Small
Participant 3	Large	Small	Small
Participant 4	Large	Small	Large
Participant 5	Large	Small	Small

These discrepant findings for action and perception can be readily explained by the two-visual system model. The dorsal system operates relatively fast (online adjustments) without the actor being conscious of how they move or what information they use; movement control is implicit. In contrast, the explicit perceptual judgments depend on the workings of the ventral system.

Although the 'deflating ball' studies provided evidence for the involvement of tau, they also suggested the contribution of additional binocular sources of information (i.e., the effects of the deflating ball were larger under monocular as compared to binocular viewing, see footnote 1). We therefore conducted a series of experiments examining the role of binocular sources of information in the control of catching (Bennett, Van der Kamp, Savelsbergh and Davids, 1999, 2000; Van der Kamp, Bennett, Savelsbergh and Davids, 1999; Van der Kamp, Savelsbergh, and Bennett, 1998). In these studies we used the telestereoscope to manipulate binocular information (figure 3). Von Helmholtz (1896) developed the telestereoscope in order to be able to perceive depth at large distances.

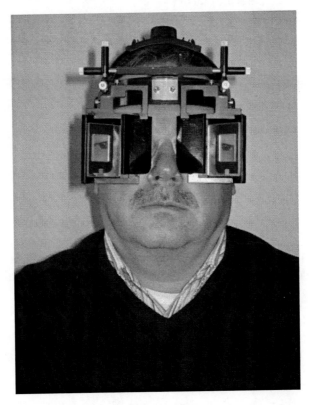

Figure 3. The telestereoscope, the mirrors increase the effective interocular separation between the left eye and the right eye.

The telestereoscope consists of two pairs of mirrors positioned parallel to each other. By displacing the line of sight of each eye laterally, the telestereoscope increases the interocular distance (IO) between the two eyes. An increased IO results in a larger angle subtended by the ball and the two eyes, resulting in a decrease of the perceived distance of an object. When wearing the telestereoscope, participants closed their hand much earlier than when they did under normal binocular viewing without the telestereoscope (Bennett et al., 1999, 2000; Van der Kamp et al., 1999). Most participants closed their hand so early that they failed to grasp the ball. This provided strong evidence for the contribution of binocular information when controlling the timing of a one-handed catch. Informal post-experimental interview, however, also showed that many of the participants saw the ball farther away under telestereoscopic viewing compared to normal viewing (Van der Kamp et al., 1998). Again, this discrepancy between action and perception is easily understood in terms of the two-visual system model. It is not unlikely that the dorsal system, which controls the catching action, uses binocular disparity information that is increased under telestereoscopic viewing. In contrast, the perceptual judgment of object distance, which engages the ventral system, might have been based on optical angle information, which is smaller under telestereoscopic viewing. We performed another experiment to substantiate these informal observations (unpublished data). The participants were presented with three different ball sizes under telestereoscopic and normal binocular viewing. They carried out two tasks: a perceptual judgement of ball size, in which the participants were asked to match hand aperture to the size of the ball, and a catching action. Table 2 reports the outcomes.

Table 2. Perceptual Judgment of Ball Size (mm) and Maximal Hand Aperture during Catching (mm) as a Function of Ball Size and Viewing

	Ball size					
	60 mm		80 mm		100 mm	
	Judgment	Catch	Judgment	Catch	Judgment	Catch
Viewing						
Normal	79	98	85	101	100	108
Telestereoscopic	75	99	78	101	82	108

The participants were able to perceptually discriminate the different sized balls, but consistently perceived the ball as smaller under telestereoscopic viewing. Also the maximal hand aperture during catching was adjusted to ball size, but contrary to the perceptual judgments, it was not affected by telestereoscopic viewing. Again, these differential effects for action and perception support Milner and Goodale's two visual-system model.

CONCLUSION: RAMIFICATIONS
FOR SPORTS PRACTICE AND RESEARCH

The relevance of the two-visual system model for sport is illustrated by an experiment by Johnston and co-workers (Johnston, Benton, and Nishida, 2003). They examined visual perception and action in a golfputting task. A successful putt requires the alignment of the direction of the swing through the ball with the distant target hole. Nonetheless, Johnston et al. found that even experienced golfers make systematic perceptual errors in perceiving the direction of the hole. They judged a pointer, which was placed at the ball's location, to point exactly at the hole when it was actually rotated slightly clockwise. This pointing illusion would result, if 'uncorrected', in the ball being aimed to the side of the hole. Yet, the perceptual illusion did not translate into bias when putting. There was no bias of the ball being placed to the side. Within the context of the two-visual system model this can be explained as follows: the dorsal system underlies the visual guidance of the golf swing and is not influenced by the ventral system that supports the perceptual judgment. In other words, because it uses metrically accurate information, the dorsal system is not deceived by the illusion. Interestingly, Johnston et al. (2003) reported another intriguing finding in that some, but not all golfers tended to have a big illusion at their unpractised side. Perhaps this illusionary bias in the unpractised side mirrors an increased reliance on the ventral vision for perception processes because of verbalisation (Van der Kamp et al., 2008).

When we accept the two-visual system model, then this implies that the use of visual information in sports situation consists out of a contribution of two separate visual processes. It is not the case, however, that interceptive actions are solely based upon either the dorsal or the ventral system. On the contrary, the two visual systems serve complementary functions.

Let us consider an important concept with respect to interceptive action in sport situation: anticipation.

The perception of what action to perform (i.e. what the situation affords for action) involves the contribution of the ventral vision for perception processes. The visual regulation of the action undertaken is supported by the dorsal vision for action processes. Based on this proposal, Van der Kamp and colleagues (2008) have argued that much of previous laboratory (e.g. studies using the occlusion paradigm, Abernethy and Russell, 1987) and field research (e.g., studies using liquid crystal goggles, Starkes, Edwards, Dissanayake, and Dunn, 1995) on visual anticipation predominantly required participants to make perceptual judgments about the landing location of the ball. In all likelihood, this only engaged the ventral system, whereas natural interceptive action would require the integrated contribution of the two systems. Actors not only have to perceptually judge, but must also move to intercept the ball. The use of visual information in (ball) sports involves as much action as perception. Hence, our understanding of the experts' superiority in visual anticipation is at best limited or at worst biased or even misleading (see for a detailed argument, Van der Kamp et al., 2008). Another example: coaches, on the one hand, view the game from an outsider's or third person's perspective. They see players and the ball relative to each other. The decisions made by coaches will therefore mainly rely on allocentric sources of information, which engages vision for perception processes in the ventral system. Players, on the other hand, not only view team mates, opponents and the ball relative to each other (as coaches do), but when acting to intercept the ball they must also take a first person's or egocentric perspective, which implies the involvement of the vision for action processes in the dorsal system. This raises many (as yet unanswered) questions; can coaches really provide instructions related to the first person's perspective? Are players constantly switching between ego- and allocentric viewpoints, or is this a parallel process? Can players have different degrees of expertise in tasks that rely more on the ventral system (e.g. tactical decision making) or on the dorsal system (e.g. receiving and passing balls in soccer), or does expertise always involve complementary engagement of both systems? We suspect that the experts' superiority can be found in the interaction between the vision for action and vision for perception processes.

A final issue concerns learning and practice. It has been suggested that implicit learning, in which awareness is drawn away from movement execution, 'uses' the dorsal vision for action processes (Van der Kamp, Oudejans and Savelsbergh, 2003; Abernethy, Maxwell, Masters, Van der Kamp, and Jackson, 2007). In contrast, explicit learning, which involves the accumulation of conscious knowledge about the rules and regularities of an action, is hypothesized to evoke ventral vision for perception processes. If these conjectures are true, then explicit learning would result in a greater reliance on allocentric sources of information. This may be unwise, if the goal of learning is expertise in movement control. In this case, learning may be better facilitated by letting pupils 'just do it' and minimizing the amount of explicit instructions. However, if the goal of learning is to improve perceptual judgment (or decision making), then explicit learning may indeed be more appropriate. In other words, coaches and teachers should be aware that different types of instruction or practice regimes may lead to the involvement of different types of processes. Again, if we accept that expertise involves the interaction between vision for action and vision for perception processes, then a trade-off between explicit and implicit learning should probably be pursuit. Nevertheless, whether there is trade-off and whether the trade-off changes with learning is still an open empirical question.

REFERENCES

Abernethy, B., Maxwell, J.P., Masters, R.S.W., Van der Kamp, J., and Jackson, R.C. (2007) Attention processes in skill learning and expert performance. In G. Tenenbaum and R.C. Eklund (Eds.), *Handbook of Sport Psychology*. (3rd Ed) (pp. 245-263). New York: Wiley.

Abernethy, B., and Russell, D.G. (1987). Expert-novice differences in an applied selective attention task. *Journal of Sport Psychology, 9*, 326-345.

Alderson, G.J.K., Sully, D.J., and Sully, H.G. (1974). An operational analysis of a one-handed catching task using high speed photography. *Journal of Motor Behavior, 6*, 217-226.

Bennett, S.J., van der Kamp, J., Savelsbergh, G.J.P., and Davids, K. (1999). Timing a one-handed catch: I. Effects of telestereoscopic viewing. *Experimental Brain Research, 129*(3), 362368.

Bennett, S.J., van der Kamp, J., Savelsbergh, G.J.P., and Davids, K. (2000). Discriminating the role of binocular information in the timing of a one-handed catch. The effects of telestereoscopic viewing and ball size. *Experimental Brain Research, 135*, 341-347.

Caljouw, S., van der Kamp, J., and Savelsbergh, G.J.P. (2004). The fallacy of the time-to-contact assumption in catching and hitting. In H. Hecht and G.J.P. Savelsbergh (Eds.), *Theories of time-to-contact* (pp. 443-474). Amsterdam: Elsevier Science Publishers.

Gibson, J.J. (1979). *The ecological approach to visual perception*. Boston, MA: Houghton Mifflin.

Goodale, M.A., and Milner, A.D. (1992). Separate pathways for perception and action. *Trends in Neurosciences, 15*, 20-25.

Goodale, M.A., and Milner, A.D. (2004). *Sight unseen*. Oxford, UK: Oxford University Press.

Goodale, M.A., and Westwood, D.A. (2004.). An evolving view of duplex vision: Separate but interacting cortical pathways for perception and action. *Current Opinion in Neurobiology, 14*, 203-211.

Johnston, A., Benton, C.P., and Nishida, S. (2003). Golfers may have to overcome a persistent visualspatial illusion. *Perception, 32*, 1151-1154.

Lee, D.N. (1976). A theory of visual control of braking based on information about time-to-collision. *Perception, 5*, 437-459.

Milner, A.D., and Goodale, M.A. (1995). *The visual brain in action*. Oxford: Oxford University Press.

Milner A.D., and Goodale, M.A. (2008). Two visual systems re-viewed. *Neuropsychologia, 46*, 774-785

Otto-de Haart, E.G., Carey, D.P., and Milner, A.B. (1998). More thoughts on perceiving and grasping the Müller-Lyer illusion. *Neuropsychologia, 37*, 1437-1444.

Rossetti, Y., and Pisella, L. (2002). Several 'vision for action' systems: A guide to dissociating and integrating dorsal and ventral functions. In W. Prinz and B. Hommel (Eds.), *Attention and Performance XIX: Common mechanisms in perception and action,* (pp. 62-119). Oxford: Oxford University Press.

Savelsbergh, G.J.P., Whiting, H.T.A., and Bootsma, R.J. (1991). 'Grasping' Tau. *Journal of Experimental Psychology: Human Perception and Performance, 19*, 315-322.

Savelsbergh, G.J.P., Whiting, H.T.A., Pijpers, J.R., and van Santvoord, A.M.M. (1993). The visual guidance of catching. *Experimental Brain Research, 93,* 146-156.

Starkes, J.L., Edwards, P., Dissanayake, P., and Dunn, T. (1995). A new technology and field test of advance cue usage in volleyball. *Research Quarterly for Exercise and Sport, 66,* 162-167.

Sharp, R.H., and Whiting, H.T.A. (1974). Exposure and occluded duration effects in a ball-catching skill. *Journal of Motor Behavior, 3,* 139-147.

Turvey, M.T. (1990). Coordination. *American Psychologist, 45,* 938-953.

Van Doorn, H., van der Kamp, J., and Savelsbergh, G.J.P. (2007). Grasping the Müller-Lyer illusion: The contributions of vision for perception in action. *Neuropsychologia, 45,* 1939-1947

Van der Kamp, J., Bennett, S. J., Savelsbergh, G.J.P. and Davids, K. (1999). Timing a one-handed catch: II. Adaptation to telestereoscopic viewing. *Experimental Brain Research, 129*(3), 369-377.

Van der Kamp, J., Oudejans, R., and Savelsbergh, G.J.P. (2003). The development and learning of the visual control of movement: An ecological perspective. *Infant Behavior and Development, 26,* 495-515

Van der Kamp, J., Rivas, F., van Doorn, H., and Savelsbergh, G.J.P. (2008). Ventral and dorsal system contributions to visual anticipation in fast ball sports. *International Journal of Sport Psychology, 39* (in press).

Van der Kamp, J., Savelsbergh, G.J.P., and Bennett, S.J. (1998). Do we report what we see and do?. In B. Bril, A. Ledebt, G. Dietrich and A. Roby-Brami (Eds.), *Advances in perception-action coupling* (pp. 45-49). Paris: Editions EDK.

Von Helmholtz, H. (1896). Handbuch der Physiologischen Optik (2nd edition). Hamburg-Leipzig: Verlag von Leopold Voss.

Whiting, H.T.A., and Sharp, R. H. (1974). Visual occlusion factors in a discrete ball catching task. *Journal of Motor Behavior, 6,* 11-16.

In: Perspectives on Cognition and Action in Sport
Editors: D. Araújo, H. Ripoll and M. Raab

ISBN: 978-1-60692-390-0
© 2009 Nova Science Publishers, Inc.

Chapter 3

INTERPERSONAL COORDINATION TENDENCIES, DECISION-MAKING AND INFORMATION GOVERNING DYNAMICS IN RUGBY UNION

Pedro Passos [1,2], *Duarte Araújo* [1], *Keith Davids* [4],
Luís Gouveia [3], *João Milho* [2] *and Sidónio Serpa* [1]

[1] Faculty of Human Kinetics, Technical University of Lisbon, Portugal
[2] Lusófona University of Humanities and Technologies, Portugal
[3] Faculty of Pharmacy, University of Lisbon, Portugal
[4] Queensland University of Technology, Australia

ABSTRACT

In this chapter, ideas from ecological psychology and nonlinear dynamics are integrated to characterize decision-making as an emergent property of self-organization processes in the interpersonal interactions that occur in sports teams. A conceptual model is proposed to capture constraints on dynamics of decisions and actions in dyadic systems, which has been empirically evaluated in simulations of interpersonal interactions in team sports. For this purpose, co-adaptive interpersonal dynamics in team sports such as rugby union have been studied to reveal control parameter and collective variable relations in attacker-defender dyads. Although interpersonal dynamics of attackers and defenders in 1 vs 1 situations showed characteristics of chaotic attractors, the informational constraints of rugby union typically bounded dyadic systems into low dimensional attractors. Our work suggests that the dynamics of attacker-defender dyads can be characterized as an evolving sequence since players' positioning and movements are connected in diverse ways over time.

INTRODUCTION

This chapter analyses how the emergence of cognition, decision-making and actions supports intentional behavior in complex, adaptive systems functioning in dynamic performance environments (see also van Orden, Holden and Turvey, 2003; Araújo, Davids and Hristovski, 2006, Araújo, Davids, Bennett, Button, and Chapman, 2004).

In team sports, a most important source of information constraining the perceptions and actions of individuals is provided by other interacting players (see Marsh, Richardson, Baron and Schmidt, 2006). Interpersonal coordination tendencies[1] between players (captured by an attacker's dribbling action to pass a defender or a tackle by a defender) can emerge in team sports regulated through inherently perceptual processes, founded on the interpersonal dynamics of players cooperating or competing in a dyad or sub-group (Araújo et al., 2004; McGarry et al., 2002; Schmidt, O'Brien and Sysko, 1999; for a theoretical overview see Warren, 2006). In this ecological dynamics perspective, the behavior of interacting players in team games is interpreted as an emergent process resulting from the spatio-temporal relations established during competitive performance sub-phases of team sports. In offensive and defensive sub-phases of team sports, specific modes of interpersonal coordination tendencies can emerge under the influence of specific contextual (e.g., number and characteristics of team supporters), personal (e.g., emotions, cognitions, technical and tactical skills) and task (e.g., rules of the game) constraints (Araújo et al., 2004) (see also Davids, Chapter 1).

In this chapter, we propose and evaluate a conceptual model of pattern, forming interpersonal dynamics in team sports to describe processes of emergent decision-making and actions of players. We exemplify these processes with data from studies of 1 vs 1 interpersonal dynamics in attacker-defender dyads in the team sport of rugby union. Our aim is to describe the theoretical basis of this ecological dynamics model, illustrating how it can be influential in understanding the emergent nature decision-making and action in team sports, captured as a multi-agent, complex adaptive system. The emergent interactions between components of complex adaptive systems under constraints have been studied for some time. For example, Kauffman's (1993) modeling of evolutionary processes from the perspective of spontaneous self-organizing system dynamics has provided valuable insights for understanding interpersonal dynamics in complex social systems. In such systems rich and varied patterns of behavior can emerge as individual agents (e.g., players) subtly co-adapt their actions to achieve specific system outcomes or goals (e.g., in rugby union to score a try or to tackle an opponent). It has been observed that interpersonal coordination tendencies can spontaneously emerge when the activity of previously uncorrelated agents, for example team players, suddenly becomes interrelated under constraints (Juarrero, 1999).

Modelled as dynamical systems, multi-agent systems like sports teams also reveal important characteristics like complexity and metastability due to the high level of system connectivity and the potential for interactions to emerge between system components (i.e., performers) over time (Araújo et al., 2006; Passos, Araújo, Davids, Gouveia, and Serpa, 2006), on how to formalize dynamics of attacker-defender dyads in rugby union). The behavior of sub-systems in team sports (e.g., attacker-defender dyads) is bounded by two categories of hierarchically-organised constraints that are influential in shaping the decisions and actions of players over time. These include *first order constraints* (Juarrero, 1999) defined as any environmental constraint that decreases randomness of agent behavior and

---

[1] In this chapter, the term *coordination tendencies* is adopted as terminology to describe interpersonal dynamics between attackers and defenders after Kelso's (1995) description of coordination dynamics of complex systems. He used the term to show that the parts of a complex system can operate independently much of the time, but come together to exhibit rich patterns of behavior when under constraints. As we report in this chapter, this is exactly what happens in attacker-defender dyads.

simultaneously increases the potential of system agents to explore new sources of information. In team sports, the actions and decisions of dyadic sub-systems are externally regulated by boundaries of the information fields geared by first order constraints, such as specific performance area dimensions, initial interpersonal distance between players, boundary markings (e.g., the side lines; the goal line), equipment, and rules of the game. In line with Juarrero's (1999) insights on the nature of *first order* constraints on complex systems, in the performance context of team sports they initially define the perceptual-motor space where a particular action takes places. Due to their specificity to particular team sport contexts, these constraints increase the probability that specific actions will emerge, such as an attacker selecting a particular running trajectory in order to make a score, instead of running randomly across a playing area, or a defender committing to an interceptive action at a specific location when defending a goal or target area.

Over time, team players' actions become so systematically related that their specific intentions make little sense if separated from each other's actions. In this way, the probability of an event depends on and is altered by localized emergent interactions between performers (Araújo et al., 2006; see Araújo et al., Chapter 10). This context dependency of initial sub-system interactions leads to the emergence of the other category of constraints: *Second order constraints* which reveal the self-organization tendencies of complex social systems' emergent behavior (Juarrero, 1999). Under *second order* constraints, random interactions between system components can suddenly change into more organized forms of interactions as one key system parameter (a control parameter, i.e., an important system parameter that moves the system to its different states) changes in value. When critical control parameter values are achieved, relevant variations of behavior in complex systems can emerge and at these values it is considered that the system enters a region of self-organizing criticality (SOC; Bak, 1996).

For example, in this region, initial states of system organization in team games can dissolve, with new rich states of organization emerging. For example, a commonly observed initial state of organization in team games (e.g., rugby union, basketball, ice hockey) occurs when a defender is positioned between an attacker and the goal/target. When this attacker-defender dyadic system enters the SOC region, a new state of order might emerge, exemplified when an attacker passes a defender and becomes the closest player to the goal or scoring target, or when a defender recovers the projectile from an attacker. In both these situations the dyadic system's initial state of organization dissolves to re-form into another state of coherence. In SOC regions interactions between players and nearest neighbours (i.e., team mates and opponents) become coupled, in a type of domino effect, capturing global system interactions and leading to a sudden reduction from multiple options to one. In this critical state a slight change in circumstances (e.g., an increase in the attacker's speed) characterizing near neighbour interactions will break the balance of equally poised options leading to a transition in system order. Criticality in the behavior of complex, adaptive social systems provides the platform for a functional mix of variability and stability to support decision-making in dynamic performance environments.

A MODEL OF EMERGENT DECISION MAKING IN RUGBY UNION DYADS

These key insights of Kauffman (1993) and Juarrero (1999) led us to conceptualise how behavior might emerge from two players mutually coupled in a team sport sub-system (e.g., attacker and defender dyad). In this chapter, we capture the ideas in the performance context of rugby union. We conceptually modeled a team sports dyad as a complex dynamical system characterised by chaotic behavior with three potential attractor states (i.e., preferred tendencies of coordination amongst attacker and defender) towards which system agents (i.e., the players) might converge over time. Notwithstanding different individual constraints (e.g., technical and tactical skills, cognitions, emotions), both players in a dyadic sub-system in rugby union are attracted to the space available in front of them. This is a key first order constraint in Juarreros'(1999) terminology. Despite the individual trajectories that each player might adopt, a 1 vs 1 sub-system will always converge toward one of the three attractor states. In the initial stable state of a dyadic sub-system in rugby union, the defender starts closest to the try line and if the attacker passes the defender, the current sub-system organization is broken. At this point, both players' decisions and actions are bounded by first order constraints (e.g., side and goal lines; distance to try). Throughout performance players' interactions attract each other (due to decreasing interpersonal distance) to a region of SOC where the decisions and actions of each player no longer remain independent. In this region, the emergence of second order constraints results in the potential for rich variations in dyadic system behavior as attackers attempt to break system symmetry and defenders attempt to stabilise it from these perturbations.

Despite enormous variability and complexity of behavior (i.e., expressed in players' individual trajectories) in dynamic performance environments, theory and experimental evidence points to the existence of pattern forming dynamics in interpersonal interactions (e.g., Schmidt et al., 1999). In line with ideas of Schmidt and colleagues we suggest that the significant variability of trajectories undertaken by dyadic system agents might be shaped by second order constraints (i.e., each player's decisions and actions depends on the immediate opponent's decisions and actions). The dynamics that emerge during this phase typically moves the attacker-defender sub-system towards one of three possible outcome attractor states: i) *physical contact takes place but the attacker does not pass the defender* and initial system organization is preserved. Nevertheless, the type of connection between the dyad components changes (from non-physical to physical) resulting in the system entering a new phase in the self-organizing, emergent process; ii) *physical contact takes place and the attacker passes the defender*. Due to physical contact, the type of connection between the dyad components changes but the main difference between this new emergent state and the previous one is that a change in within-system organization occurs, and the attacker is now the player closest the try line; or iii) *the attacker passes the defender without physical contact* and the connection between the two players remains non-physical. However, the dyad undergoes a phase transition since the within-system structural organization changes with the attacker now closer than the defender to the try line.

This conceptual modelling shows how cognition, decision-making and action in a dynamic performance context might emerge due to the self-organizing, pattern-forming dynamics (shared interactions) of coupled players in a dyad. Self-organization under constraints is characterized by system agents becoming systematically re-organized in qualitatively novel ways with changes in connection type or organization amongst them (Juarrero, 1999). However, a conceptual model needs to be grounded on empirical data. This perspective on the dynamics of interpersonal interactions led us to empirically investigate the conceptual model in a study of dyadic system behavior in 1 vs 1 sub-phases of the team sport of rugby union.

CAPTURING DYNAMIC DYADIC BEHAVIOR

The first step in model evaluation was identifying a collective variable or order parameter that accurately captures the rich behavioral dynamics of two interacting players in an attacker-defender dyad in rugby union. For this purpose we needed a variable indicating whether the dyadic system had maintained its initial structure (i.e., the defender remained the player closest to the try line), and also capable of showing whether initial system structure was broken by the attacker moving closer to the try line than the defender. The proposed collective variable was calculated based on the angle observed in the defender-attacker vector with an imaginary horizontal line parallel to the try line. This analysis method resulted in an angle close to +90 deg before the attacker reached the defender and close to -90 deg if the attacker successfully passed the defender, with a zero crossing point emerging exactly when the attacker reached the defender (see figure 1). As a result of player interactions, the defender-attacker vector varied over time, with values of this angular relationship providing a potential collective variable to capture system behavior (i.e., immediate information on the players' relative positioning) (Passos, Araújo, Davids, Diniz, Gouveia, Serpa and Milho, 2008a).

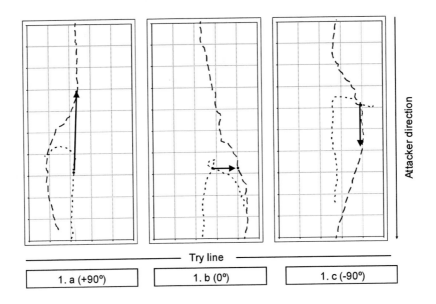

Figure 1. Defender-attacker vector. Attacker trajectory (dashed line), the defender trajectory (pointed line). Three different positions (figure 1.a, 1.b, 1.c, for angles of +90°, 0° and -90° respectively) of the collective variable which is represented by the continuous black arrow.

A *continuous* decline in angle values, up to approximately -90 degrees, reflected that the attacker passed the defender and moved towards the try line without further contact. This behavior was typically associated with try scoring outcomes. However, fluctuations in angle values over time could be observed when contact between the players occurred. This fluctuation stopped when a tackle occurred or alternatively when an attacker managed to avoid contact with a defender.

If angle values did not reach 0 (zero) degrees, this measure of system coordination tendencies signified that the attacker did not pass the defender, an outcome usually associated with an effective tackle by the defender. The collective variable can be examined on two levels: i) identification of different phases of a self-organized process; and ii), to describe three different outcome situations that could emerge from a dyad's interpersonal coordination tendencies in rugby union. In graphical format (figure 2) four phases of a self-organized process can be recognized: i) the approach phase; ii) the critical fluctuation phase; iii) a phase transition; and iv) an emergent phase.

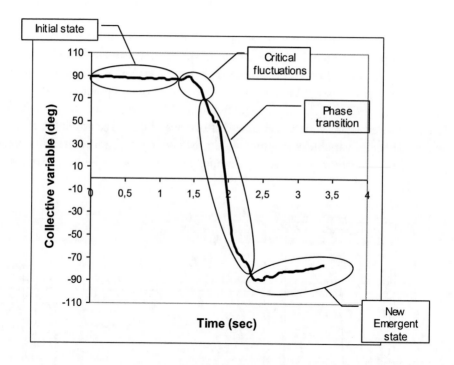

Figure 2. Four phases of a self-organized process. Angle of defender-attacker vector values in degrees (black line). a) Approach phase; b) Critical fluctuations phase; c) Phase transition phase; d) Emergent phase.

Our observations showed that the approach phase was characterized by preservation of defender-attacker horizontal angle values, since attacking players kept their running lines straight. In the critical fluctuations phase, there was evidence that a decrease in interpersonal distance led to some changes in running line, with the attacker aiming to avoid contact with the defender and using technical skills to explore the sub-system's stability. This is an emergent process constrained by the information field created by a decrease in interpersonal distance between the attacker and defender (for further information see Araújo et al., Chapter 10, concerning emergent tactical solutions in attacker-defender interactions).

The non-linear interactions that occurred in the attacker-defender system created fields of information that moved the dyadic system to a basin of attraction (i.e., players trajectories created a region on the field that attracted the dyadic system and where an abrupt change in system structural organization took place) with three possible attractor states (figure 3). The attractor states in this region of SOC were demonstrated behaviourally by: i) a clean try where contact between an attacker and a defender did not occur; ii) a tackle situation where the attacker passed the defender; and iii), an effective tackle by the defender to stop the attacker. By plotting the evolution of the collective variable patterns from the attacker-defender interactions we could observe what happened at each moment in time, as well as characterizing the type of phase transition that occurred (i.e., changes in system organization or changes in the dyadic components' connection).

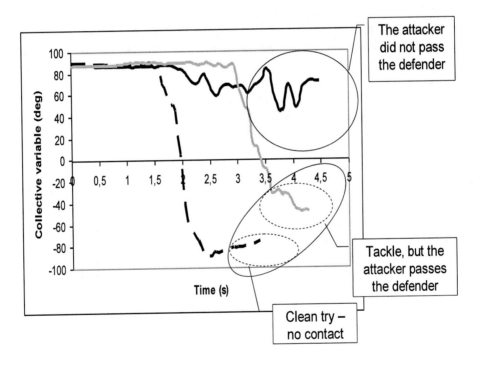

Figure 3. Three different performance situations in 1 vs 1 dyads. Angle of defender-attacker vector values with an imaginary line parallel to try line in degrees. Clean try situation (black dashed line); Tackle, but the attacker passes the defender (gray line); Effective tackle (black line).

In a clean try situation, the potential inside the basin of attraction was not powerful enough to maintain system stability (i.e., the defender remaining the closest player to the try line) and the attacker-defender dyadic system flowed to the edge of the basin of attraction.

This observation signified that, after the attacker passed the defender, values of interpersonal distance tended to increase. In this event the probability of the defender tackling the attacker decreased and the system neared desegregation as the attacker reached the try line. That particular tendency seemed to be predicated on the velocity of each player inside the basin of attraction, which altered the players' relative positioning. On the other hand, if system transition was characterized by a change in connection among players (i.e., from non-physical to physical in the attacker-defender interactions), the potential (i.e., the strength of the coupling) created by agents of the dyadic system would be strong enough to maintain the system inside the basin of attraction. However, for both situations, (i.e., try or tackle) the fluctuations that occurred in the values of the collective variable due to the emergence of second order constraints (i.e., players' decisions and actions dependency), led the system to the region of self-organizing criticality, poising it for a transition.

Rate of Change in Players' Positioning

To analyze the rate of change of the relative positioning between an attacker and defender in a dyadic system, we plotted the first derivative of the collective variable over time (figure 4). When an attacker achieved higher values of relative velocity of movement than a defender, the first derivative values increased with distance to the minimum. On the other hand, when a defender's relative velocity was higher than an attacker's, the first derivative values tended towards the minimum. When there were no differences between the players' relative positions, the first derivative values tended towards zero.

An increase in the magnitude of first derivative fluctuations suggested that the system was approaching a region of SOC, which signified that the system was poised for a transition. An abrupt decline in first derivative values indicated that the players were changing their relative positions very quickly, which was consistent with clean try situations. Every time first derivative values approached 0 deg/s, it signalled that the players maintained their relative positions. This situation is usually consistent with successful tackles where defenders are able to counterbalance the attacker's decisions and actions and preserve system stability. The lowest value achieved is the inflection point, signifying the moment when an attacker passed a defender. Approximate to 0 deg/s the defender maintained system stability by successfully counterbalancing the attackers' decision and actions, an example of co-adaptive moves in the interpersonal dynamics of agents coupled in a complex, adaptive system (Kauffman, 1993). Alternatively, when values were far from 0 deg/s, players had altered their relative positions. In these situations the attacker had the ability to increase locomotion velocity to create the fluctuations needed to de-stabilize the system, allowing the defender to be passed.

These observations were supported by additional non-linear time series analyses. As suggested by (Stergiou et al., 2004) we used non-linear analysis methods, such as measuring system state space, to analyze differences in the structural variability of each specific dyadic interpersonal interaction. Juarrero (1999, p. 152) defined state space as a representation of a system's current potential. Each possible state of the system is represented as an intersection of coordinates, a point or region in two, three or, more likely, multidimensional space. Over time, the string of new points can be traced by a smooth line displaying the trajectory of the dyadic system in state space.

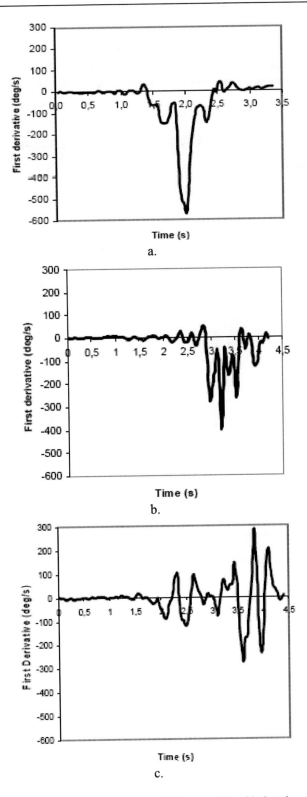

Figure 4. First derivative of the collective variable. a) clean try; b) tackle but the attacker passed the defender; c) effective tackle.

Figure 5 shows three different coordination structures in state space: i) a try situation (figure 5, black dashed line); ii) when a tackle occurred and the attacker passed the defender (figure 5, continuous grey line); and iii) when the attacker did not pass the defender because an effective tackle took place (see figure 5, continuous black line).

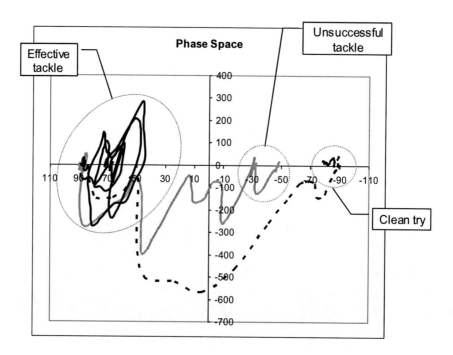

Figure 5. Phase Space Plot of Collective Variable. x-axis represents the defender-attacker vector values (i.e., collective variable); y-axis represents the first derivative. Black line represents an effective tackle; grey line represents a tackle where the attacker passes the defender; the black dashed line represents a clean try when no contact occurred.

In these exemplar trials, it is apparent that in a dyadic system, slight differences in initial conditions (as portrayed in figure 3) led to major differences in final system state. These data are harmonious with Kauffman's (1993) observations that complex systems often display chaotic behavior in the form of high sensitivity to initial conditions. Observing signs of chaotic behavior means that the dyadic system displayed nonlinear characteristics, where micro variations in the initial state of the system (e.g., players' relative position) and the consequent interdependence of decisions and actions of both agents involved in the dyad, led to an unpredictable final state (i.e., outcome).

A second observation is that despite attacker-defender sub-systems in rugby union existing in a high dimensional state space, where they can be influenced by a huge number of variables (i.e., technical, physical and physiological characteristics of dyad members; emotions and cognitions; eye movements, game states; weather conditions; playing surface), typically system behavior always flowed to a low dimensional attractor captured by the three coordination tendencies presented. That is the system was boxed into a small region of state space by the first and second order constraints impinging on it during performance.

In our analysis of the non-linear time series, the approximate entropy data (a measure of complexity of a system; Pincus, 1991) for the three coordination tendencies, revealed that system complexity increased with intensity of physical contact among the interacting players (i.e., in a tackle where the attacker is forced backwards by a defender, physical contact is usually more intense than in a tackle where the attacker passed the defender). In this event richness of dyadic system behaviour increased with intensity of physical contact between an attacker and defender.

Nested Control Parameters: The Information Governing Dynamics

Based on their research, Araújo and colleagues have previously suggested interpersonal distance as a candidate control parameter for moving attacker-defender dyads in 1 vs 1 sub-phases of basketball through different states organisation (Araújo et al., 2002, 2004). However more recent work on rugby union (e.g., Passos, Araújo, Davids, Gouveia, Serpa, and Milho, 2008b) revealed that interpersonal distance as a potential control parameter did not contain sufficient information to move a dyadic interpersonal system to all its states. In other words, solely relying on interpersonal distance it was not possible to explain why collective variable values can suddenly change from +90° to -90° as occurred in the clean try situations, or why the collective variable values remained close to +90° in the effective tackle situation. Passos et al. (2008a) suggested the influence on interpersonal dynamics of another potential control parameter: the "relative velocity" between attacker and defender in a dyad. Relative velocity was defined as the difference between the running line velocity of an attacker and defender in a dyad. Under the specific task constraints of rugby union, it was observed how attackers used velocity to create fluctuations leading to phase transitions (e.g., when an attacker passed the defender) in attempts to de-stabilize dyadic systems. These data implied that the control parameter influencing system structural organization in sub-phases (e.g., 1 vs 1) of different team sports might alter due to different task constraints.

The results suggested that interpersonal distance can operate as an initial potential control parameter that drives a dyadic attacker-defender system to a region of SOC where system phase transitions, such as a clean try situation, might occur (Passos et al., 2008b). However, it was observed that relative velocity gained greater influence on dyadic behavior as values of interpersonal distance decreased. It is within this region of SOC (i.e., within 4m of interpersonal distance) that changes in the value of the relative velocity between an attacker and defender appeared to exert an informational, second order constraint on dyadic system coordination tendencies. Within this region affordances for actions become bounded and the dyadic system evolved to a single solution that was expressed in one of the three possible outcome attractor states of the system. It was observed that, when relative velocity values increased, the magnitude of the attacker's velocity was higher than that of the defender. In contrast, when the rate of increase of the defender's velocity was greater than that of the attacker, relative velocity values decreased. These results suggested that, in both tackle situations the defender was able to counterbalance the attackers' actions, and prevented the attacker from de-stabilizing the dyadic system.

These findings supported the existence of critical periods in the social interactions of dyadic complex systems. Critical periods have been identified as brief windows of time and space during which a complex system's organisation is most open to modification from external and internal influences (Anderson, 2002). Our results suggested that in the dynamic social interactions of attacker-defender dyads, a critical period disturbing the stability of the dyadic system over short timescales (i.e., seconds or fractions of a second during performance) emerged at around 4 m of interpersonal distance during which changes in relative velocity had greatest effects on pattern forming dynamics.

Indeed, our findings pointed to the existence of two preferred zones (attractors) in the region of SOC to which the dyadic system evolved (see figure 6). These attractors captured how the two candidate control parameters functioned in a nested manner to provide informational constraints on system dynamics. In this critical region, relative velocity values embedded within a particular interpersonal distance value were most capable of influencing dyadic system organisation.

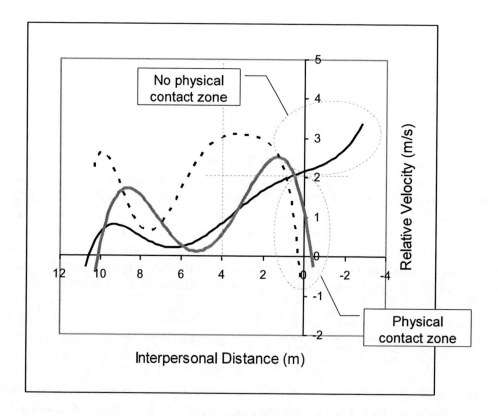

Figure 6. Two preferred zones to where the dyadic system evolves. Clean try situation (black line); Tackle but the attacker passed the defender (grey line); Effective tackle (black dashed line).

In sum, due to individual movement trajectories of both players in an attacker-defender dyad, the specific values achieved by the collective variable accurately captured the behavioral dynamics of the dyadic system revealing the specific coordination tendencies within the basin of attraction. However, due to slight differences in initial conditions, the final state achieved by the system was quite different, again signalling how collective performance outcomes (decisions and actions of players) are challenging to prescribe in advance during coaching sessions. These findings are consistent with our suggestion that the decisions and actions of sub-systems in large organizations could be modelled as a chaotic attractor, suggesting that organizational decision-making and planning in multi-agent systems such as team sports should be predictive and adaptive in nature and not static.

Training system design to improve decision-making in multi-agents interpersonal dynamics should be predicated on a good understanding of the unique first- and second-order constraints that shape coordination tendencies of the system in particular performance environments. In fact, these constraints could outline the basis of 'realism' in designing specific decision-making training simulations. Team sport coaches should avoid attempting to 'control the uncontrollable' by trying to eradicate variability in decision-making and actions of individual players (see also Passos, Araújo, Davids and Shuttleworth, 2008). Rather collective team performance is more likely to be enhanced by developing adaptive behaviors of performers by specifying the amount of variability included in training environments of players (see also, Chapter 10 to understand how variability enhances sport performance). Ideally, this pedagogical strategy would result in 'noisy' practices that include just the right amount of variability to move the players to the region of self-organising criticality where rich patterns of behaviour might emerge during practice. This approach would provide a platform for players to learn how to make decisions and perform actions that stabilise or de-stabilise sub-system interactions (e.g., 1vs1; 2vs2; 3vs3) so that they can work in a collective manner or independently to achieve task goals.

CONCLUSION

In this chapter, we presented data demonstrating that changes in the interpersonal interactions between an attacker and defender in the team sport of rugby union can be explained by the coupling of two nested potential control parameters: interpersonal distance and relative velocity. It was observed how the former control parameter shaped the coordination tendencies of dyadic system behavior over time, with a critical period in the pattern forming dynamics of attacker-defender interactions emerging within 4 m of interpersonal distance. From an applied perspective the data highlighted the need to improve attackers' decision-making by helping them to create a velocity differential that allows them to succeed in de-stabilising an 'unwanted' dyad with a marking defender (i.e., one player increased velocity while the other maintained or decreased running line velocity). Conversely, defenders can be helped to use relative velocity to counter an attacker's perturbing movements and maintain system stability. Figure 7 summarizes the main conclusions of this chapter regarding the predictive utility of interpersonal distance and relative velocity as potential control parameters in attacker-defender dyadic systems in rugby union.

Future research is needed on different levels such as extending this method to situations that involve more agents in sub-system interactions of team sports (e.g., sub-phases of 2 vs 1; 3 vs 2; 4 vs 3). This aim involves examining a general question: how the information shared in a competitive setting by the players of a micro unit allows them to decide and act successfully. A potentially useful methodology to address this issue has been used in previous work on biological systems by Couzin, Krause, Franks, and Levin (2005). Their work with schools of fish accounted for the ability of grouping organisms to modify their motion on the basis of local interactions (social interactions). Within such complex biological systems, a proportion of individuals provide information to others to maintain a preferred direction towards a goal direct behavior. Collective decisions in team sports demand a share of the information available in the performance context, and social interactions amongst team members may propagate that information.

These investigations are required because, Kauffman (1993) pointed out that, as the number of complex system degrees of freedom increases, the potential for interaction increases and the likelihood of phase transitions increases. Regardless of complex system organizational context, one common feature needs to be addressed: the discovery of relevant collective variables.

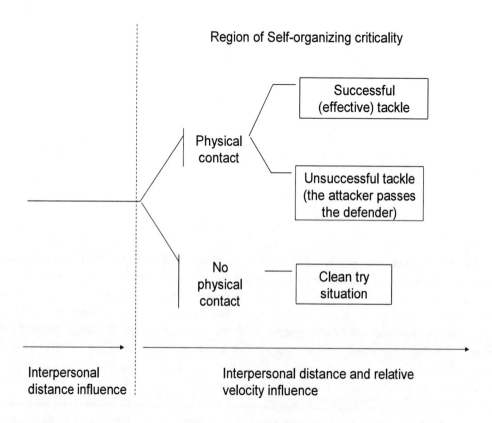

Figure 7. Schema showing the Interpersonal distance and relative velocity influence as control parameters.

Finally, the model and data presented in this chapter highlighted the value of interpreting the subtle variability in the interpersonal dynamics of players' behaviors to understand decision-making processes in organizations as complex systems. The chaotic features of dyadic system behavior in our conceptual model, and the nested control parameters that moved the system to regions of self-organized criticality are underlying signatures of complexity in team sports.

REFERENCES

Anderson, D.I. (2002). Do critical periods determine when to initiate sport skill learning? In F.L. Smoll and R.E. Smith (Eds.), *Children and Youth in Sports: A Biopsychosocial Perspective (2nd Ed., pp. 105-148)*. Indianapolis: Brown and Benchmark.

Araújo, D., Davids, K., Sainhas, J., and Fernandes, O. (2002). Emergent decision-making in sport: a constraints-led approach. In L. Toussaint and P. Boulinguez (Ed.), *International Congress "Movement, Attention and Perception"* (p. 77). Poitiers, France: Université de Poitiers.

Araújo, D., Davids, K., Bennett, S., Button, C., and Chapman, G. (2004). Emergence of Sport Skills under Constraints. In A. M. Williams and N.J. Hodges (Ed.), *Skill Acquisition in Sport: Research, Theory and Practice* (pp. 409-433). London: Routledge, Taylor and Francis.

Araújo, D., Davids, K., and Hristovski, R. (2006). The ecological dynamics of decision making in sport. *Psychology of Sport and Exercise, 7*, 653–676.

Bak, P. (1996). *How Nature Works. The science of self-organized criticality*. Copernicus. Springer-Verlag. NY.

Couzin, I., Krause, J., Franks, N., and Levin, S. (2005). Effective leadership and decision-making in animal groups on the move. *Nature, 433*, 513-516.

Juarrero, A. (1999). *Dynamics in Action. Intentional Behavior as a Complex System*. Massachusetts: MIT Press.

Kauffman, S. (1993). *The Origins of Order. Self-organization and selection in evolution*. NY: Oxford University Press.

Kelso, J.A.S. (1995). *Dynamic patterns: The self-organization of brain and behaviour*. Cambridge, MA: MIT Press.

Marsh, K.L., Richardson, M.J., Baron, R.M., and Schmidt, R.C. (2006). Contrasting approaches to perceiving and acting with others. *Ecological Psychology, 18*, 1-38.

McGarry, T., Anderson, D., Wallace, S., Hughes, M., and Franks, I. (2002). Sport competition as a dynamical self-organizing system. *Journal of Sports Sciences, 20*, 771-781.

Passos, P., Araújo, D., Davids, K., Gouveia, L. and Serpa, S. (2006). Interpersonal Dynamics in Sport: The Role of Artificial Neural Networks and Three-dimensional Analysis. *Behavior and Research Methods. 38*, 683–691.

Passos, P., Araújo, D., Davids, K., Diniz, A., Gouveia, L., Serpa, S., and Milho, J.(2008a). Decision Making in Team Sports: Data, model and applied perspective. *116th Annual Convention of American Psychological Association*. 14-17 August 2008, Boston, MA.

Passos, P., Araújo, D., Davids, K., Gouveia, L., Serpa, S., and Milho, J. (2008b). Information governing dynamics of attacker-defender interactions in youth level rugby union. *Journal of Sports Sciences. 26*, 1421-1429.

Passos, P., Araújo, D., Davids, K., and Shuttleworth, R. (2008). Manipulating Constraints to Train Decision Making in Rugby Union. *International Journal of Sports Sciences and Coaching. 3*, 125-140.

Pincus, S. (1991). Approximate Entropy as a measure of system complexity. *Proceedings of the National Academy of Science USA. 88*, 2297-2301.

Schmidt, R.C., O'Brien, B. and Sysko, R. (1999). Self-organization of between-persons cooperative tasks and possible applications to sport. *International Journal of Sport Psychology, 30,* 558-579.

Stergiou, N., Buzzi, U, Kurz, M. and Heidel, J. (2004). Nonlinear Tools in Human Movement. In N. Stergiou (Ed.), *Innovative Analyses of Human Movement* (pp. 63-87). Champaign, IL: Human Kinetics

Van Orden, G., Holden, J.G. and Turvey, M. (2003). *Self-Organization of Cognitive Performance. Journal of Experimental Psychology: General, 132,* 331-350.

Warren, W. (2006). The Dynamics of Perception and Action. *Psychological Review, 113,* 358-389.

In: Perspectives on Cognition and Action in Sport
Editors: D. Araújo, H. Ripoll and M. Raab

ISBN: 978-1-60692-390-0
© 2009 Nova Science Publishers, Inc.

Chapter 4

Information for Regulating Action in Sport: Metastability and Emergence of Tactical Solutions under Ecological Constraints

Robert Hristovski[1], Keith Davids[2] and Duarte Araújo[3]

[1] Faculty of Physical Education,
University of Ss. Cyril and Methodius, Republic of Macedonia
[2] Queensland University of Technology, Australia
[3] Faculty of Human Kinetics, Technical University of Lisbon, Portugal

Abstract

The aims of this chapter are twofold. First, we show how experiments related to nonlinear dynamical systems theory can bring about insights on the interconnectedness of different information sources for action. These include the amount of information as emphasized in conventional models of cognition and action in sport and the nature of perceptual information typically emphasized in the ecological approach. The second aim was to show how, through examining the interconnectedness of these information sources, one can study the emergence of novel tactical solutions in sport; and design experiments where tactical/decisional creativity can be observed. Within this approach it is proposed that perceptual and affective information can be manipulated during practice so that the athlete's cognitive and action systems can be transposed to a meta-stable dynamical performance region where the creation of novel action information may reside.

INTRODUCTION

Some of the basic issues in research on cognition and action in sport are related to problems on the nature and use of information by athletes. Key questions concern the meaningful information that athletes perceive to organize their solutions to a tactical problem or the relation between the *amount* of information present in the performance environment and the decision-making behavior of athletes. In some investigations it has been proposed that environmental information is available in advance to performers. In many experiments information has usually been held constant over trials so that the athletes have to merely make a decision and respond accordingly. For example, in traditional cognitive science approaches to the study of reaction time (RT) (e.g., Schmidt and Wrisberg, 2004) the main emphasis has been on the relation between the *amount* of unpredictability (i.e., information content) of environmental events and RT measures of athletes treated as a decision-making performance variable. From this perspective a challenging question has been: How is this information created in sport contexts? A particular concern has been that the amount of information designed into these experiments had to be introduced in an *ad hoc* manner by experimenters, and was not a constituent derived from explanatory models of cognition and action in sport.

In contrast to this approach, some empirical effort has been directed towards unraveling understanding of the *nature* of the information used to support actions. For example, in the ecological approach it is assumed that a rich informative structure in the optical array already exists waiting to be picked up by the athlete's perception systems while moving within the performance environment (e.g., Davids, Savelsbergh, Bennett and Van der Kamp, 2002). The skill of picking up the relevant informational variables sometimes needs a prolonged period of time to educate the attention of learners (Jacobs and Michaels, 2002). Hence, within the ecological approach to cognition and action, it is proposed that the exploratory movements of athletes can maintain or change the nature and amount of meaningful information sources needed for successful decision making and action by their movements. Meaningful informational variables are obtained by perceiving affordances or invitations for action. These variables are meaningful to athletes by supplying them with information from which an action is afforded for a particular behavioral goal. In this respect, interesting research relates to the early pick-up of information from the preparatory actions of opponents by performers (e.g., Abernethy, 1993; Ward, Williams, and Bennett, 2002). These studies showed how preparatory movement kinematics from the movements of an opponent may contain information invariants, which can be used for action anticipation. Thus, perceptual information for action is not internalized as in the conventional information-processing approach but is distributed inside and outside the athlete and bridges the gap between the athlete and the properties of the environment. In this sense a further basic question arises: How can these separate parameters of cognition and action in sport (i.e., the *nature* and *amount* of information available in a performance context) be unified in a theoretical framework that will enable them to be studied as interdependent qualities?

One way to achieve this aim is by extending principles and concepts of nonlinear dynamical systems theory to the study of information for action in sport. In the last two decades insights from the nonlinear dynamical systems theory have provided an alternative theoretical rationale for explaining how processes of perception, cognition, decision making and action underpin intentional behaviors in complex, self organizing neurobiological systems functioning in dynamic environments (e.g., van Orden, Holden, and Turvey, 2003; Turvey and Shaw, 1995, 1999). Within this theory, or more precisely its *synergetics* variant (see Haken, 1983), there are two types of parameters that can constrain action. The first type involves non-specific parameters whose change constrains the stability of ongoing actions. Candidate variables for modifying ongoing actions include perceptions, especially affordances (i.e. invitations for actions), emotions, intentional aims not directly focused on the specific action structure itself, ideas and morphological and physiological properties of the body. In other words non-specific parameters are those which do not specifically constitute the mode of action itself, but which form an influential background performance context for action. The second type includes order parameters (i.e., collective variables), which do define the mode of action. Inherent degeneracy of neurobiological systems and the nonlinear interactions between system components enable the existence of more than one stable solution to a particular task, termed *multistability* (see Kelso, 1995; Edelman and Gally, 2001; Araújo, Davids and Hristovski, 2006). Multistable systems can also exhibit a property known as *meta-stability*. Meta-stability in movement systems always arises when modes of action are weakly stable or weakly unstable (i.e., close to an instability point) and manifests itself in the switching between two or more modes of action (see Fingelkurts and Fingelkurts, 2004; Kelso, 2002). This framework proposes that the most relevant information for producing tactical solutions and controlling action in dynamic environments is emergent during performer-environment interactions (see Araújo et al., 2006; van Orden et al., 2003; Passos, Araújo, Davids, Gouveia, Milho, and Serpa, Chapter 3). From this viewpoint, cognitive and action systems of athletes exhibit purposive behavior based on the spontaneous patterns of interactions between system components.

This rationale for explaining cognition, perception and action proposes that order parameters guide the emergent collective cooperative behavior of the athlete's system components (degrees of freedom) and serve two roles. First, order parameters inform the relevant components of the athlete's movement system (e.g., an attacker in the martial arts) how to behave cooperatively. Second, they inform other perceivers (e.g., the defender in a martial arts dyad) about the mode of action of an attacker. Through skilled observation of the collective behavior of an opponent's movement system, an individual can pick up meaningful information, which can be used to regulate ongoing action. Order parameters of an opponent's action can act as relevant essential information that athletes use for anticipating opponents' actions. It is no coincidence that order parameters or collective variables have been termed an *"informator"* (Haken, 1999). In previous work, by adopting concepts from the ecological approach to cognition and action we have attempted to connect these two informational variables. We identified affordances, which, once picked up, could inform athletes about alternatives for action. Other work has investigated order parameters of action modes that express information about the macroscopic behavior of an athlete. In this chapter we describe experimental findings that exemplify how the change and emergence of novel information in tactical solutions are dependent on changing ecological constraints of practice (non-specific parameters of dynamics), specifically perceptual and emotional constraints on individual athletes that influence the emergent dynamics of their actions (see Hristovski, Davids, and Araújo, 2006a; Hristovski, Davids, and Araújo, 2006b; Hristovski, Davids, Araújo, and Button 2006; Hristovski, Davids, and Araújo, 2007; Chow, Davids, Button, Rein, Hristovski, and Koh, M., 2009).

EMERGENCE OF NOVEL TACTICAL INFORMATION
IN A HEAVY – BAG PUNCHING TRAINING TASK

One of the most fundamental functions of complex cognitive systems in sport is to coordinate responses such as defensive or offensive behavior with environmental events (see also Vereijken, Chapter 6). Recent work (e.g., Hristovski, Davids, and Araújo, 2006a) has provided insights into perception-action dynamics of cognitive and action systems in athletes characterized as dynamic pattern-forming entities. For example, in one study, 8 novice boxers, unfamiliar with a heavy-bag punching task, were asked to strike a heavy bag 60 times from various distances scaled to their arm lengths. The angle of fist-target collision was treated as an order parameter (i.e. as an informator about the boxer – target coordination state in Haken's sense). The manipulated control parameter was the boxers' perception of scaled distance to the target. It was observed that the perception - action system of boxers was highly sensitive to small changes of scaled distance from the heavy-bag. These small perceptual alterations induced continuous and abrupt changes (i.e. bifurcations)[1] in the set of possible actions as the control parameter was continuously varied (see figure 1).

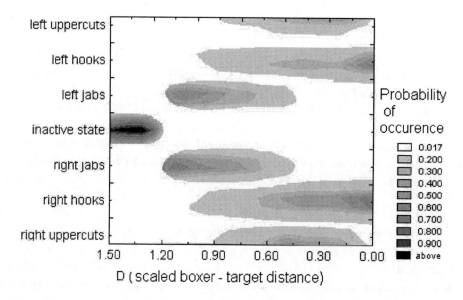

Figure 1. Continuous and abrupt changes (bifurcations) of the occurrence probability of action modes in boxers as a function of the scaled boxer - target distance D (with kind permission from the journal *Nonlinear Dynamics, Psychology and Life Sciences*).

Also, the whole dynamical landscape of actions changed with small variations in the perceptual control parameter, which led to continuous and abrupt changes of action unpredictability and diversity as captured by entropy (H) values depicted on figure 3. For example, the emergence of a novel action influenced future system behavior by changing the probability of occurrence of the whole set of remaining actions. The continuous switching

---

[1] Abrupt changes of the behavior of the system are called bifurcations (i.e. branchings), since typically they signify change of the number of possible action modes of the system.

between modes of action suggests that under the constraints of the training task, the dynamical landscape of the boxers was highly meta-stable. Small variations in the perceptual control parameter led to emergence of new affordances (i.e. invitations for action) manifested in new action modes and sharp increases in entropy measures, that is, sharp increases in the information content of the athletes' actions. This finding demonstrated the inextricable link between an individual's perceptual and action systems. The amount of information present in an athlete's actions (i.e., the number of action choices and associated probabilities) was dynamically created by changes in the perceptual systems responsible for detecting the 'strike-ability' affordance. The maximum of the entropy value H (i.e. amount of the information content of striking actions) around the scaled distance D = 0.6 signified a minimal coupling, that is, tendency towards decoupling, between each pair of striking actions and a transition from a predominant use of straight arm jabs to exclusively 'arced' actions (i.e., hooks and uppercuts). This context dependent creation and change of the information content of actions is depicted on figure 3.

Results showed that boxers were able to discover new modes of tactical solutions for the task goal through intentional changes of the scaled distance parameter D. These decisions led to increased exploratory activity and changes in the perceptual context, with boxers consequently altering, sometimes drastically, the informational content of their actions.

This characteristic was also apparent when we analyzed the dynamics of sequential actions (Hristovski, Davids, and Araújo, 2006b). The coupling between the left and right arm modes of action, as assessed by the conditional probabilities,[2] was also highly sensitive to small perceived changes in the scaled boxer - target distance. Analogously, this effect produced continuous and abrupt changes in the amount of conditional informational content of temporally juxtaposed actions.

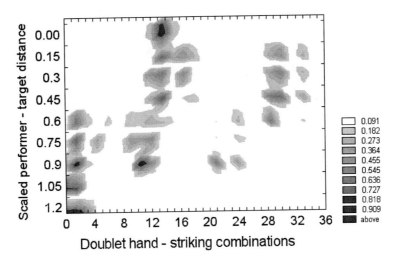

Figure 2. The conditional probability landscape of the hand-striking combinations as a function of the scaled boxer - target distance D. (with kind permission from the journal *Nonlinear Dynamics, Psychology and Life Sciences*)

---

[2] Conditional probabilities tell the probabilities of the rest of the actions given one already performed. For example: If a left jab is already performed what are the probabilities of the other actions? These probabilities can be considered as coupling strength. Larger conditional probability means larger coupling strength and vice versa.

In figure 2 one can observe the existence of islands of highly coupled and less coupled actions immersed in a sea of undiscovered sequential combinations spreading between them. This graphic illustrates how the evolutionary stabilized action combinations (such as left-right hand strikes) dominated over the other combinations, reducing the degree of flexibility in sequential behavior, and the amount of information content, in novice boxers. It is apparent how perceptual information induces metastability as a generic dynamical mechanism for producing diversity of actions and the discovery of new action modes and the extinction of others, which leads to changes in the nature and the amount of action information content in the practice task.

On the level of inter-personal coupling, the intra-personal action information content H (see figure 3) has another role (Hristovski, Davids, Araújo, and Button 2006). In figure 3 it can be seen that the space (i.e., scaled boxer-boxer distance) is split into two metastable action regimes (the minimal values of the H curve). These areas are metastable, because for the time scale of one observation (1 round for example) the inter-personal dynamics will switch many times between those regimes.

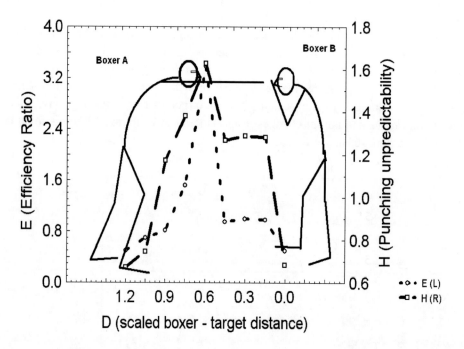

Figure 3. Boxer – boxer coordination (i.e. sparring) spontaneously emerges. The amount of punching information content *(H)* (dashed line) and efficiency ratio *(E)* (dotted line) minima, located around *D* =1.2 and *D* = 0 are the attractive states, and their maxima located around *D* = 0.6 are the unstable states of the coordination. The global minimum is located around *D* =1.2 and represents the optimal strategic position area in which boxers continually spend the most of time since it minimizes the unpredictability, efficiency ratio and consequently the global efficiency of the opponents punching actions (with kind permission from the Journal of Sport Science and Medicine).

The first regime (the location of boxer A) closely matches the distance of the arm length away from the target (i.e., boxer B) and the other is the clenched position where opponent boxers lean against one another, for example when boxer A moves to the position D = 0). In both cases the unpredictability of actions (the H function) is at a minimum because of the paucity of actions possible from those distances, as demonstrated in the experiment. The maximum of the information content (maximum unpredictability peak located at the scaled boxer - target distance = 0.6) is an unstable region for inter-personal dynamics since it is a location in which boxers spend very short periods of time. It is a region of maximal uncertainty in anticipating the type of action that might be used by an opponent (all actions are almost equally possible). In this way, the behavior of boxers is dynamically guided by the information landscape depicted on figure 3. In other words the amount of information (the H function) present has a dynamical role in constraining action. Whereas on the level of intra-personal dynamics scaled distance D has a role as a perceptual control parameter (figures 1 and 3), on the level of inter-personal dynamics, due to the nature of the information landscape H, scaled distance D has a role as an order parameter with two metastable states (the minima of H function) and one unstable (the maximum of H function) located at D = 0.6. In other words, interpersonal dynamics in boxing is spontaneously formed in a self-organizing fashion due to the influence of the informational dynamical landscape. This is an elegant example of the interchanging roles that parameters of the system can have: a non-specific perceptual parameter (i.e. scaled distance) can change its nature and become an order parameter (i.e. action informator) and vice versa. This observation is also valid for the information content H: on an intra-personal level it is dynamically created by continuous and particularly abrupt creations of novel modes of action (i.e., bifurcations) and is dependent on the scaled distance D as depicted in figure 1 and 3. On the higher level of inter-personal coupling, however, it plays a dynamical role in spontaneously forming the most probable strategic positioning of boxers (the minima of H), expressed in units of the scaled distance D. To summarize, the significance of these findings: on the one hand information content (H) was dynamically formed as a function of the scaled distance to target D, and on the other hand it dynamically controlled the strategic scaled distance positioning of boxers.

Metastability as a generic mechanism of varying information content was also present in the sequential hand-striking behavior as revealed by partial autocorrelation analysis (see figure 4).

Negative partial autocorrelation of lag 1 sequences were dominant in the observations of the boxers' actions, corresponding to left-right or right-left striking couplings. However, other short-range memory[3] sequences were also present in the data, including purely random (i.e. memory-less) sequences, up to those with lag 4 (i.e., action sequence motifs). This observation implied that the action system of individual boxers was highly diverse during the production of striking behavior. Changes in the sequence memory length, illustrating the versatility of the strength and length of the temporal couplings between actions, was another characteristic of meta-stable functioning and of the varied amount of information content of perception-action systems in boxers.

---

[3] The term *memory* refers to the range of dependence of the current strike on the past strikes. Memory-less sequence means that there is no dependence between the subsequent strikes. The current strike is not influenced by the type of previous strikes. Memory of lag 4 means the current strike is influenced by the type of the past 4 strikes. Partial autocorrelations show the average *net* influence of the past strikes to the current one.

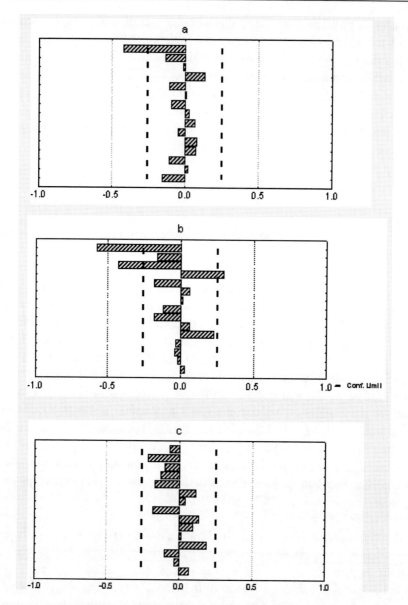

Figure 4. The partial autocorrelation functions for one of the boxers. Production of striking sequences with different memory (information) content is obvious. A. Short range memory of lag 1 corresponds to dominant left ↔ right strikes. B. More elaborate striking motif with memory lasting to lag 4. C. A purely random memory-less punching sequence. The dashed line is the p = .05 level of significance.

EMERGENCE OF NOVEL TACTICAL INFORMATION IN ATTACK – DEFENCE DYAD PERFORMING MODIFIED FOCUSERS TRAINING TASK

In another of our experiments six participants formed three attacker-defender dyads. The attackers were asked to increase and decrease their jab striking frequency in time with computer-generated sound signals presented through earphones that they wore. The frequency regimes were divided into 6 frequency groups with a frequency 1 group experiencing the lowest frequencies and a frequency 6 group the highest. Defenders had to try to evade the attackers' hand strikes with their arms in two modes: (i) under 90 deg. with respect to the direction of attack i.e. left-right-left arm movements in a horizontal plane, and collect points (collecting defensive mode) and (ii) they were allowed to withdraw the hand close to their shoulder (under 0 deg. with respect to the attacking direction) to save the scored points (saving defensive mode). Obviously, this second performance characteristic was a possible alternative *pre-planned* action. The angle of defense was treated as an order parameter (i.e., informator) that contained the information about the dyad collective coordination modes. The 3 tasks were differentiated in the degree of motivation (affective significance) for the defenders to stay untouched, by manipulating a 'perceived harm constraint'. In the first task there was no motivation for the defenders to stay untouched, since they collected points without regard to whether they were hit or not. In the second task the collected points by the defender, due to successfully evading the attacker's strikes, were transferred to the attacker if he hit the defender's arm. In the third task the motivation for staying untouched was made extreme by asking the defenders to imagine that the attacker was attempting to strike them with a sharp object. The defenders had to express behaviorally their defensive decision. The 'perceived harm constraint' was introduced as a non-specific control parameter and was scaled by the athletes on a scale $0 - 5$ (0 = no harm and 5 = extreme harm). Perceived harm was treated as affective information, and in coalition with the striking – evading frequency control parameter, as a source of perceptual information it was expected to produce different dynamical effects in the three experimental tasks.

In task 1, since all boxers assessed the harm variable as $h = 0$, the only action observed was the collecting mode of action (see figure 5).

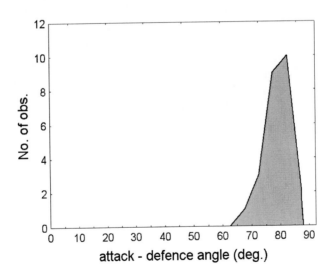

Figure 5. For task 1 coalition of constraints ($h = 0$) the only stable mode was the collecting one. The probability of actions condensed close to the 90 deg. defensive mode. This is a case of intra-mode variability with informational content arising solely from the non-zero dispersion around the mean.

For all increasing and decreasing striking frequencies the dyadic interaction stabilized the evading actions at approximately 90 deg. with respect to the attacking line. The intra-mode variability of actions produced almost a constant information amount for all frequency groups (see figure 8). Under the task 3 constraints, which contained high perceived harm values, the only stable behavior was the saving mode as depicted in figure 6. The information content of the actions was lowest under these task constraints (see figure 8).

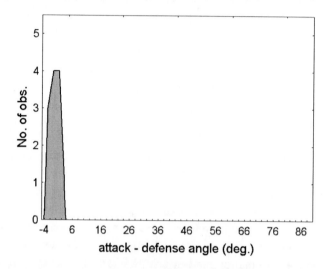

Figure 6. For task 3 coalition of constraints (h = 4 and 5) the only observed action mode was the saving mode. The low variability (i.e. dispersion) around the mean point to the high stability of this mode of action. A case of low intra-mode variability and low information content.

The dyadic interaction produced much more versatile behavior for harm values h = 1 and 2 present under task constraints 2 (see figure 7). For lower striking frequencies of the attacker the more probable state of defense was the collecting mode. For medium striking frequencies the probability of observing the defender's collecting or saving mode was approximately equal and for high striking frequencies the predominantly observed mode was the saving one (see figure 7 under A, B and C respectively).

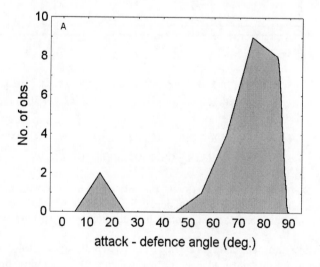

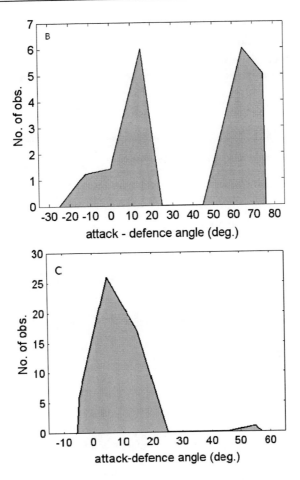

Figure 7. For task 2 coalition of constraints (h = 1 and 2) a meta-stable dynamics occurred (i.e. switching from the collecting to saving mode and vice versa). The probability condensed around two modes of action forming a bi-modal distribution. The minimum between the two peaks corresponds to an unstable (rarely visited or unvisited) region of attacker – defender coordination. This is a case of high intra and inter-mode variability (i.e. diversity) of actions with high information content. As the striking frequency increases the probability of observing one of the actions changes. A. striking frequency group 1;. B. group 3; C. group 5.

For task 2 the information content of actions was highest and there was a maximum for medium attacking striking frequencies. The maximization of entropy through producing a meta-stable state is a hallmark of phase transitions of the first kind (Kondratyev and Romanov, 1992). Meta-stability arose as a consequence of the increase in probability of the decoupling between the attacker's and defender's actions. Although not instructionally imposed by experimenters as a prescribed task solution, the constant switching between the collecting and saving modes was a robust observation. That is, defenders discovered a new mode of action, i.e. a combination of collecting and saving actions, to satisfy the interacting perceptual, affective and goal constraints. It is important to note that this new mode of action combination emerged as a *novel* solution to the tactical problem (i.e., task goal) of collecting more points and winning. Whereas during the first and third task constraints the perception – action system of the performers was trapped into stable extremes, under task 2 constraints the perception – action system was most creative and diverse (as indexed by the entropy measure) around the transition regions where meta-stability resided (i.e., between the two extremes). Intermittently combined actions of collecting and saving points induced a high amount of information from actions, that is, greater diversity and unpredictability in the tactical actions of the defender (see figure 8).

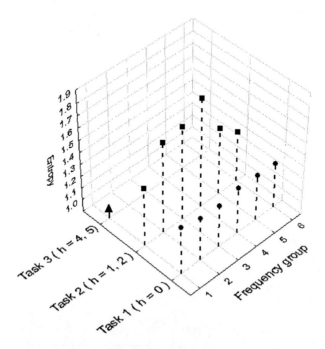

Figure 8. The change of the entropy (amount of information content of actions) as a function of the striking frequency group and degree of harm (h) of attacker's actions.

The pre-planned intention (i.e., the saving mode of action) introduced multi-stability as a necessary condition for spontaneous change of actions in dynamic performance environments. Although the saving mode of action was a pre-planned alternative, instructionally imposed as a possible mode of behavior in all three tasks, it emerged (i.e., contributed to the action information amount) only under the task 2 and 3 coalition of constraints. This observation signified that the pre-planned intention was immersed in the overall dynamical decision-action landscape and was shaped by the ongoing interactions of the manipulated constraints. In task 2 it was stabilized, that is, it became a sole tactical solution, emerging only above a specific range of striking frequencies (see figure 7 and 8) after the system passed through a meta-stable 'collect-save' regime and was intimated by the maximum of the entropy value (i.e., information amount). In other words, it appears that consciously-imposed, pre-planned intentions and the spontaneity of their execution may not be irreconcilable concepts, as intuitively believed (see Davids, Chapter 1). The final stabilization of the intended alternative pattern (i.e., saving mode) spontaneously arose, driven by systematic changes in the non-specific affective and perceptual parameters. Thus, organizational states in athletes, created by intending and decision making, can be construed as various phases of the global intentional aim spread over time. Within the framework of this research program, intentions, even when consciously imposed, emerged as decisions and were non-specifically (emotionally and environmentally) driven events. Both, the specific (i.e.

conscious) and the non-specific (i.e., emotional and environmental) constraints cooperated to create the change from the ongoing collecting to the intended alternative withdrawal (saving) decision-action complex. Specific constraints (intentions) introduced virtual instabilities in the decision landscape, while non-specific parametric influences enhanced them and enabled spontaneous transitions among the collecting and saving tactical decisions as a novel combined form of action.

CONCLUSION

In this chapter, we discussed how perceptual and affective information sources can create and change, sometimes abruptly, through creation of new action modes, the information contained in the order parameter (i.e., the informator) that shapes emergent movement patterns. We showed how ecological information and information entropy influence each other and are interdependent. These findings can be considered under a unified theoretical framework offered by nonlinear dynamics. Empirical work demonstrated how information sources have biological meaning in performance contexts like sport precisely because they are able to provide the basis for creating new, more adaptive, modes of action with respect to emerging task and goal constraints of athletes. Experiments demonstrated that practice task constraints (i.e. instructional, emotional and perceptual context) can be organised in a way that enables maximization of dynamic metastability affording athletes maximal ease and flexibility of discovering and switching between novel action combinations. These action modes were not instructionally imposed on athletes but simultaneously increased the intra- and inter-mode variability of their movements. Therefore, putting the athlete's perceptual, cognitive and action systems in the metastable (i.e., weakly stable or weakly unstable) region by adjusting the instructional, affective and perceptual constraints could be a natural way to amplify the stochastic perturbations and movement variability needed to enhance the diversity of actions and exploratory behavior in athletes (see the Schöllhorn, Michelbrink, Welminski, and Davids, Chapter 5). Context dependent metastability of the perceptual, cognitive and action systems is a viable generic dynamical mechanism of creativity in sport.

Another important observation was that pre-planned intentions became stable and emerged as decisions only under a well defined coalition of constraints. Inter alia this observation signifies that coaches should be aware of the moment when athletes simply do not act as prescribed. Pre-planned intentions emerging from externally- or internally-imposed instructions become relevant only when task (including the goal), personal and environmental constraints afford the emergence of that intention. The coach's third person perspective and the athlete's first person perspective might not match, especially during competition, and putting too much emphasis on prescribing individual tactical solutions might be somewhat counterproductive.

Moreover, while the amount of action information content may be dynamically formed by changes in some non-specific control parameter (i.e., perceptions of scaled distances, affective influences or striking frequency of the attacker), on another level it may create the dynamics of that parameter. This is a hallmark of the circular causality that operates on different levels in complex systems. The empirical observations discussed in this chapter showed how the *amount* of information and the *nature* of information interact and can bring about a self-organization of strategic interactions between athletes without instructional intervention. One research direction that should persist in future should be ascertain answers to issues such as: when and why instructional constraints are required and when and why athletes should be released to follow her/his self-organizing capacities (Savelsbergh and van der Kamp, Chapter 2).

REFERENCES

Abernethy, B. (1993). Searching for minimal essential information for skilled perception and action. *Psychological research, 55*, 131–138.

Araújo, D. Davids, K., and Hristovski, R. (2006). The ecological dynamics of decision making in sport. *Psychology of Sport and exercise, 7,* 653 -676.

Chow, J.Y., Davids, K., Button, C., Rein, R., Hristovski R., and Koh, M. (2009). Dynamics of Multi-articular Coordination in Neurobiological Systems. *Nonlinear Dynamics, Psychology and the Life Sciences, 1*, 27-52.

Davids, K., Savelsbergh, G., Bennett, S.J. and Van der Kamp , J. (2002). Interceptive actions in Sport. Theoretical perspectives and practical applications. In D. Keith, G. Savelsbergh, S. Bennett and J. Van der Kamp (Eds.), *Interceptive Actions in Sport. Information and Movement* (pp. 225-240). London: Routledge.

Edelman, G.M., and Gally, J. (2001). Degeneracy and complexity in biological systems. *Proceedings of the National Academy of Sciences, 98,* 13763-13768.

Fingelkurts, An.A., and Fingelkurts, Al.A. (2004). Making complexity simpler: multivariability and metastability in the brain. *International Journal of Neuroscience, 114,* 843-862.

Haken, H. (1983). *Synergetics. An Introduction.* Series in Synergetics (3rd ed., Vol 1). Heidelberg, Germany: Springer–Verlag.

Haken, H. (1999). Information and Self-Organization. A Macroscopic Approach to Complex Systems (2nd ed). *Springer.*

Hristovski, R., Davids, K., and Araújo, D. (2006a). Affordance – controlled bifurcations of action patterns in martial arts. *Nonlinear Dynamics, Psychology and the Life Sciences, 4,* 409–440.

Hristovski, R., Davids, K., and Araújo, D. (2006b). Bifurcations in motor solutions to the continuous boxing hand – striking task: Some spatial, sequential and temporal characteristics. *Journal of Biomechanic, 39,* Supplement 1, S35, Abstract 5301.

Hristovski, R., Davids, K., Araújo, D., and Button, C. (2006). How boxers decide to punch a target: Emergent Behaviour in Nonlinear Dynamical Systems. *Journal of Sports Science and Medicine (2006) CSSI, 60-73.*

Hristovski, R., Davids, K., and Araújo, D. (2007). Emergent tactical solutions in an attack-defence hand striking game. *Proceedings of the12th European Congress of Sport Psychology* 4-9 September, Halkidiki, Greece, p. 151.

Jacobs, D.M., and Michaels, C.F. (2002). On the apparent paradox of learning and realism. *Ecological Psychology, 14,* 127-139.

Kelso, J.A.S. (1995): Dynamic Patterns. The Self-Organization of Brain and Behavior. MIT Press.

Kelso, J.A.S. (2002). The Complementary Nature of the Coordination Dynamics. *Nonlinear Phenomena in Complex Systems, 5/4,* 364–371.

Kondratyev, A.S., and Romanov, V.P. (1992*). Exercises in Statistical Physics (In Russian).* Nauka. Moscow.

Schmidt, R.A., and Wrisberg, C.A. (2004). *Motor Learning and Performance* (3rd ed). Human Kinetics.

Turvey, M.T., and Shaw, R.E. (1995). Toward an ecological physics and a physical psychology. In R.L. Solso and D.W. Massaro (Eds.), *The science of the mind:2001 and beyond* (pp. 144-169). New York: Oxford University Press.

Turvey, M.T., and Shaw, R.E. (1999). Ecological foundations of cognition: I Symmetry and specificity of animal-environment systems. *Journal of Consciousness Studies, 6*(11-12), 95-110.

Van Orden, G.C., Holden, J.G., and Turvey, M.T. (2003). Self-organization of cognitive performance. *Journal of Experimental Psychology: General, 132,* 331–350.

Ward, P., Williams, A.M., and Bennett, S.J. (2002). Visual search and biological motor perception in tennis. *Research Quarterly for Sport and Exercise, 73*(1), 107–112.

In: Perspectives on Cognition and Action in Sport
Editors: D. Araújo, H. Ripoll and M. Raab

ISBN: 978-1-60692-390-0
© 2009 Nova Science Publishers, Inc.

Chapter 5

INCREASING STOCHASTIC PERTURBATIONS ENHANCES ACQUISITION AND LEARNING OF COMPLEX SPORT MOVEMENTS

Wolfgang Schöllhorn[1], Maren Michelbrink[1], Daniela Welminsiki[2] and Keith Davids[3]

[1] University of Mainz, Germany
[2] University of Münster, Germany
[3] Queensland University of Technology, Australia

ABSTRACT

Traditionally, the acquisition of skills and sport movements has been characterized by numerous repetitions of a presumed model movement pattern to be acquired by learners. This approach has been questioned by research identifying the presence of individualized movement patterns and the low probability of occurrence of two identical movements within and between individuals. In contrast, the differential learning approach claims advantages for incurring variability in the learning process by adding stochastic perturbations during practice. These ideas are exemplified by data from a high jump experiment which compared the effectiveness of classical and a differential training approach with a pre-post test design. Results showed clear advantages for the group with additional stochastic perturbations during the acquisition phase in comparison to classically trained athletes. Analogies to similar phenomenological effects in the neurobiological literature are discussed.

INTRODUCTION

Commonalities and differences in traditional motor learning approaches and the question of how to become skilled at everyday actions or sport movements have been addressed by a large variety of theoretical approaches. Traditional motor learning approaches have included the constant repetition of a to-be-learned target movement (Gentile, 1972), progression towards a target skill by performing a methodical series of exercises (Gaulhofer and Streicher,

1924), variability of practice (Schmidt, 1975) and contextual interference learning (Shea and Morgan, 1979). The constant repetition approach is based on the idea that the enhancement of movement skill is only effected by repeating a target movement as often as possible, and learning by means of methodical series of exercise is founded on exercises that have a structural similarity to specific parts of a target movement.

In the variability of practice approach, derived from Schmidt's schema theory (1975), the representation of movement classes is based on invariant programs and variable parameter features. A practical consequence of this assumption is that, if a single invariant is trained in combination with several variable parameters, the program for a specific movement within a given movement class becomes more stable. In spite of this view, it is worth noting that experimental support for the variability of practice hypothesis has mainly been provided from a specific range of movement tasks (Wulf and Shea, 2002) that have primarily required the production of muscular forces, but which have tended to minimize the influence of gravitational forces and moments of inertia (Schneider, Zernicke, Ulrich, Jensen, and Thelen, 1990). Additionally, weaknesses in experimental designs have led to indeterminate evidence in favour of the advantage of variable practice in comparison to constant practice (van Rossum, 1990).

While the variability of practice approach has emphasized investigation of the role in practice of variation of movement elements, the contextual interference (CI) approach maintains a stronger focus on the variation of the practice conditions with respect to the sequential order of different movements. The CI approach, was originally transferred from language learning experiments (Battig, 1966) into movement sciences (Shea et al., 1979). It occurs when at least two types of movements are learned in parallel (Goode and Magill, 1986; Lee and Magill, 1983). The more randomized (high CI) is a sequence of movement tasks during the acquisition period, the greater are expectations that the movements will interfere with each other in comparison to a less randomized (blocked) sequence (low CI). It has been observed that in retention or transfer tests high CI (alternating sequence) groups display smaller decreases in performance than low CI groups (blocked sequence). Meta analyses (e.g., Brady, 2004; Magill and Hall, 1990) have provided evidence for these effects primarily if the learned movements stem from different movement classes with different invariant features (e.g. different relative timing). The effect is assumed not to occur in children (Wulf and Shea, 2002) and less experienced participants (Smith, Gregory, and Davies, 2003), leading to a recommendation that learning new skills should begin with blocked training before random practice follows on a more experienced level (Wulf et al., 2002).

A most intriguing phenomenon was identified when the methodical series approach was interpreted in terms of contextual interference learning (Smith and Davies, 1995). By learning a single movement through different sequences of preparation exercises, facilitation, rather than interference, was predicted during the acquisition period. When movements have been learned in most variable environments, higher rates of improvement have been observed in the acquisition phase when high CI was applied. For instance, in one case water served as variable environment for acquiring a pawlata role in kayaking (Smith and Davies, 1995) while in another case snow texture created a variable environment for learning snowboarding skills (Smith, 2002).

In these traditional motor learning approaches, despite some fundamental distinctions between the contextual-interference, the variability-of-practice, and the repetition approaches, all commonly rely on the implicit assumption of the need for learners to acquire a constant target movement with at least some invariant features. While the repetition approach favours the stability of a movement by simply repeating all parts of the movement as often as possible, the variability of practice approach rather assumes that invariants can be refined in different combinations with variable parameters. Furthermore, the contextual interference approach claims to improve the stability of a target movement by changing the short term (historic) associations for a target movement by preceding it with different movements with different invariants.

Another important feature common to most traditional motor learning approaches is a generic view of movement variance with respect to the target movements. Variance is considered to occur as a result of erroneous or noisy (Schmidt, 1991) movement planning or execution, requiring error minimization in learners by encouraging them to only practice a movement correctly. From this perspective, variance is accredited with a destructive character and occurs as a result of serendipitous movement errors which passively accompany the learning process. While the repetition approach favours the complete avoidance of errors, the variability of practice and CI approach concede some benefit in some movement errors in the learning process (Magill, 1993, p. 363) since they enhance performer awareness of deviations from a target movement to facilitate conscious corrections for future executions. From this perspective, a certain amount of variance in the target movement is mainly conceived and tolerated as a source of inherent system error. In traditional approaches, variance in the target movement is only considered to play a passive, destructive role because it is included implicitly in the explanation of CI-effects within the Elaboration and Reconstruction hypothesis.

DIFFERENTIAL LEARNING APPROACH

In contrast to these traditional views, the differential learning approach contains several alternative assumptions based on ideas from dynamical systems theory, artificial neural net research, and stochastic resonance phenomena. Furthermore, differential learning can be explained by focusing on differences between consecutive movements while avoiding movement repetitions to exploit the constructive role of fluctuations during the learning process. In the remainder of this chapter, we outline the differential learning approach in more detail. An important idea in the differential learning approach is the enlargement of differences between subsequent movements in order to produce additional information for the system. This idea is mainly anchored in philosophical approaches to cognition (Heidegger, 1957; Derrida, 1982; Spencer-Brown, 1997), and can be comprehended by understanding how the visual and auditory sensory systems function in the nervous system. In the visual system the difference between an object's image from the left and right eye on the retina provides observers with information on its distance. In the auditory system the difference in the time delay of an acoustic signal received in the left and right ear is perceived as information for the spatial orientation of a signal. Additionally, from a physical point of view, information production is based on a choice between at least two different states (= 1 bit; Shannon, 1948).

The fundamental idea, that movement variability is considered a necessity for adaptive system function, can be traced back to the dynamical systems perspective, where fluctuations are considered as necessary for functional adaptations to changing environmental contexts and the prevention of loss of system complexity as constraints change (Button, Davids, and Schöllhorn, 2006; Kelso, 1995; Schöner and Kelso, 1988). Deviations from an intended movement are not considered as errors but rather as fluctuations and intermittencies in system organization (Tumer and Brainard, 2007). When applied to the study of motor control, fluctuations are particularly important in the adaptive process of switching between stable movement patterns during goal directed behaviour. Fluctuations also seem to govern motor learning processes (Zanone and Kelso, 1992) playing an active role during the acquisition phase.

A similar active and constructive role is ascribed to noise in robotics and artificial neural network (ANN) research. When a robot is confronted (trained) with noisy stimuli within a constantly changing environment during the training or learning phase, much better orientation to different environmental conditions can be observed in the application phase in comparison to a robot that has been trained within a constant environment (Miglino, Lund, and Nolfi, 1995). Training of ANNs with noisy data results in better recognition rates in the application phase as well (Bishop, 1995). A transfer of ANN research to the study of motor learning was undertaken by Horak (1992). In his work, the training phase in ANNs was assigned to the acquisition phase in motor learning and the test phase was aligned with the transfer test. The simulation of different training schedules by Horak (1992) on the basis of three simulated data sets led to a smaller error rate for the blocked condition in an acquisition phase, whereas random and the serial training schedules resulted in smaller error rates for the transfer test. In this context insights into the simulated transfer abilities may be of specific interest for motor learning in humans. Within artificial neural nets the quality of transfer depends highly on the mapping of the transfer task to the nodes' weights, relative to the nodes' weights of the trained tasks. When a transfer task is mapped to an area within the range of the trained area then the ANN will interpolate well, as ANNs are typically quite successful in performing this task. In contrast, a transfer task that is mapped outside the trained area leads to extrapolation which results in larger error rates (Haykin, 1994). Here interpolation corresponds to an estimation towards a region located between two known measurement values, whereas extrapolation is an estimation towards a region that is outside known measurement values.

These characteristics of ANNs are consistent with the idea of the elaboration hypothesis which was developed for explaining phenomena in contextual interference experiments and mainly relies on the assumption of the two processing modes: intra-task and inter-task processing. The elaboration hypothesis proposes that superior retention results during random practice are enhanced due to comparisons of multiple tasks in working memory (Shea and Morgan, 1979). In consequence, during training of ANNs a large neuron space should be covered (by the input data) in order to allow as much interpolation as possible in the transfer phase. From a connectionist point of view it is not only the number of influencing neurons but also the density and distribution of training stimuli that influences the quality of the net in the test phase. Typically, the area of interest should be covered optimally by stimuli that lead to a lattice-like distribution over the ANN neuron space with optimal expansion and influence on the neurons (Hertz, Krogh, and Palmer, 1994; Nguyen and Widrow, 1990). A transfer to neurobiological learning would correspond to an increased variability in content and sequences during the acquisition phase in order to enlarge the neuron space of mesh size of the lattice (Kohonen, 2001).

In a similar way, the differential learning approach (Schöllhorn, 1999) suggests that motor learning could benefit from adding stochastic perturbations in the form of random or variable movement components to a target movement pattern. In this context, stochastic perturbations can be understood as fluctuations which naturally occur during multiple repetitions of the target movement. The term stochastic is used to denote fluctuations in movement repetitions that do not seem to follow any deterministic structure or rule, although they could also be chaotic instead of noisy (Riley and Turvey, 2002). Traditionally, perturbations have been interpreted as the arbitrary execution of erroneous movements whereby the errors are always changing.

The differential learning approach mainly relies on the assumption that each movement trial has to be considered as individual (Schöllhorn and Bauer, 1998; Schöllhorn, Nigg, Stefanyshyn, and Liu, 2002) and unrepeatable (Bernstein 1967; Hatze, 1986). Empirical evidence for the individuality of movement patterns exists in analyses of world class javelin throwers, in which individual throwers could be identified over several years by means of their throwing pattern during the last 200ms of their final throwing phase (Schöllhorn and Bauer, 1998). Furthermore, analysis of several steps of female walkers allowed the recognition of individuals by means of their ground reaction forces and lower limb kinematics (recognition rates > 95%) (Schöllhorn et al., 2002). In order to find an individual's situational optimum, motor learning is not considered as the acquisition and storage process of different movement parameters. Learning is rather characterized as the improvement of internal adaptation processes which is achieved by means of adding stochastic perturbations to a so called "ideal movement" (Schöllhorn, Michelbrink, Beckmann, Trockel, Sechelmann, and Davids, 2006).

There is wide ranging assumption of the existence of 'common optimal movement patterns' in the study of human movement behaviour, which is an example of 'biological determinism' in science, particularly manifesting itself in the cognitive sciences, biomechanics and perceptual-motor disorders (Davids, Bennett, and Newell, 2006). For example, this assumption has been promulgated in the biomechanics optimization literature where a consuming challenge has been to identify optimal techniques for the performance of a wide range of movement activities. The implicit assumption is that identification of optimal patterns for performing specific movements could lead to improvements in sport performance while preventing the occurrence of injuries through dysfunctional movement patterning (e.g., Glazier and Davids, 2009; Hatze, 1986). From this perspective, an "ideal movement" can be understood as a person-independent model of a movement that fulfills momentarily, from the standpoint of science, on average the most effective solution of a given movement task. Typically, an "ideal movement" is defined within relative narrow borders and remains constant over time. In the cognitive sciences, as we noted earlier, increasing expertise has been proposed to lead to movement invariance and the construction of a single motor program, as argued in some traditional theories of motor control.

The misconception of 'common optimal movement patterns' also exists in the motor control literature where theoretically cogent arguments have been proposed as a rationale for studying how individuals satisfy unique interacting task and personal constraints coordination solutions in order to maintain functionality in dynamic environments (Brisson and Alain, 1996; Davids, Bennett, and Newell, 2006). As Latash and Anson (1996) argued, the "phenomena of variability of voluntary movements by themselves indicate that "correct" peripheral motor patterns may form a rather wide spectrum" (p. 65).

In the study of movement disabilities, the implicit 'medical model' or 'disability as tragedy model', used by many clinicians provides a unitary, biologically determined perspective of health and movement behaviour in which variability, viewed as deviation from an 'accepted' norm, is seen as dysfunctional and an index of abnormality (Davids, Shuttleworth, Button, Renshaw, and Glazier, 2003; Latash and Anson, 1996).

The addition of randomly fluctuating movement components to a target skill (such as high jumping) could result in emergent movement solutions changing even after thousands of performance trials because of dynamic performance conditions (Davids et al., 2003; Hatze, 1986; Schöllhorn, 1998). As a consequence of random new elements to movement repetitions, resonance effects might be instrumental in enhancing the ability of performers to adapt to these new elements and engage in a process of performance differentiation through exploring individualized movement solutions (Schöllhorn and Bauer, 1998; Schöllhorn et al., 2002). Resonance effects are typically characterized by an increase in amplitude of oscillations of a signal exposed to an external force. While two anti-phase signals would lead to mutual extinction, two in-phase signals are accompanied by alternate amplification. During differential learning, the fluctuating dynamics of the athlete's performance are assumed to get in resonance with the external force of stochastic perturbations that are provoked by the movement tasks. In this context the finding of the most effective motor learning approach that is operationalized by a maximum learning rate can be assumed as finding the optimum task noise for each individual in each situation.

Historically, the differential training approach is a practical application of the findings of fundamental research on dynamical systems and artificial neural nets research. In both areas the theoretical influence of fluctuations and noise has been described independently from each other. In contrast to dynamical systems research that mainly considers fluctuations as natural and passive characteristics of primarily cyclic movement systems with different amplitudes in stable and instable modes (Haken, Kelso, and Bunz, 1985; Schöner and Kelso, 1988), ANN research has inserted/applied different amplitudes of noise actively for improving the effectiveness of mathematical models of neurons. In combining both aspects, the differential learning approach considers fluctuations as a specific form of noise and applied amplified fluctuations to movement learning in general. Due to the problem of quantifying the frequency content of amplified fluctuations in ballistic movements, these signals have been termed 'stochastic perturbations' in differential learning.

EXPERIMENTAL EVIDENCE FOR DIFFERENTIAL LEARNING

To investigate these theoretical ideas there is an ongoing program of work to quantitatively examine the effects of the differential learning approach with more traditional approaches to pedagogy in sports such as shot put (Beckmann and Schöllhorn, 2003), football (Schöllhorn et al., 2006), tennis (Humpert and Schöllhorn, 2006) and high jumping. In this chapter we consider research on high jumping to illustrate our arguments. Because high jump includes technical and conditioning elements to training, the effects of differential training on vertical jumping performance were also examined.

In the research program, 36 male and 21 female (22.8 ± 2.2y) novices were categorized into two experimental and one control group according to the results of a high jump pre-test.

A pre-post test design was used with a subsequent retention test conducted 10 days after the posttest. Every test phase included performance of a Fosbury Flop, which has high technical requirements, and a conditioning test related to high jump performance, in the form of a jump-and-reach-test. The Fosbury Flop test was accomplished according to IAAF rules. The jump-and-reach test was carried out standing beside a wall and measured the difference between reach height in a standing position and reach height after a two legged vertical jump (figure 1).

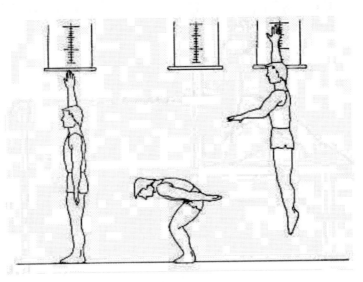

Figure 1. Jump and reach test (Weineck, 2000; p. 322).

The two experimental groups participated in a training intervention program over 4 weeks with 2 training sessions per week. One experimental group (T) was trained in a traditional way according to the IAAF recommendation for high jump (Jonath, Krempel, and Haag, 1995). The other experimental group (D) was trained by differential training principles. The control group (CO) did not participate in a specific jump training during the whole duration of the experiment. Group T was trained with feedback for error correction and performed a high number of repetitions. These training principles were chosen according to classical pedagogic recommendations of encouraging learner progression from easy to hard and from simple to complex exercises. In this approach, every exercise had to be repeated until movement stability was achieved before participants proceeded to the next, more complex exercise. In contrast, group D received no corrective instructions and never repeated a high jump movement twice in the same way, but rather changed their movements after every trial. For this group, different exercises were applied during the approach, take off, flight and clearance of the bar. For instance, the high jump approach could be varied by changes in stiffness at the knees, magnitude of elbow extension or trunk leaning angle. Similarly, the take off could be altered by bending the head to the left or right. All members in the D group adopted the same sequence of differential learning program. Although the exercises for the differential group were selected randomly by the coach, the existence of a latent structure cannot be excluded.

To compare effects of the different intervention methods on high jump performance, results of the two exercises (Fosbury Flop, jump-and-reach test) were analysed statistically with a two-way repeated measures ANOVA. In the case of statistical significant interaction effects of group and test phase, t-tests of pair differences were calculated to detect inter-group differences at each specific test phase. Concerning the jump-and-reach test, paired t-tests were calculated for the two experimental groups separately to evaluate if the intervention had a significant influence on rather conditional factors of high jump performance.

Results showed that the initial average high jump performance of group T amounted to 1.41m (±0.15m). Group D showed an initial performance of 1.40m (±0.16m) height and the control group reached 1.40m (±0.15m). The differences between the three groups were not significant. After 4 weeks of training the athletes of group D improved their high jump performance and reached an average of 1.45m (±0.17m), while group T achieved 1.42m (±0.15m). The performance and variance of the control group did not change. After a break of 10 days, both experimental groups improved high jump performance by 1 cm on average (group T: 1.43m; group D: 1.46), while the control group did not change its performance (see figure 2).

The improvement of high jump performance averaged across the groups was significant between pre and post test (F (2,108) = 11.077; p= .000; η^2 = .170). The test of contrasts of the within-participant factor shows that the significant change happened between pre and post test (F (1,54) = 11.771; p = .001; η^2 = .178). The difference between the group performances averaged across the three test phases as the main factor group was not significant (F (2,54) = .278; p = .758; η^2 = .010). However, the change from one test phase to another was significantly different in at least two groups, as the interaction between the within-participant factor and the main factor group was significant (F (4,108) = 5.885; p = .000; η^2 = .179). Again, contrasts show that improvement differences appeared between the pre and the post test phase which can be seen in figure 2, too. The improvement from pre- to post test between group T and group D was significantly different (t (36) = -2.058; p = .046). Additionally, differences between performance changes of group D and the control group were highly significant (t (36) = 4.082; p < .001). The comparison of performance changes between group T and the control group was not significant (t (36) = 1.748; p = .089). However, these p-values were not alpha-corrected. Concerning the T-tests of pair differences between post and retention test values we did not find any significant results.

High Jump Performance [m]

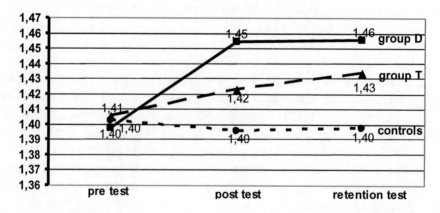

Figure 2. High Jump Performance.

Initial values for the jump-and-reach test averaged between 0.40m (±0.06m) for group T and the control group and 0.41m (±0.05m) for group D. After 4 weeks of intervention, both experimental groups improved their performance in jump-and-reach by about 2 cm, while the controls rested at their starting level on average. After a break of 10 days, group T degraded again to 0.41m while the other groups maintained their performance level (see figure 3).

The improvement of jump-and-reach performance averaged across the groups was significant between pre- and post-test (F (2,108) = 4.591; p = 0.012; η^2 = .078). The test of contrasts of the within-participant factor shows that the significant change happened between pre and post test (F (1,54) = 6.610; p = .013; η^2 = .109). We did not find any difference between the group performances averaged across the three test phases as the main factor group was not significant (F (2,54) = .713; p = .495; η^2 = .026). The change from one test phase to another was not statistically significant different between the groups as the interaction between the inner subject factor and the main factor group was not significant (F (4,108) = 1.227; p = .304; η^2 = .043).

To evaluate, if the experimental groups significantly improved their jump-and-reach performance during the intervention, we applied paired t-tests. Performance changes from pre to post test in group T were not significant (t (18) = -1.458; p = .162 and t (18) = 1.268; p = .221), although the improvement from pre to post test of group D was (t (18) = -2.317; p = .032). As the control group did not change its jump-and-reach performance, there was no significant improvement. Note, these differences do not mean that group D improved its jump-and-reach performance significantly differently from group T as the interaction effect was not significant.

Jump-and-reach test performance [m]

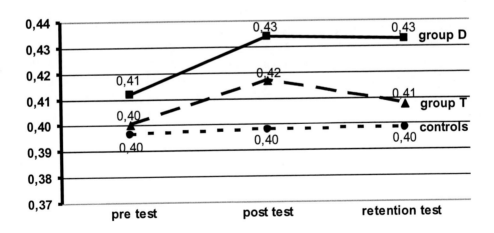

Figure 3. Jump-and-reach performance.

Performances (1.40m-1.60m) and changes in high jump (0.06m) and jump and reach (0.05m) within the training period of 4 weeks were within the range observed in comparable investigations in the literature (Rhea, Peterson, Lunt, and Ayllon, 2008). Both experimental groups were able to improve their fosbury flop performance after 4 weeks of intervention although their training was totally different: The differential learning group D never repeated a movement twice but was characterized by randomly adding stochastic perturbations to the Fosbury Flop technique, while the classical training group was trained by means of error correction and lots of numerous repetitions of perceived correct movements. Most intriguingly, the differential learning group D improved their performance the most during the acquisition phase and was able to maintain its performance advance after the 10-day break. Interactions showed that the improvement rate from pre to post test of group D was significantly different from that of group T and CO. Since it can be assumed that both groups improved their conditioning by a comparable amount during this period, it can also be assumed that the larger performance improvements of the differential learning group were mainly due to technical or coordinative improvements. Here, the interaction of test phase and intervention was not significant.

In interpreting these results two explanations can be considered. The first explanation is related to the performance of errors during the realization of the traditional approach and is thus a question of intervention accomplishment. Note, this explanation has got a negative nuance. The second one is oriented towards feasible advantages of an alternative approach and is rather a question of principle concerning the intervention method. This explanation tends to be more positive. In the first case, it can be argued that the ideal technique proposed to the traditional training group T was not correct. This explanation can be rejected, because all the students of this group were informed in advance about the technique by means of photographs of world class high jumpers. Furthermore, all error corrections were given according to the IAAF recommended literature that are based on world class athletes as well and therefore are oriented on the same model (Jonath, Krempel, and Haag, 1995). The possibility that the corrections were given with the wrong instructions e.g. body related or metaphorically (Schmidt and Wulf, 1997), can be excluded because both groups received the same amount of body and metaphorically oriented instructions.

The consequence of the second explanation is to question the traditional understanding of model learning. Model learning is based on the assumption of a performer-independent ideal technique and thereby neglects individual sources of variance. Alternatively, the differential learning approach offers a systems dynamic model for the explanation of the observed phenomena that has been tested analytically in artificial neural nets (Horak, 1992). Similarly to successfully trained ANNs, it seems that the athlete has to be confronted by "noisy" data during the acquisition process in order to optimize not only the next movement but also subsequent movement trials for solving movement problems. The noise that is applied in an ANN corresponds to randomly adding stochastic perturbations to the model movement of high jump in the differential training group. In the differential training group athletes were confronted with all kinds of additional tasks that forced them to adapt consistently to new tasks. Therefore, athletes not only experienced a broader area of possible solutions, but they also seemed to learn to adapt to new situations more individually and more quickly. Within this explanation the results of the traditional group can also be interpreted. The variations that can be observed within the repetitions of the traditional group seemed to be too small to allow the system to follow performance changes over time, consequently leading to less rapid performance improvement.

Fundamental differences exist between these models at the level of learning principles, based on the phenomenon that consecutive movement repetitions will always be unequal (Bernstein, 1967). According to the assumptions of the differential learning approach no movement repetition will be identical (Bernstein, 1967). Despite the clustering of movement classes by means of hypothetical generalized motor programs, their small variations (Heuer, 1988a,b; Heuer and Schmidt, 1988) still lead to an infinite number of combinations of muscle activation patterns and joint momentums. The implicit assumption of such motor program structures is that similar movement outcomes are the result of the same motor program with added noise in the periphery. This assumption can be associated with the principle of strong causality. Strong causality is typically associated with similar effects that follow similar causes. With respect to boundary conditions this understanding of causality demands much more than the understanding of weak causality where only similar causes lead to similar effects. Mathematically it needs more boundary conditions in order to fulfill this strong causality which is actually associated with much more parameters to control (Cramer, 1980). Overall it seems to be neither the most adequate model for describing the variation or noise phenomena or to provide the basis for learning recommendations. However, over a longer time scale the 'repetition without repetitions' approach is associated with a change in the movement system, underpinned by reactions at the cellular level. When the movement system, in this case the athlete, is changing all the time, it seems plausible to provide a training regime that allows the athlete to cope with the same problem under changed conditions as well (Schöllhorn, Mayer-Kress, Newell, and Michelbrink, in press).

Due to the abstract and general level of the underlying theory of fluctuations, with its emphasis on system stability and instability, there is significant potential for understanding how stochastic perturbations function at different levels of description (Verejken, Chapter 6). The application of stochastic perturbations to the acquisition of catching movements is particularly interesting, because in this case the interaction of several fluctuating sub-systems like the visual perception system, the oculo-motor system, and the limb system used for catching, have to be scaled to each other (Savelsbergh and van der Kamp, Chapter 2). Similarly, investigations have revealed that the influence of coupled fluctuations between several athletes for tactical behaviour can also be considered (see Hristovski, Davids, and Araújo, Chapter 4, and Passos, Araújo, Davids, Gouveia, Milho, and Serpa, Chapter 3).

CONCLUSION

To summarise, we have described some data from a program of work that has verified other results on differential learning, where adding stochastic perturbations to a to-be-learned movement led to higher improvement rates than traditional learning approaches. In combination with findings of other investigations on differential learning (e.g., Beckmann and Schöllhorn, 2003; Humpert and Schöllhorn, 2006) all traditional learning approaches exemplify levels of stochastic perturbation which merely differ in amplitude and frequency. Accordingly, the search for a most effective learning approach can be considered as the search for optimum noise since a decrease in learning rate can be observed when too much noise is put into the system. With the same argument, the findings of Wulf and Shea (2002) can be explained whereby children show better learning rates with low contextual interference while adults are more successful with higher levels of contextual interference. It is probable that movement repetitions of children have a larger level of variability or noise that would lead to a detrimental effect when additional noise is applied to the learning experience. On the other hand more advanced athletes have reduced the levels of variability within their movement repetitions leading only to suboptimal learning progress and therefore requiring the combination of additional noise. In principle, the results implied that pedagogists should think about the typical model oriented understanding of learning, since the addition of random stochastic perturbations led to at least the same learning progress as in the highly systematic traditional approach. Future research should be aimed at examining the size and number of stochastic perturbations during the acquisition phase and according to Frank et al. (2008) to the noise during the retention phase as well.

REFERENCE

Battig, W. F. (1966). Facilitation and Interference. In E.A. Bilodeau (Ed.), *Acquisition of skill* (pp. 215-244). New York: Academic Press.

Beckmann, H., and Schöllhorn, W.I. (2003). Differential Learning in Shot Put. In W. I. Schöllhorn, C. Bohn, J. M. Jäger, H. Schaper and M. Alichmann (Eds.), *Mechanics, Physiology, Psychology - Conference Proceedings of the 1st European Workshop on Movement Science* (pp. 68-69). Köln: Sport and Buch Strauß.

Bernstein, N.A. (1967). *The Coordination and Regulation of Movements*. London: Pergamon Press.

Bishop, C.M. (1995). *Neural Networks for Pattern Recognition*. Oxford: Oxford University Press.

Brady, F. (2004). Contextual interference: a meta-analytic study. *Perceptual and Motor Skills, 99*, 116-126.

Brisson T.A., and Alain, C. (1996). Should common optimal movement patterns be identified as the criterion to be achieved? *Journal of Motor Behavior 28*, 211-223.

Button, C., Davids, K., and Schöllhorn, W.I. (2006). Coordination profiling of movement systems. In K. Davids, S. Bennett, and K.M. Newell (Eds.), *Variability in Movement Systems* (pp. 133-152). Champaign; Ill.: Human Kinetics.

Cramer, J.G. (1980). Generalized absorber theory and the Einstein-Podolsky-Rosen paradox. *Physics Review D, 22*(2), 362-376.

Davids, K., Bennett, S.J. and Newell, K.M. (Eds.) (2006). *Variability in Movement Systems*. Champaign; Ill.: Human Kinetics.

Davids, K., Shuttleworth, R., Button, C., Renshaw, I., and Glazier, P. (2003). "Essential noise"-enhancing variability of informational constraints benefits movement control: a comment on Waddington and Adams. *British Journal of Sports Medicine, 38*, 601-605.

Derrida, J. (1982). Differance. In J. Derrida (Ed.), *Margins of Philosophy*, pp. 3-27. Chicago: The University of Chicago Press.

Frank, T.D., Michelbrink, M., Beckmann, H., and Schöllhorn, W.I. (2008). A quantitative dynamical systems approach to differential learning: self-organization principle and order parameter equations. *Biological Cybernetics, 98*, 19-31.

Gaulhofer, K. and Streicher, M. (1924). Grundzüge des österreichischen Schulturnens. Fundamentals of austrian school gymnastics. Wien.

Gentile, A.M. (1972). A working model of skill acquisition with application to teaching. *Quest, 17*, 3-23.

Glazier, P., and Davids, K. (2009). Constraints on the complete optimization of human motion. *Sports Medicine* 39, 15-28 .

Goode, S., and Magill, R. A. (1986). Contextual Interference Effects in Learning Three Badminton Serves. *Research Quarterly for Exercise and Sport, 57*, 308-314.

Haken, H., Kelso, J.A.S. and Bunz, H. (1985). A Theoretical Model of Phase Transitions in Human Hand Movements, *Biological Cybernetics, 51*, 347–356.

Hatze, H. (1986). Motion Variability – its Definition, Quantification, and Origin. *Journal of Motor Behavior, 18*, 5-16.

Haykin, S. (1994). *Neural Networks*. New York: Macmillan College Publishing Company.

Heidegger, M. (1957). *Identität und Differenz* (Bd. 10). Stuttgart: Neske.

Hertz, J., Krogh, A., and Palmer, R. G. (1994). *Introduction to the theory of neural computation*. (9th ed., Vol. 1) Reading: Addison-Wesley Publishing Company.

Heuer, H. (1988a). Adjustment and readjustment of the relative timing of a motor pattern. *Psychological Research, 50*, 83-93.

Heuer, H. (1988b). Testing the invariance of relative timing: Comments on Gentner (1987). *Psychological Review, 95*, 552-557.

Heuer, H., and Schmidt, R.A. (1988). Transfer of learning among motor patterns with different relative timing. *Journal of Experimental Psychology: Human Perception and Performance, 14*, 241-252.

Horak, M. (1992). The utility of connectionism for motor learning: A Reinterpretation of contextual interference in movement science. *Journal of Motor Behavior, 24*, 58-66.

Humpert, V., and Schöllhorn, W.I. (2006). Vergleich von Techniktrainingsansätzen zum Tennisaufschlag. In Ferrauti,A. and Remmert,H. (Eds.), *Trainingswissenschaft im Freizeitsport - Symposium der dvs-Sektion Trainingswissenschaft* (pp. 121-124). Hamburg: Czwalina.

Jonath, U., Krempel, R., and Haag, E. (1995). *Leichtathletik: Springen (Track and field: Jumping)*: Vol. 2. Reinbek bei Hamburg: Rowohlt.

Kelso, J.A.S. (1995). Dynamic patterns - The Self-Organization of Brain and Behavior. Cambridge: MIT Press.

Kohonen, T. (2001). *Self-Organizing Maps*. (3rd ed., Vol. 30) Berlin: Springer.

Latash, M.L., and Anson, J.G. (1996). What are "normal movements" in atypical populations? *Behavioural and Brain Sciences, 19*, 55-106.

Lee, T.D. and Magill, R.A. (1983). The Locus of Contextual Interference in Motor-Skill Acquisition. *Journal of Experimental Psychology: Learning, Memory, and Cognition, 9*, 730-746.

Magill, R.A. (1993). *Motor learning - concepts and applications*. Dubuque, IA: Brown Communications.

Magill, R.A., and Hall, K.G. (1990). A review of the contextual interference effect in motor skill acquisition. *Human Movement Science, 9*, 241-289.

Miglino, O., Lund, H.H., and Nolfi, S. (1995). Evolving mobile robots in simulated and real environments. *Artificial Life, 2*, 417-434.

Nguyen, D. and Widrow, B. (1990). Neural Networks for Self-Learning Control Systems. IEEE *Control Systems Magazine, 10*(3), 18-23.

Rhea, M.R. Peterson, M.D. Lunt, K.T. and Ayllon, F.N. (2008). The effectiveness of resisted jump training on the VertiMax in high school athletes. *Journal of Strength and Conditioning Research, 22*(3), 731-4.

Riley, M., and Turvey, M. (2002). Variability and determinism in motor behavior. *Journal of Motor Behavior, 34*(2), 99-125.

Schmidt, R.A. (1975). A schema theory of discrete motor skill learning. *Psychological Review, 82*, 225-260.

Schmidt, R.A. (1991). *Motor learning and performance.* Champaign, IL: Human Kinetics.

Schmidt, R.A., and Wulf, G. (1997). Continuous concurrent feedback degrades skill learning: implications for training and simulation. *Human Factors, 39*, 509-525.

Schneider, K., Zernicke, R.F., Ulrich, B.D., Jensen, J. L., and Thelen, E. (1990). Understanding movement control in infants through the analysis of intersegmental dynamics. *Journal of Motor Behavior, 22*, 493-520.

Schöllhorn, W.I. (1998). Systemdynamische Betrachtung komplexer Bewegungsmuster im Lernprozess. Frankfurt: Peter Lang.

Schöllhorn, W.I. (1999) Individualität - ein vernachlässigter Parameter? *Leistungssport, 2*, 5-11.

Schöllhorn, W.I. and Bauer, H.-U. (1998). Identifying individual movement styles in high performance sports by means of self-organizing Kohonen maps. In H.J. Riehle and M. Vieten (Eds.), *Proceedings of the XVI Congress of the ISBS 1998.* (pp. 574-577). Konstanz University Press.

Schöllhorn WI, Mayer-Kress G, Newell KM, Michelbrink M. (in press). Time scales of adaptive behavior and motor learning in the presence of stochastic perturbations. Human Movement Science. 2008 Dec 3. [Epub ahead of print]

Schöllhorn, W.I., Michelbrink, M., Beckmann, H., Trockel, M., Sechelmann, M., and Davids, K. (2006). Does noise provide a basis for the unification of motor learning theories? *International Journal of Sport Psychology, 37*, 186-206.

Schöllhorn, W.I., Nigg, B.M., Stefanyshyn, D., and Liu, W. (2002). Identification of individual walking patterns using time discrete and time continuous data sets. *Gait and Posture, 15*, 180-186.

Schöner, G. and Kelso, J.A.S. (1988). A Dynamic pattern theory of behavioral change. *Journal of Theoretical Biology, 135*, 501-524.

Shannon, C.E. (1948) A Mathematical Theory of Communication. *The Bell System Technical Journal, 27*, 379-423, 623-656.

Shea, J.B., and Morgan, R.L. (1979). Contextual Interference Effects on the Acquisition, Retention, and Transfer of a Motor Skill. *Journal of Experimental Psychology: Human Learning and Memory, 5*, 179-187.

Smith, P.J.K. (2002). Applying contextual interference to snowboarding skills. *Perceptual Motor Skills, 95*, 999-1005.

Smith, P.J.K., and Davies, M. (1995). Applying contextual interference to the Pawlata roll. *Journal of Sports Sciences, 13*, 455-462.

Smith, P.J.K., Gregory, S.K., and Davies, M. (2003). Alternating versus blocked practice in learning a cartwheel. *Perceptual and Motor Skills, 96*, 1255-1264.

Spencer-Brown, G. (1997) *Laws of form.* Lübeck: Bohmeier.

Tumer, E.C., and Brainard, M.S. (2007). Performance variability enables adaptive plasticity of 'crystallized' adult birdsong. *Nature, 450*(7173), 1240-4.

van Rossum, J.H.A. (1990). Schmidt's Schema theory: the empirical base of the variability of practice hypothesis. *Human Movement Science, 9*, 387-435.

Weineck, J. (2000). *Bewegung und Sport - wozu?* Editio Zenk.

Wulf, G. and Shea, C.B. (2002). Principles derived from the study of simple skills do not generalize to complex skill learning. *Psychonomic Bulletin and Review, 9*, 185-211.

Zanone, P.G. and Kelso, J.A.S. (1992). Learning and transfer as dynamical paradigms for behavioral change. In G.E. Stelmach and J. Requin (Eds.), *Tutorials in motor behavior II* (pp. 563-582). Amsterdam: North Holland.

In: Perspectives on Cognition and Action in Sport
Editors: D. Araújo, H. Ripoll and M. Raab

ISBN: 978-1-60692-390-0
© 2009 Nova Science Publishers, Inc.

Chapter 6

LEVELS OF COMPLEXITY IN PERFORMANCE

Beatrix Vereijken

Human Movement Science Programme,
Faculty of Social Sciences and Technology Management,
Norwegian University of Science and Technology,
Trondheim, Norway

ABSTRACT

For any physical performance to be proficient, be it in sports or in activities of daily life, many factors at many different levels need to come together in a coordinated effort. When performing or coaching performance, one often concentrates on one or two factors at a time, trying to improve the contribution of that factor towards the overall performance on the assumption that this will improve overall performance as well. In research alike, we mostly concentrate on factors residing at a single or a few levels, trying to understand how each factor contributes to the overall outcome on the assumption that this also will improve our understanding of the overall outcome. Ultimately, however, exclusive focus on separate levels will fall short in either endeavor, and we need to assemble the levels again in order to create or understand overall performance. This chapter takes a look at the complexity of performance and the complexity of some of the levels, reviews their fundamental properties, and discusses how each level is connected to the level above and below. Both theoretical approaches and implications for practice will be discussed. Two levels are elaborated upon in particular, the behavioral level and the level of joint movements. The levels will then be assembled again, discussing what is involved in sports performance to achieve such an assembly. Proficiency at many levels simultaneously will be illustrated with a more detailed example taken from ski jumping. Finally, implications for learning and coaching performance will be discussed.

INTRODUCTION

Watching high-level athletes performing their sports, one is easily struck by the apparent ease with which they seem to accomplish their feat. Gymnasts tumbling through the air, soccer players outsmarting a series of opponents, and swimmers cutting through the water all display a grace that appears effortless. Similarly, the ultimate goal in different sports can often be expressed by a deceptively simple statement as well, such as jump over the bar, kick the soccer ball behind the goal line, or drive the golf ball towards a far away hole. Yet, the medley of body movements required to accomplish any of these goals is far from simple. For example, in order to set a world record in the high jump, all of the athlete's body parts necessarily have to cooperate and contribute to clear the bar. In a similar vein, it is not just the kicking foot responsible for a goal in soccer, or just the hands executing a successful golf swing. On the contrary, closer inspection of each of these actions reveals that the entire body contributes to the performance, combining efforts to produce fluency, efficiency, and ultimate success. This is not just the case for performance in high-level athletics. For any physical performance to be proficient, be it in sports or in activities of daily life, many factors at many different levels need to come together in a coordinated effort.

In contrast to the holistic nature of performing a physical activity, the study of physical performance is often limited to a subset of factors on a single or a few levels. The underlying assumption is that understanding of the parts will accumulate to an understanding of the whole. This so-called reductionist approach to science was inherited from René Descartes, who argued in the 17th century that the world was like a machine that could be understood by taking apart and studying its pieces. Although movement scientists and sports scientists are aware of the necessity to relate across factors and across levels, attempts to formulate a grand theory of performance are few and far between. As a result, we have a collection of sub-theories that largely describe specific aspects of performance from a specific perspective. Movement science has, for example, separate theories to explain motor learning and motor development, discrete versus continuous movements, and the speed-accuracy trade-off, to name but a few. As another example, muscle and muscle function are described differently from the perspectives of physiology, functional anatomy, biomechanics, and motor control. This focus on pieces of performance, however, has not made research into a simple and straightforward exercise. On the contrary, detailed analyses of even the smallest piece on a single level highlight the complexity of individual factors, their interactions, and their assembly across levels.

In this chapter, I will take a look at the complexity of performance from both a scientific and a practical viewpoint. I will peel away some of the levels, describing some of the factors at these levels in more detail. I will also discuss how the levels relate to each other and how they can be assembled in performance. I will concentrate on two levels in particular, the levels of behavior and of joint movements. Together with the environmental level, these levels are most intuitively linked to sports performance and coaching. The environmental level is dealt with more closely in the chapters on visual regulation of ball catching (Savelsbergh and van der Kamp, Chapter 2), team dynamics and decision making in rugby (Passos, Araújo, Davids, Diniz, Gouvela, and Serpa, Chapter 3) and emergent tactics in combat sports (Hristovski, Davids, and Araújo, Chapter 4). At each level, I will illustrate what the major issues are at that level, and how these challenges are dealt with or accomplished. In the final section, I will re-assemble the levels, describing how control over multiple levels can be mastered in a learning process, and illustrate the intricate end result using ski jumping as an example.

LEVELS OF COMPLEXITY IN SCIENCE

Inspired by the reductionist approach, movement science typically divides performance in different levels. This has resulted in various levels of analysis, the typical focus of researchers, and various levels of control, the typical domain of the performer. A common division in levels is from the general, macro, to the specific, micro. At the macro level we find the environmental level where interactions between people take place, as well as interactions between people and the environment. This is the level where perception and behavior interact, where team dynamics unfold, and where tactics are played out. The next level towards micro is the behavioral level of overall performance. This is the level of one person and the multiple degrees of freedom (or movement possibilities) of this person's body (Bernstein, 1967). Sports performance is often defined at this level. Another level down, we find the joint movements, such as a simple knee bend at the start of a vertical jump, or plantar flexion of the foot at the end of it. Each joint is set in motion by a muscle ensemble flexing, extending, or rotating the joint, which is the next level down. One can also focus on the properties of a single muscle, or the muscle fibers constituting a muscle, or even further down to the cell level or molecular level. Traditionally, the relationship between different levels was thought to be hierarchical, with organizations at the macro levels constraining patterns at micro levels.

As indicated above, complexity of performance resides both within the levels and across the levels. Furthermore, many phenomena first emerge when components within or across levels interact. Examples of emergent patterns are traffic jams, human culture, and flocking of animals. Although each car, person, and animal contributes to the overall pattern, no single one has created it or can be said to be 'home' to the pattern. The same goes for team dynamics or the interaction between opponent players in sports, neither can be predicted nor understood from an exclusive focus on the individual. As emergent patterns are often impossible to predict from knowledge of the separate components, their existence flies directly in the face of reductionism. The whole can be, and often is, much more than the sum of its parts. Furthermore, it is becoming increasingly clear that interactions at micro levels can give rise to organizational patterns at macro levels, arguing against strict hierarchical models. In other words, interactions between for example cells or joints give rise to self-organized properties that in turn can affect organ function or lead to coordinated action at the behavioral level, respectively. This overall complexity no matter where one looks has contributed to the reluctance to study performance at the full scale of complexity and to the difficulty to formulate a grand theory of performance. One class of theories forms a notable exception to this general rule, namely non-linear dynamic systems theories (e.g., Costa, Goldberger, and Peng, 2005; Haken, 2000; Kauffman, 1993; Yates, 1987). These theories have an explicit focus on complexity within and across levels, self-organization, emergent phenomena, the relationships between different levels, and scale invariants, i.e., characteristics that do not change despite reduction or enlargement of scale, i.e., zooming in or out. This latter characteristic of symmetry across different scales, also called self-similarity, has led to the definition of fractals (e.g., Mandelbrot, 1982). Examples of fractals are the leaves of ferns, snowflakes, and coastlines. In each of these examples, turning up the magnifying glass reveals new details that bear geometrical similarity to lower levels of magnification. Although once the domain of mathematics and physics, fractal analyses are increasingly applied to the study of biological systems (e.g., Iannaccone and Khokha, 1995) in general, and the study of cardiodynamics (e.g., Stanley, Amaral, Goldberger, Havelin, Ivanov, and Peng, 1999) and gait dynamics (e.g., Hausdorff, Purdon, Peng, Ladin, Wei, and Goldberger, 1996) in particular. In the remainder of this chapter, the focus will not lie on multi-scale analyses, but on knowledge within and across levels that is relevant for sports.

BEHAVIORAL LEVEL

As mentioned above, the behavioral level is the level of the overall performance. This level is often characterized by whole-body movements, consisting of multiple degrees of freedom that have sheer endless possibilities for accomplishing a task. The organization of the many degrees of freedom that need to be controlled is the major issue at this level (Bernstein, 1967). For example, a child bouncing a ball around an obstacle course has to control many body parts: the joints and muscles of the arm bouncing the ball, the joints and muscles of the lower body navigating around the obstacles, and the joints and muscles involved in maintaining posture and balance. Control of the relevant body parts is further complicated by the redundancy, or more accurately degeneracy (Edelman and Galley, 2001), of the movement system. Degeneracy means that the movement system has more degrees of freedom and possible movement organizations than are necessary to solve a motor problem. In other words, more than one combination of body parts and movement organizations will accomplish the task, so that one has many possibilities to choose from to get the job done. For example, which hand to bounce the ball with, the many possible trajectories around the obstacles, the speed of walking, the frequency of bouncing, and so on. How does one organize the control over all body parts? And how does one choose between many possible solutions?

Nikolai Bernstein, a Russian physiologist, suggested a 3-stage learning process for the acquisition of motor control. In these stages, the body's mechanical degrees of freedom are progressively constrained, explored, and exploited, respectively (Bernstein, 1967). From the first to the third stage, both complexity and proficiency of the movement increase. An earlier study on a so-called ski apparatus illustrated the changing degrees of freedom during a learning process (Vereijken, van Emmerik, Whiting, and Newell, 1992a). The performer stands on a platform that can be moved sideways over bent rails. Springs assure that the platform returns towards the resting position in the centre after a deviation sideways. The task of a novice performer is to make large, fluent sideways movements, which entails learning when to exert how much force on the platform, while maintaining balance. At the first stage, novices typically reduce their movement possibilities, and thereby the control problem, by allowing only few body parts to be actively involved in the performance and introducing fixed couplings between these body parts. Hip, knee, and ankle joints are kept at fairly rigid angles, and they move mostly in concert. This allows the performer to remain balanced, but the sideways movements are small and far from fluent. At the advanced stage, the performer gradually increases the number of degrees of freedom involved in the performance, and fixed couplings gradually give way to functional couplings. This increases the output of the system, resulting in larger and more fluent sideways movements. At the expert stage, the entire body is involved in the performance (Vereijken et al., 1992a) and efficient use is made of existing reactive forces (Vereijken, Whiting, and Beek, 1992b), thereby reducing the need for active muscle forces (Vereijken, van Emmerik, Bongaardt, Beek, and Newell, 1997). This decreases energy-consumption while increasing performance (Almåsbakk, Whiting, and Helgerud, 2001). This line of research illustrates why performers bother exploring and exploiting degrees of freedom in endless cycles of practice in order to reach expert levels of performance when constraining degrees of freedom gets the job done as well. The answer lies in the effect of performing an activity with the contribution of only a few and tightly coupled degrees of freedom. Such performance lacks flexibility, complexity, fluency, and often proficiency. When one wants to excel at a performance, it is the exploitation of movement possibilities and available energy that makes the difference between a gold medal and no medal at all.

Although several studies have provided support for each of the stages of learning as proposed by Bernstein (e.g., Haehl, Vardaxis, and Ulrich, 2000; Ko, Challis, and Newell, 2003; Paavolainen, Häkkinen, Hämäläinen, Nummela, and Rusko, 1999; Vereijken et al., 1992a, 1992b), evidence for all three stages is rarely found in a single learning study. More typically, evidence for two out of three stages is found in both empirical studies and in examples from daily life. For example, many people engage in many activities for which they will never reach (or need to reach) the third stage of expert performance where reactive forces are skillfully exploited and performance is fluent and efficient. They lack the practice, experience, opportunity, or motivation to achieve the expert level. Similarly, the first stage of learning is often skipped when one does not need to stay in control of all degrees of freedom or all reactive forces (Vereijken and Adolph, 1999). This was illustrated in a study on infant crawling, in which infants that started to crawl on their belly explored rather than constrained their movement possibilities (Adolph, Vereijken, and Denny, 1998). They advanced to the expert stage when they embarked on crawling on hands and knees, where a stable, diagonal movement pattern across the four limbs allowed for fast and efficient crawling (Adolph et al., 1998). Furthermore, progression through different stages of learning may deviate from the serial fashion suggested by Bernstein, as was illustrated in a study by Chow, Davids, Button, and Koh (2008) on adults practicing a kicking task. Their results highlighted the influence of individual characteristics on observed coordination changes. Finally, patterns of change in movement organization with experience are often strongly task specific rather than task independent, as illustrated in a cross-sectional study of ball bouncing by Broderick and Newell (1999). The latter authors question the generality of Bernstein's model as a global task coordination principle, suggesting instead that it is the interaction between performer, task, and environment that gives rise to specific coordination patterns. Despite this lack of consensus, the concepts of degrees of freedom, exploration, and exploitation have demonstrated their benefit for coaching pupils through motor learning processes, in particular when combined with the manipulation of organismic, task, and environmental constraints (e.g., Bjerke and Vereijken, 2007; Corbetta and Vereijken, 1999; Newell, 1985, 1986).

LEVEL OF JOINT MOVEMENTS

Instead of looking at whole-body movements, one can also concentrate on the individual joint movements. Some of the issues at this level are the anatomical, biomechanical, and neuronal differences that exist between different joints. Anatomical differences are reflected in the different movement directions of the joints and differences in the muscle ensemble moving the joints. The knee, for example, has only one movement direction: flexion-extension. The elbow has an additional movement direction: pronation-supination. The shoulder, in contrast, has three movement directions: flexion-extension, adduction-abduction, and internal rotation-external rotation. Differences in the muscle ensemble creating motion in the joints are reflected in the number of muscles working on a joint, and in whether they are mono-articulate or multi-articulate. Bi-articulate muscles, for example, span two joints, such as the hamstrings which crosses both hip and knee joint, or gastrocnemius which crosses both knee and ankle joints. Multi-articulate muscles actively couple joints, which improves the coordination of movements and reduces the redundancy of the degrees of freedom of the system (van Ingen Schenau, 1989). In addition to the anatomical differences there are biomechanical differences, reflected in differences in lever arms, muscle masses, and so on. Neuronal differences are found in differences in innervation of muscles of proximal versus distal joints. For example, the distal muscles of the wrist and digits are controlled by the lateral descending pathways that cross in the lower part of the brainstem. Proximal muscles of the shoulder, on the other hand, are controlled by descending ventromedial pathways that do not cross (Kandel, Schwartz, and Jessell, 2000; Kolb and Whishaw, 2003). How do these anatomical, biomechanical, and neuronal differences influence joint movements and the control hereof?

Several studies in our lab are tackling this question from diverse angles. One of the angles focuses on accuracy and control of simple pointing movements in proximal versus distal joints (Aune, Vereijken, and Ettema, manuscript in preparation). Questions in this study are related to whether lateral versus ventromedial control of joint muscles is related to differences in spatial and temporal accuracy of joint movements, and to possible differences in speed-accuracy trade-off. Another angle of our research focuses on force control and force modulation in isometric contractions such as arm flexion, arm extension, and plantar flexion. We investigate this in a wide variety of subjects, such as young adults, elderly, adolescents, and children and adults with Cerebral Palsy (CP). The maximum voluntary contraction (MVC) of these subjects differs widely, with adults typically having higher MVC than children, and healthy younger subjects having higher MVC than subjects with CP or elderly. The relationship between force control, force modulation, and the level of MVC is studied by comparing subjects' ability to maintain a steady force level at 20% and 40% of their MVC, their ability to increase and decrease force in ramp and sinus contractions, differing rates of force development, and differences in the ability to learn to track a force curve through isometric contractions.

Both these lines of research beg the question how muscles work together in creating and controlling movement in a joint. How do they stabilize a joint? When are muscles working together, or in opposition of each other, or in an alternating fashion? How is this influenced by age or disease? These questions belong to the next level down, that of muscle functioning, and will not be further elaborated upon here.

ASSEMBLING THE LEVELS

As indicated above, researchers often study phenomena on one particular level while ignoring the others. Such phenomena can be the interaction between perception and action at the environmental level, the changing number of degrees of freedom during a learning process on the behavioral level, the relationship between the accuracy and speed of movements at the joint level, the organization of muscle activation patterns at the muscular level, and so on. One can also focus on the explanation of a phenomenon in terms of the next level up or down. For example, how does perception-action coupling at the environmental level influence the number of degrees of freedom at the behavioral level? How can specific properties of joint movements be explained by the muscle ensemble creating motion at the joint? How do characteristics of muscle functioning influence the possibilities of joint motion and overall performance? By focusing on one or two levels, the researcher considerably simplifies the investigation at hand. The disadvantage is that outside the laboratory, all levels contribute to coordinated movements and goal-directed actions. Furthermore, additional phenomena emerge in the interaction between different components. Building theories of movement control on research restricted to certain levels necessarily leads to fragmented theories that can explain some of the phenomena, but typically do poorly at others or exclude them explicitly from their scope. As a result, we lack a unified theory of movement, having instead multiple hypotheses, models, and principles of parts of the movement problem. Examples of this are the equilibrium-point hypothesis (λ-model) for single muscle control (Feldman, 1966, 1986), the minimum jerk model for multijoint movements (Flash and Hogan, 1985), the vector-integration-to-endpoint model of arm movements (Bullock and Grossberg, 1988) and the adaptive model theory of central nervous system processing (Neilson, 1993; Neilson and Neilson, 2005).

In performance, one does not have the luxury of focusing on just a few levels and ignoring the others. More often than not, performance would fail under such conditions. On the contrary, one has to assemble many levels simultaneously in order to get the body to move as intended. For example, if a baseball player stretches out an arm to catch a fly ball, postural control systems need to be active as well in order to avoid balance loss. When a race walker increases both step length and step frequency, upper body rotations need to increase also to counteract disruptive reactive forces. In elite sports, the relevant processes on all levels have to be in place in order to be able to compete at the highest level. How does one achieve this? How does one bring the different levels together? The answer is through a gradual learning process, which already starts before we are born. Even a fetus displays bouts of activity, and the chain of events leading to and following the resulting movements contributes to the functional development of the brain and the gradual control over movements. The process of learning continues after we are born and speeds up as we start interacting with our environment. As Sheets-Johnstone (1999) put it so aptly, we all start out apprentices of our own bodies. We have to learn what kind of body we have, how we can activate it, how we can control its movements, and what the consequences are of our movements. Later learning builds on these early foundations and extends the level of our control and achievements. Our genetic make-up, our personality and ambitions, our environment, and available opportunities all serve as boundary conditions for what we want to achieve, what it takes to be able to reach our goal, and the probability for achieving our goal. Although there is little the outside world can do at the earliest stages of learning, that of a fetus and newborn, coaches and trainers can help older children and athletes to improve their performance. They can point out what factors and what levels need to be focused upon and improved. This way, an athlete can get proficient at an appropriate level before focusing on another level. This is not to say that learning should necessarily proceed bottom-up (Vickers, Livingston, Umeris-Bohnert, and Holden, 1999) or that a complex skill should always be broken down into its components that a learner must acquire separately and in sequence. It is more likely a combination of approaches, including training at the full complexity of the skill, that results in long-lasting, flexible movement skills.

EXEMPLIFYING ASSEMBLED LEVELS

Let us take a look at a more elaborate example of a complex skill, ski jumping, that illustrates the interplay within and between levels. A ski jump can be divided in four different phases, namely the in-run, the take-off, the flight, and the landing. In order to set a world record, many factors at many levels need to be in place, securing proficient performance in each of the four phases. The important sub-tasks for the athlete during the in-run are to maintain symmetric medio-lateral balance on both feet and to have proper anterior-posterior weight distribution, which is slightly forward (Ettema, Bråten, and Bobbert, 2005). Both these behavioral demands must be implemented by appropriate force production around the joints of upper body, upper limbs, and lower limbs. This can to a large extent be practiced indoors on a force plate that is mounted on the floor or on a movable platform rolling down a slope, giving the athlete and the coach immediate feedback about actual weight distribution. Furthermore, in-run speed should be maximized by minimizing air resistance. The proper body posture for this can be established in a wind tunnel and is again implemented at the level of joints and muscular activity.

With a proper in-run on the largest hills, the athlete will approach the take-off board at speeds of over 100 km/h. In order to take-off properly, the athlete needs to produce equal force with both legs and create a slight forward rotation (Ettema et al., 2005), all within a time span of about 300 ms. This too can be practiced indoors with the help of force plates. This allows the athlete to check the result of adjustments at the muscle level on the outcome level of behavior. Furthermore, exploiting existing aerodynamic forces at take-off is an important prerequisite for achieving a good flight position (Virmavirta, Kivekäs, and Komi, 2001). These characteristics as well lie at the behavioral level.

During the flight phase, which can last for about 7 seconds on the largest ski flying hills, the athlete needs to keep an appropriate angle between body and skis to balance optimally between lift and drag. This angle should start at about 10^0 at the beginning of the flight and rapidly decrease to about 7^0 on average (Seo, Murakami, and Yoshida, 2004). With extended practice and many jumps, the best jumpers also learn to 'ride the air' by continually making small adjustments in ski and body positions according to environmental conditions. Again, changes at the behavioral level are brought about by fine-tuning at the muscular level. Here, the coach and video playback can help the athlete pinpoint potential factors for improvement. Finally, at the landing, jumping legislation dictates that the feet should be in split position and the arms straight out from the side of the body. This latter posture aids balance, while the distance between the feet (anterior-posterior) and the skis (medio-lateral) gives a smooth glide through the out-run radius. Again, the coach and video playback can help the athlete improve the landing and receive higher scores from the judges.

Apart from the obvious complexity of the skill, ski jumping was chosen as example for an additional reason. Although scientists can study and describe separate components of the skill at will, it is not possible for the jumper to practice one phase of the jump only while ignoring the other three. Although parts of the task in each phase can be focused on and fine-tuned in simulation jumps, an actual jump will necessarily encompass all four phases. This means that practice as well has to include actual jumps on actual hills at full scales of complexity.

CONCLUSION

As described in this chapter, performance is created by many factors at many different levels. Observing the process of acquiring a new skill, in children and adults alike, provides a unique window for researchers how the different levels of performance are assembled by the performer. Although one can attempt to either study or acquire skilled performance factor by factor, level by level, proficient performance requires all factors to be in place, both within and across levels. Each level does not operate independently, but is both coupled to and restricted by the level below and the level above. Furthermore, additional complexity arises as self-organized, emergent properties in the interaction between factors and between levels that cannot be studied or created by breaking down the skills in components. For example, the challenge at the behavioral level is to get all the body parts to function together in a coordinated manner. This is guided by the perception-action couplings at the environmental level, and achieved by the creation of the proper moments at the joint level. To achieve the proper moments, the challenge at the muscle level is to provide the appropriate contractions at the appropriate time. Depending on the goal, the overall challenge can be to achieve maximum efficiency, maximum output, minimum effort, to score a goal, and so on. Training and learning do not start at all levels at once, but build up gradually with steadily increasing complexity. As not all levels are accessible to either the coach or the athlete, one of the middle levels is often a good starting point, for example the joint level or the behavioral level. From each of these levels, increased competence paves the way for incorporating additional factors and additional levels, allowing more complex phenomena to emerge in the process. As several chapters in this book highlight, high-level athletes are a rich source of information for researchers regarding the complexity within and across levels, just as much as researchers can inform athletes about how to come to terms with complexity.

REFERENCES

Adolph, K.E., Vereijken, B., and Denny, M.A. (1998). Learning to crawl. *Child Development*, *69*, 1299-1312.

Almåsbakk, B., Whiting, H.T.A., and Helgerud, J. (2001). The efficient learner. *Biological Cybernetics*, *84*, 75-83.

Aune, T.K., Vereijken, B., and Ettema, G.J.P. Spatial and temporal precision of pointing movements in proximal versus distal joints. Manuscript in preparation.

Bernstein, N.A. (1967). *The coordination and regulation of movement*. London: Pergamon Press.

Bjerke, Ø., and Vereijken, B. (2007). Promoting motor skills in school children and adolescents. In J. Liukkonen, Y. Vanden Auweele, B. Vereijken, D. Alfermann and Y. Theodorakis (Eds.), *Psychology for physical educators – Student in focus* (pp. 219-237). Champaign, IL: Human Kinetics.

Broderick, M.P., and Newell, K.M. (1999). Coordination patterns in ball bouncing as a function of skill. *Journal of Motor Behavior, 31*, 165-188.

Bullock, D., and Grossberg, S. (1988). Neural dynamics of planned arm movements: Emergent invariants and speed-accuracy properties during trajectory formation. *Psychological Review, 95*, 49-90.

Chow, J.Y., Davids, K., Button, C., and Koh, M. (2008). Coordination changes in a discrete multi-articular action as a function of practice. *Acta Psychologica, 127*, 163-176.

Corbetta, D., and Vereijken, B. (1999). Understanding development and learning of motor coordination in sport: The contribution of dynamic systems. *International Journal of Sport Psychology, 30*, 507-530.

Costa, M., Goldberger, A.L., and Peng, C.-K. (2005). Multiscale entropy analysis of biological signals. *Physical Review E, 71*, 1-17.

Edelman, G.M., and Galley, J.A. (2001). Degeneracy and complexity in biological systems. *Proceedings of the National Academy of Sciences, USA, 98*, 13763-13768.

Ettema, G.J.C., Bråten, S., and Bobbert, M.F. (2005). Dynamics of the in-run in ski jumping: A simulation study. *Journal of Applied Biomechanics, 21*, 247-259.

Feldman, A.G. (1966). Functional tuning of the nervous system with control of movement or maintenance of a steady posture - II. Controllable parameters of the muscles. *Biophysics, 11*, 565-578.

Feldman, A.G. (1986). Once more on the equilibrium-point hypothesis (λ-model) for motor control. *Journal of Motor Behavior, 18*, 17-54.

Flash, T., and Hogan, N. (1985). The coordination of arm movements: An experimentally confirmed mathematical model. *Journal of Neuroscience, 5*, 1688-1703.

Haehl, V., Vardaxis, V., and Ulrich, B. (2000). Learning to cruise: Bernstein's theory applied to skill acquisition during infancy. *Human Movement Science, 19*, 685-715.

Haken, H. (2000). *Information and self-organization: A macroscopic approach to complex systems*. New York: Springer-Verlag.

Hausdorff, J.M., Purdon, P., Peng, C.-K., Ladin, Z., Wei, J.Y., and Goldberger, A.L. (1996). Fractal dynamics of human gait: Stability of long-range correlations in stride interval fluctuations. *Journal of Applied Physiology, 80*, 1448-1457.

Iannaccone, P.M., and Khokha, M.K. (1995). *Fractal geometry in biological systems: An analytical approach*. New York: CRC Press.

Kandel, E.R., Schwartz, J.H., and Jessell, T.M. (2000). *Principles of neural science*. New York: McGraw-Hill.

Kauffman, S. (1993). *The origins of order: Self-organization and selection in evolution*. New York: Oxford University Press.

Ko, Y.G, Challis, J.H., and Newell, K.M. (2003). Learning to coordinate redundant degrees of freedom in a dynamic balance task. *Human Movement Science, 22*, 47-66.

Kolb, B., and Whishaw, I.Q. (2003). *Fundamentals of human neuropsychology* (5th ed). New York: Worth Publishers.

Mandelbrot, B.B. (1982). *The fractal geometry of nature*. San Fransisco: W.H. Freeman.

Neilson, P.D. (1993). The problem of redundancy in movement control: The adaptive model theory approach. *Psychological Research*, *55*, 99-106.

Neilson, P.D., and Neilson, M.D. (2005). An overview of adaptive model theory: Solving the problems of redundancy, resources, and nonlinear interactions in human movement control. *Journal of Neural Engineering*, *2*, S279-S312.

Newell, K.M. (1985). Coordination, control and skill. In D. Goodman, R.B. Wilberg and I.M. Franks (Eds.), *Differing perspectives in motor learning, memory, and control* (pp. 295-317). Amsterdam: North-Holland.

Newell, K.M. (1986). Constraints on the development of coordination. In M.G. Wade and H.T.A. Whiting (Eds.), *Motor development in children: Aspects of coordination and control* (pp. 341-360). Dordrecht: Nijhoff.

Paavolainen, L., Häkkinen, K., Hämäläinen, I., Nummela, A., and Rusko, H. (1999). Explosive strength training improves 5-km running time by improving running economy and muscle power. *Journal of Applied Physiology*, *86*, 1527-1533.

Seo, K., Murakami, M., and Yoshida, K. (2004). Optimal flight technique for V-style ski jumping. *Sports Engineering*, *7*, 97-104.

Sheets-Johnstone, M. (1999). *The primacy of movement*. Amsterdam: John Benjamins Publishing Co.

Stanley, H.E., Amaral, L.A.N., Goldberger, A.L., Havelin, S., Ivanov, P.C., and Peng, C.-K. (1999). Statistical physics and physiology: Monofractal and multifractal approaches. *Physica A*, *270*, 309-324.

van Ingen Schenau, G.J. (1989). From rotation to translation: Constraints on multi-joint movements and the unique action of bi-articular muscles. *Human Movement Science*, *8*, 301-337.

Vereijken, B., and Adolph, K.E. (1999). Transitions in the development of locomotion. In G.J.P. Savelsbergh, H.L.J. van der Maas and P.C.L. van Geert (Eds.), *Non-linear developmental processes* (pp. 137-149). Amsterdam: Elsevier.

Vereijken, B., van Emmerik, R.E.A., Bongaardt, R., Beek, W.J., and Newell, K.M. (1997). Changing coordinative structures in complex skill acquisition. *Human Movement Science*, *16*, 823-844.

Vereijken, B., van Emmerik, R.E.A., Whiting, H.T.A., and Newell, K.M. (1992a). Free(z)ing degrees of freedom in skill acquisition. *Journal of Motor Behavior*, *24*, 133-142.

Vereijken, B., Whiting, H.T.A., and Beek, W.J. (1992b). A dynamical systems approach to skill acquisition. *Quarterly Journal of Experimental Psychology*, *45A*, 323-344.

Vickers, J.N., Livingston, L.F., Umeris-Bohnert, S., and Holden, D. (1999). Decision training: The effects of complex instruction, variable practice and reduced delayed feedback on the acquisition and transfer of a motor skill. *Journal of Sports Sciences*, *17*, 357-367.

Virmavirta, M., Kivekäs, J., and Komi, P.V. (2001). Take-off aerodynamics in ski jumping. *Journal of Biomechanics*, *34*, 465-470.

Yates, F.E. (1987). *Self-organizing systems: The emergence of order*. New York: Plenum Press.

SECTION 2. WHAT IS THE INFLUENCE OF KNOWLEDGE ON PLAYER'S BEHAVIOUR?

In: Perspectives on Cognition and Action in Sport
Editors: D. Araújo, H. Ripoll and M. Raab

ISBN: 978-1-60692-390-0
© 2009 Nova Science Publishers, Inc.

Chapter 7

WHAT IS THE IMPACT OF KNOWLEDGE ON PLAYER'S BEHAVIOUR?

Hubert Ripoll

Information and System Science Laboratory & Sport Sciences Faculty,
Aix-Marseille Universities, France

ABSTRACT

A comparison of cognitive and noncognitive models raises two questions: Are the behaviors of athletes -- particularly in team sports -- guided by knowledge, or do they emerge during action? And beyond this question, is it possible to study the behavior of athletes outside of the playing context? The author examines these questions through the chapters in this section, and proposes his point of view.

INTRODUCTION

Are the behaviors of athletes -- particularly in team sports -- guided by knowledge, or do they emerge during action? And beyond this question, is it possible to study the behavior of athletes outside of the playing context? Specialists have been asking these fundamental questions since the appearance of cognitive models, from the second part of the XIX century, and the noncognitive models such as Gibson's (1979) ecological approach, and Kugler, Kelso, and Turvey's (1980) dynamic approach. In this introduction, I analyze the stance taken on this issue by the authors of each chapter in this section, and I provide a possible answer.

The chapter by Williams and North (Williams and North, Chapter 8) studies expert knowledge stored in memory: its nature, its representation format (local or global, static or dynamic), and how it is activated in accordance with task constraints and the subject's level of expertise. The authors conclude that knowledge governs players' expectations and perceptions, and enables them to produce suitable responses despite the heavy constraints involved in sports. To the question "knowledge or emergence?" they answer "knowledge" and to the question "is it possible to scientifically identify a world-class player outside of his or her sport context?" their answer is clearly "yes".

The chapter by Laurent and Ripoll (Laurent and Ripoll, Chapter 11) deals with how the cognitive system adapts to the constraints of sports situations, notably, time pressure and the amount of information to be processed, both of which counter reasoning and decision-making processes. They show that a perceptual categorization process activates perceptual knowledge in a quasi-automatic way, and this allows players to cope with the extreme conditions found in sports. The authors bridge the gap between their own approach and Araújo et al.'s view by suggesting a direct perception-decision coupling that frees the system of the heavy processing load incurred by reasoning. To the question "knowledge or emergence?" they answer "knowledge" and to the question "is it possible to scientifically identify a world-class player outside of his or her sport context?" their answer is clearly "yes".

Köppen and Raab's chapter (Köppen and Raab, Chapter 9) looks into how task constraints, particularly complexity and time pressure, affect decision-making. They postulate the existence of heuristics for producing not the ideal response, but a satisfycing one, given the constraints of the task and the decision-maker's resources. The idea of limited rationality provides these authors with a fruitful theoretical framework for understanding how actors make decisions in such contexts. To the question "knowledge or emergence?" they answer "knowledge" and to the question "is it possible to scientifically identify a world-class player outside of his or her sport context?" their answer is clearly "yes".

The chapter by Araújo, Davids, Cordovil, Ribeiro, and Fernandes (Araújo, Davids, Cordovil, Ribeiro, and Fernandes, Chapter 10) describes the interaction between two offense and defense players, each seeking to gain a favorable position with respect to the goal. They describe the moves of two such players in terms of physics laws, using the ecological approach to account for perceptual-motor interactions and the dynamic approach to account for physical interactions between players, seen as systems functioning as a whole. The fact that sports behaviors can be described by the laws of physics, in the end quite simple, leads these authors to answer "emergence" to the question "knowledge or emergence?" And their answer to the question "is it possible to scientifically identify a world-class player outside of his or her sport context?" is clearly "no".

These different points of view appear totally contradictory. But is this incompatibility well-founded? I don't think so, for in my mind, two different components of a player's actions are at stake: one that controls what I call local behaviors, and another that controls global behaviors (for a discussion of these concepts, see Ripoll and Ripoll, 2004). "Local behaviors" are seen here as direct interactions between players as they attempt to get the advantage; global behaviors are interactions of the entire team. In this view, local behaviors are determined by simple physics principles that regulate confrontations between players; global behaviors result from combining local behaviors in accordance with a frame of reference shared by all players, i.e., a playing system.

It is obvious that mental representations guide the behavior of players. Playing systems are social conceptions devised by coaches. In 1930 in Uruguay, the players competing for the first soccer World Cup did not adopt the same playing systems as in the German competition in 2006, which is proof if there is one that these systems do not emerge spontaneously. Simply watch a group of beginners playing soccer -- they'll manage their local spaces on their own, but they'll never get organized according to a conventional playing system. Have them play regularly together and you'll see evolved forms of interaction appear, but you'll never see a conventional playing system emerge.

We tackled this issue in a study currently under way[1] where we administered a soccer recognition task to coaches, trained players (with more than 10 years of training), untrained players (who had been playing soccer as a recreational activity, without formal coaching, at least once a week for more than three years), and nonplayers. The last two groups were avid spectators of soccer games, either live or on television. The experiment consisted of judging the similarity ("same" or "different") of two soccer configurations presented in succession on a video screen. The source situation was presented for 4 seconds, followed by a mask and then the to-be-judged target. Three types of situations were presented: prototypical configurations like those found in a conventional soccer-playing system, coherent configurations that followed the internal logic of the game but were not prototypical, and incoherent configurations that did not obey the logic of soccer. The response-accuracy results (<.05) showed that (i) only coaches and trained players recognized prototypical configurations and coherent configurations, and (ii) prototypical configurations were processed more effectively than coherent ones. The response-time results showed that coaches and trained players processed prototypical and coherent configurations faster than incoherent ones. These findings indicate that soccer training triggers the storage of perceptual knowledge in memory, whereas informal playing and soccer-game watching on television do not. It thus seems that untrained players only learn how to handle local interactions; they apparently do not have access to complex playing systems or even to general knowledge about the structure of the team. The fact that during action, only trained players reproduce the elaborate forms of play that constitute playing systems clearly leads to the idea that a team's behavior is determined by representations shared by team members; these representations act as a cognitive background. The question that arises is whether reliance on this cognitive background is incompatible with the extreme time constraints encountered during play. This is what Laurent and Ripoll bring to the fore in this section by showing that perceptual knowledge is activated automatically whenever known categories are involved. Indeed, it has been shown that categorical perception processes trigger a low-level, feedforward type of activity (corresponding to sensory encoding) as early as 75ms post-stimulus, and a decision-related high-level activity (corresponding to categorization) starting at 150ms post-stimulus (Fei-Fei, VanRullen, Koch, and Perona, 2005). So what we have here are highly automated processes facilitated by visual attention (Hillyard and Anllo-Vento, 1998) in the low-level phase and by categorical knowledge in the high-level phase.

Do these results go against Araújo et al.'s (this section)? Certainly not. As stated above, control of local behaviors (interactions between individual players) and control of global behaviors (the way the team operates as a whole) are rooted in different modes of functioning. Local interactions imply managing optical flow to permit effective use of playing spaces and to organize one's moves within those spaces. In the ecological and dynamic approaches, the adjustments players make to occupy or defend these spaces is naturally governed by physics principles, so it follows that these principles are well-suited to describing such interactions. But, even though the combination of all local spaces -- which we will call the location space -

---

[1] Research in collaboration with Vincent Ferrari (CReA – Salon-de-Provence, France) and Mohamed Sebanne (LSIS - University of Mostaganem, Algeria)

- can result in a homogeneous organization of space, it will never lead to the construction of a global space -- which we will call the form space -- made up of evolved forms of play.

The distinction between location space (the space of actions) and form space (the space of representations) was proposed by Paillard back in 1971, so it is not new. It is related to the functioning of the central nervous system in general, and of the visual system in particular. Accordingly, locating functions, which are in charge of physical relations between an organism and its environment, serve to construct the location space and are processed at the subcortical level, whereas functions in charge of form recognition or activation serve to build the form space and are processed at the cortical level. Dancers, for example, use their locating functions to move around, while their form-reproducing functions act as the "signature" of their movement. In the same manner, the motricity of team-sports players is determined both by optical laws and the principles of system dynamics, which allow players to manage the local action space, and by their cognitive background, i.e., the conventional space of prototypical playing forms into which conventional playing systems are incorporated. In my mind, these findings suggest that a player's local space is controlled at a more superficial level and in a more automatic way than the global space. The latter space would be controlled by more elaborate processes, although potentially automated too, as shown by Poplu, Baratgin, Mavromatis, and Ripoll (2003) and Laurent and Ripoll (Chapter 11).

It is not surprising, then, that the interactions of two players, one competing to occupy a space and the other competing to keep that space, can be perfectly described by the ecological and dynamic models. Similarly, it is not surprising that if we change the players' physical properties (by modifying their size) or their symbolic representations (by modifying the task instructions), the functional characteristics of the pair change too, and -- borrowing the concepts of nonlinear dynamic systems -- we freeze the relation onto a new stable state which is the response adopted by the system to satisfy task constraints.

To conclude, I contend that the approaches presented in this section are complementary, to the extent that they delineate different facets of sports playing. To the question "Knowledge or emergence?" my answer is "knowledge and emergence". And to the question "Is it possible to scientifically identify a world-class player outside of his or her sport context?" my answer is clearly "yes".

Let the readers decide for themselves.

REFERENCES

Fei-Fei, L., VanRullen, R., Koch, C., and Perona, P. (2005). Why does natural scene categorization require little attention? Exploring attentional requirements for natural and synthetic stimuli. *Visual Cognition, 12*(6), 893-924.

Gibson, J.J. (1979). *The ecological approach to visual perception.* Hillsdale, New Jersey: Lawrence Erlbaum Associates.

Hillyard, S.A., and Anllo-Vento, L. (1998). Event-related brain potentials in the study of visual selective attention. *Proceedings of the National Academy of Sciences, 95,* 781-787.

Kugler, P.N., Kelso, J.A.S., and Turvey, M.T. (1980). On the concept of coordinated structures as dissipative structures. I: Theoretical lines of convergence. In G. Stelmach, and J. Requin (Ed.), *Tutorials in Motor Behavior* (pp. 3-45). Amsterdam: North Holland.

Paillard, J. (1971). Les déterminants moteurs de l'organisation spatiale. *Cahiers de Psychologie, 14,* 261-316.

Poplu, G., Baratgin, J., Mavromatis, S., and Ripoll, H. (2003). What kinds of processes underlie decision-making in soccer simulation? An implicit memory test. *International Journal of Sport and Exercise Psychology, 14,* 390-405.

Ripoll, H. and Ripoll, T. (2004). Le raisonnement. In J. Larue and H. Ripoll (Eds.), *Manuel de Psychologie du Sport. Tome 1: Bases psychologiques de la performance sportive* (pp. 269-280). Paris: Editions Revue EP.S, Collection Recherche et Formation.

In: Perspectives on Cognition and Action in Sport
Editors: D. Araújo, H. Ripoll and M. Raab

ISBN: 978-1-60692-390-0
© 2009 Nova Science Publishers, Inc.

Chapter 8

SOME CONSTRAINTS ON RECOGNITION PERFORMANCE IN SOCCER

A. Mark Williams[1] and Jamie. S. North[2]

John Moores University, Liverpool, England, United Kingdom
Sheffield Hallam University, England, United Kingdom

ABSTRACT

We examine key factors influencing the ability of skilled players to recognise patterns of play in soccer. Our findings suggest that skilled soccer players perceive and process displays based on structural relations between critical features such as team-mates, opponents and the ball. In particular, relative motion information arising from only a few select features such as the central attacking players appears crucial. Although the most likely scenario is that players pick up relative motions between the central attacking players, perhaps in conjunction with the ball and other offensive players, it is not possible at this stage to dismiss the importance of absolute motion information arising from these players. It is also apparent that relevant 'structure' or motion information may only emerge in the final few moments before a critical event such as a penetrative pass or shot at goal. The relationship between recognition and anticipation skill remains unclear, with anticipation most likely being dependent on a range of perceptual-cognitive skills rather than merely on pattern recognition per se. Implications for research, theory and practice are discussed.

INTRODUCTION

The ability to anticipate the intentions of an opponent or the opposing team is essential to performance in many sports. This ability is likely to be particularly important in team ball sports such as soccer where the speed of play often dictates the need to be proactive rather than reactive in deciding on a suitable course of action (Williams, Davids, and Williams, 1999). Numerous published reports exist to document that skilled performers in these sports demonstrate superior anticipation than their less-skilled counterparts (e.g., see Savelsbergh, van der Kamp, Williams and Ward, 2002; Williams, Davids, Burwitz, and Williams, 1994;

Williams and Davids, 1998). Moreover, anticipation skill has been reported to increase in importance at higher levels of competition, with the suggestion that performance on such perceptual-cognitive tests is more sensitive in predicting eventual attainment level compared to physiological and anthropometric measures (Ward and Williams, 2003; Williams and Reilly, 2000).

Skill-based differences in anticipation are well-reported, yet there remains considerable debate as to the mechanisms underpinning effective performance (Williams and Ericsson, 2005; Williams and Ward, 2007). The proposal is that as a result of extended engagement within the sport (e.g., see Ward, Hodges, Starkes, and Williams, 2007) skilled performers developed a range of perceptual-cognitive skills that facilitate anticipation. These skills include the ability to: a) pick up anticipatory cues from an opponent's postural orientation; b) more effectively and efficiently use the visual system to pick up relevant information from the display; c) recognise structure and patterns within the display; d) more accurately predict likely event probabilities (for a detailed review, see Carling, Reilly, and Williams, 2008; Stratton, Reilly, Williams, and Richardson, 2005). Less clear is the extent to which the importance of these skills differs from one situation to the next. It is likely that their relative importance varies from one sport and/or situation to another and that one or more of these skills may be pivotal in guiding the anticipation process at any given moment in time (Williams and Ward, 2007).

When compared to the significant number of reports focusing on advance cue utilisation and visual search behaviours, few researchers have examined recognition performance in sport. The ability to recognise sequences of play is usually inferred from performance on the 'classical' recall or recognition paradigms imported from cognitive psychology (see Chase and Simon, 1973; Goldin, 1978). In the recall paradigm, participants are required to recall players' positions after viewing structured (i.e., a typical offensive move) and unstructured (e.g., players warming up before a match) filmed sequences of play lasting 3-10 seconds. An error score is calculated by comparing each player's actual position with that recalled by participants. A skill effect is usually observed on the structured sequences only (e.g., see Ward and Williams, 2003; Williams and Davids, 1995; Williams et al., 1994).

In the recognition paradigm, players are typically presented with film clips involving structured and unstructured sequences of play lasting 3-10 seconds. In a subsequent recognition phase, players are presented with a similar sample of sequences some of which have been presented in the earlier viewing phase and others of which are novel. Players are required to indicate which sequences are new and which were presented earlier. The accuracy with which players are able to recognise previously viewed clips is taken as the dependent measure. Skilled players are usually more accurate than less-skilled players in recognising structured sequences only (e.g., see Smeeton, Ward, and Williams, 2004; Ward and Williams, 2003; Williams and Davids, 1995).

Although skill-based effects have been commonly reported in the literature, there has been limited progress in identifying the mechanisms underpinning recall or recognition skill. No efforts have been made to record process measures during performance on these tests and consequently, we have limited knowledge of the key sources of information employed when making recall or recognition judgements (i.e., 'what'?) or the time periods for information extraction (i.e., 'when'?). We need to answer the 'what' and 'when' questions in order to better understand superior performance on these tasks and how elite performers within the domains perceive structure and meaning. A somewhat more contentious issue is the extent to which performance on recall and recognition tasks is actually related to anticipation skill. For example, it has been argued that the ability to recall and recognise patterns of play is not directly related to anticipation performance and is a by-product of extended task exposure rather than a constituent of expertise (e.g., Ericsson and Lehmann, 1996). The latter issue would impact significantly on how we should best capture perceptual-cognitive expertise as well as in the design of training programmes to enhance anticipation skill in team ball sports (Ericsson and Williams, 2007; Williams and Ericsson, 2005).

In this chapter, we summarise a recent programme of research undertaken in our laboratories to examine some of the key constraints on recognition performance in sport. We employ the recognition paradigm to identify the mechanisms underpinning the identification of sequences of play in soccer. A combination of process tracing measures are employed, such as eye movement recording and retrospective verbal reports, along with various task manipulations in an attempt to identify the 'what' and 'when' of recognition performance. Moreover, the extent to which recognition performance and anticipation skill are related is determined by recording outcome and process measures as players perform both types of tasks. We present each of the key issues in the form of a question and then attempt to answer this question with reference to recent empirical work. We conclude with a brief discussion of the implications of this work for research, theory and practice.

IS STIMULUS RECOGNITION BASED UPON THE PERCEPTION OF RELATIONAL INFORMATION OR SUPERFICIAL DISPLAY FEATURES?

Williams, Hodges, North, and Barton (2006) examined the relative importance of superficial display features and relational information between players when recognising sequences of play. Skilled and less-skilled soccer players completed a recognition test where sequences of play were presented under both film and point-light display conditions. In the point-light display condition, player positions and movements were highlighted as coloured dots against a black background with the playing area represented as white lines, whereas more superficial features such as the colour of players' uniforms, postural cues, or the condition of the playing surface and other environmental effects were removed. A typical frame of action presented in both film and point-light display format is highlighted in figure 1.

Although skilled players' recognition accuracy suffered in the point-light compared to the film condition, the decrement was less marked than for less-skilled players and, most importantly, the skill main effect was maintained across viewing conditions. The findings are presented in figure 2. Skilled performers are able to detect similarity across patterns of play based upon structural relations (e.g., positions and movements of players) and the higher-order predicates they convey (e.g., tactical significance of these relations between players), whereas less-skilled players depend almost exclusively on more superficial structural features (Gentner and Markman, 1998).

Figure 1. A frame from a typical structured trial presented in a) video and b) point-light display format.

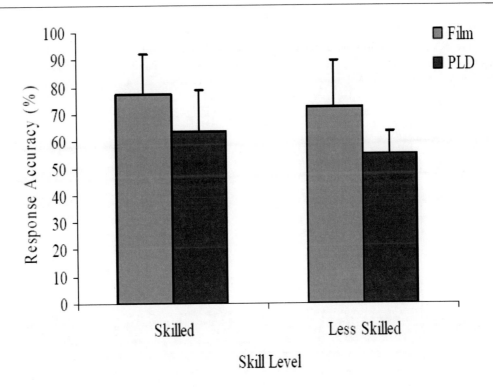

Figure 2. Mean response accuracy scores and standard deviations for the skilled and less-skilled participants on the film and point-light display conditions (data from Williams et al., 2006).

IS RELATIONAL INFORMATION PERCEIVED AS A FUNCTION OF MOTION INFORMATION OR THE POSITIONAL RELATIONSHIPS BETWEEN PLAYERS?

North and Williams (2007) examined the above question by presenting soccer action as static or dynamic sequences during the viewing phase. Skill and less-skilled soccer players were initially presented with 3-second sequences representing either dynamic patterns of play or a static image from the final frame of such a sequence. In the recognition phase, both new and old static images and dynamic film sequences were presented. Only structured stimuli were presented. Participants made familiarity judgments as to whether or not they had viewed the static and dynamic stimuli. An interaction between participant skill level and viewing condition is presented in figure 3.

The skilled players were more accurate when recognising dynamic sequences rather than static images, whereas no differences were observed across display formats for the less-skilled players. Findings suggest that skilled players rely on motion information rather than positional orientation of players when recognising sequences of play. Unfortunately, the particular source(s) of motion information that players pick up could not be identified. Although theoretically it is permissible that skilled players rely on common or absolute motion when determining the familiarity of playing sequences, it is far more likely that the key sources of information arise from the relative motions between two or more players (see also North, Williams, Hodges, Ward, and Ericsson, 2006; North and Williams, 2007).

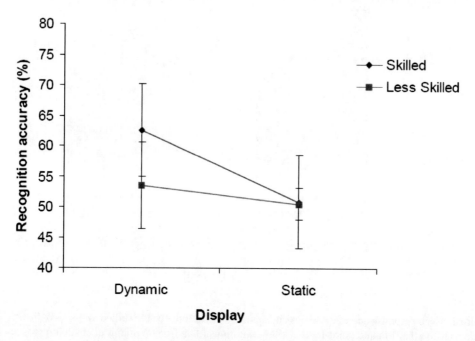

Figure 3. Mean response accuracy scores for skilled and less-skilled participants and standard deviations on the static and dynamic images (data from North and Williams, 2007).

DO SOME PLAYERS CONVEY MORE INFORMATION THAN OTHERS?

If skilled players are able to recognise patterns of play from motion information, as proposed by North and Williams (2007), a related question is whether some players convey more information than others. In order to examine this issue, Williams et al. (2006) used a spatial occlusion technique to delete certain players from the action sequences during the recognition phase. The two central attacking players and their corresponding defensive markers were occluded from the structured sequences of play, whereas in a control condition, two peripheral offensive players and their corresponding defensive markers were occluded to ensure that the deterioration in performance was not caused by the spatial occlusion procedure itself.

A decrement in performance was observed when the two central attackers and their corresponding defensive markers were occluded compared with performance under the non-occluded film and control conditions. This effect was more pronounced in the skilled compared with less-skilled players. The mean response time data for the three conditions are presented for both skill groups in figure 4.

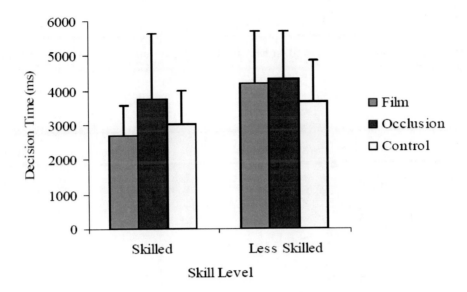

Figure 4. Mean decision times for skilled and less-skilled players in the non occluded film condition (Film), the condition where two central attackers and their corresponding markers were occluded (Occlusion), and another condition where two peripheral players and their markers were removed (Control) (data from Williams et al., 2006).

North et al. (2006) and North and Williams (2007) examined this issue using complimentary methodologies. In the former study, eye movement data were recorded as skilled and less-skilled participants made familiarity-based recognition judgments, whereas in the latter study verbal reports were gathered immediately after each trial. The skilled players recorded a higher number of fixations on central attacking players and made more fixation transitions from the ball to an attacking feature and vice versa when compared with less-skilled players. In a similar vein, skilled players made significantly more verbalisations involving the movements of offensive players 'off the ball' than less-skilled players, with the central attacking players being particularly important for the skilled players when sequences were presented in point-light format. The data suggest that when attempting to identify sequences of play the ability to pick up relative motion information between a few key features, notably the central attacking players in isolation or in conjunction with other features, is crucial.

WHEN DOES THE CRITICAL INFORMATION FOR SKILLED RECOGNITION EMERGE?

Although several researchers have attempted to identify the critical time window for information extraction in relatively closed skills such as the tennis serve or the soccer penalty kick (e.g., see Savelsbergh, van der Kamp, Williams, and Ward, 2005; Williams, Ward, Knowles, and Smeeton, 2002), this issue has not been directly examined using the recognition paradigm. However, in a recent study, North and Williams (2008) manipulated viewing duration during the recognition phase using three groups of skilled players. In the viewing phase the players viewed sequences of play high and low in structure each 5-second in duration, whereas, in the recognition phase, new and old sequences of play were presented with viewing durations that showed either the final 1-, 3- or 5-seconds. The results are presented in figure 5.

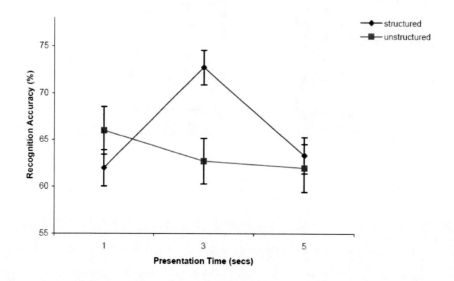

Figure 5. Mean recognition accuracy scores on structured and unstructured sequences with 1-, 3 and 5-second exposure durations respectively (data from North and Williams, 2008).

When highly structured playing sequences were presented, the skilled players were significantly more accurate in the 3-second condition when compared with the 1- and 5-second condition. In contrast, no significant differences in response accuracy were reported across the three viewing conditions on trials deemed low in structure (as determined by a panel of expert coaches). Findings suggest that in relatively chaotic sports such as soccer structure emerges only in the final moments preceding an important attacking event such as a penetrative pass. Although there is evidence to suggest that information can be extracted very quickly when viewing static images of natural scenes (e.g., see Kirchner and Thorpe, 2006), it appears that a viewing duration of 1-second is too short for players to pick up the important relational information that exists between players in dynamic soccer action sequences. In contrast, in the 5-second exposure condition the presentation of additional, non-relevant information negatively affects recognition performance. Viewing duration appears an important constraint on recognition performance in skilled soccer players.

IS PATTERN RECOGNITION A CENTRAL COMPONENT OF ANTICIPATION SKILL?

The importance of recognition performance to anticipation skill remains a somewhat contentious issue. Several researchers have proposed that the ability to recognise patterns of play is central to anticipation skill in team sports (e.g., Abernethy, Neal, and Koning, 1994; Abernethy, Baker, and Cote, 2005; Williams and Davids, 1995), whereas others have proposed that it is simply a by-product of extended task exposure and not a constituent of expertise (e.g., Ericsson and Lehmann, 1996). North et al. (2006) examined this issue statistically by running correlations between performance on separate anticipation and recognition tasks. No significant correlations were reported between anticipation and recognition performance for skilled or less-skilled players respectively, although when the two groups were collapsed a moderate correlation between anticipation accuracy and recognition sensitivity was obtained (r (24) = .39, p= .06).

An analysis of the visual search behaviours employed during anticipation and recognition provided some evidence to support the argument that recognition processes underpin anticipation judgments. For example, the skilled participants showed no differences in fixation transitions between key features across the two tasks, indicating a broad, relation-based perceptual strategy. However, in contrast, there was also evidence that the two tasks require somewhat different processing strategies. When instructed to anticipate rather than recognise film clips, participants fixated on more locations, showed an increase in the number of fixations, recorded shorter fixation durations, and spent less time fixating the ball and more time viewing the offensive team.

In a follow-up study, North and Williams (2007) provided additional data using verbal report protocols to suggest that the two tasks rely on different processes.. After play, when asked to anticipate rather than recognise sequences of play, participants verbalised more stimuli, actions, and cognitions, albeit on both tasks the skilled players made more relevant evaluations than less-skilled players. Although both anticipation and recognition tasks stimulate complex retrieval structures, the processes involved in activating these structures differ somewhat. While recognition may be involved in anticipation the latter skill is more complex, invoking different and more refined retrieval structures.

CONCLUSION

Our intention in this programme of research was to identify the mechanisms underpinning recognition performance in soccer. More specifically, we wanted to determine the key sources of information that players employ when making recognition-based judgements (i.e., what?) and whether there are key time windows for extracting this information as the action sequences unfold (i.e., when?). A secondary aim was to examine the relationship between recognition performance and anticipation skill and to ascertain whether there are differences in the processing strategies employed when completing these two tasks.

Our findings indicated that skilled soccer players perceive and process displays based on the relational information between features. In particular, the motion information arising from only a few select features would appear crucial. The likelihood is that the key information may be picked up from the motion of central attacking players. Although the most likely scenario is that players pick up the relative motion between these players, perhaps in conjunction with the ball and other offensive players, it is not possible at this stage to dismiss the importance of absolute motion information arising from the central attacking players. Further research is required to clarify this issue. It is also apparent that the key source(s) of information arise at discrete moments in time as the action unfolds and that the relevant 'structure' or motion information may only emerge in the final few moments before a critical event such as a penetrative pass or shot at goal.

Although evidence was presented to suggest that recognition and anticipation skills have common processes, in general the mechanisms underpinning these two tasks differ with anticipation and recognition performance being only modestly correlated. Anticipation is dependent on a range of perceptual-cognitive skills, with each varying in importance from one situation to the next, and while recognition may on occasion contribute, it is not fundamental to the process. Other perceptual-cognitive skills such as advance cue utilisation and knowledge of likely event probabilities may be more important in guiding anticipation judgements in certain situations (Williams and Ward, 2007). An interesting challenge would be to ascertain how the different perceptual-cognitive skills interact in a dynamic and evolving manner during performance and which skills are more important in certain situations.

If anticipation and recognition performance are not directly related then there are significant implications for how best to capture expertise in sport. Several researchers have challenged the manner in which expertise is currently captured in sport, urging the need to design representative tasks using field and laboratory based protocols that effectively and reliably capture the essence of expert performance (see Ericsson and Williams, 2007; Williams and Ericsson, 2005). Ericsson and Smith (1991) proposed a conceptual framework for the study of expertise, termed the *expert performance approach*, and a central cornerstone of this approach is the need to develop a representative task that captures the essence of expertise in the domain. Caution must therefore be exercised when employing a task that does not directly involve the same processes that are normally used during superior performance in the sport. In a soccer match, for example, players are required to anticipate future events but not necessarily to recognise evolving sequences of play.

At a conceptual level, our findings lend support to Dittrich's (1999) Interactive Encoding Model. Dittrich (1999) proposed that skilled players combine both low- and high-level cognitive processes when making recognition-based judgments. Participants initially extract low-level motion information and temporal relationships between features, before engaging in high-level processing where the relational information is judged in the context of some stored memory structure. One interpretation is that the stimulus presentation is matched with an internal semantic concept or template (Didierjean and Marmeche, 2005; Gobet and Simon, 1996). The proposal is that skilled players develop a library of encountered scenes and potential scene formations and that these are stored as semantic concepts or templates. Less-skilled players develop fewer templates and so processing is unrefined and based primarily on the recognition of distinctive surface features.

An alternative interpretation is provided by Ericsson and Kintsch's (1995) Long Term Working Memory theory. According to this theory, experts develop complex task-specific encoding skills and associated retrieval structures in long term memory. These retrieval structures, which are developed following extensive deliberate practice within the domain, allow experts to index and store information at encoding, such that features or collections of features can permit superior representation of current scenarios and facilitate both recognition and anticipation of events (Ericsson, Patel, and Kintsch, 2000). These complex information structures in long term memory are accessible through cues held in short term memory. The proposal is that long term working memory helps performers develop an encoding for a situation, which, in turn, facilitates monitoring, the formulation of planning actions, and continual evaluation of the present situation and planned actions. This same encoding dynamically integrates retrieval structures in 'real time' such that experts can anticipate future events, predict the outcome of these and develop proactive as well as reactive behaviours that enable them to cope effectively with the demands placed upon them during performance.

At a practical level, our findings have implications for those interested in developing anticipation skill in sport. It is now widely reported that the development of anticipation skill can be facilitated through training and instruction (for a recent review, see Ward, Hancock, and Williams, 2006; Williams and Ward, 2003). However, most researchers have focused on developing the ability to pick up cues from an opponent's postural orientation prior to a key event such as ball-foot or ball-racket contact. No researchers have examined whether the ability to recognise sequences of play can be facilitated through practice and instruction. The knowledge derived from the programme of research presented in this chapter would certainly provide a conceptual backdrop for the type of training successfully used to develop other perceptual-cognitive skills. For example, instruction or task manipulations that constrain learners to focus attention on the relational information between players would appear crucial as would the need to sample numerous variations of different patterns of play.

Less apparent perhaps, given the moderate correlation between recognition and anticipation performance, is whether developing the ability to recognise sequences of play would actually lead to a significant improvement in anticipation skill. However, this issue could be addressed empirically by including a transfer test to examine whether any observed pre- to post-practice improvement in recognition performance facilitates anticipation skill. Ideally, both laboratory- and field-based measures of transfer should be employed to examine this issue (see Williams and Ward, 2003).

In conclusion, it is now well established that skilled performers in team ball games such as soccer demonstrate better recognition and anticipation performance than their less-skilled counterparts. However, there have been few attempts to identify the mechanisms underpinning successful recognition or indeed the extent to which performance on anticipation and recognition tasks is related and share common processes. In this chapter, we have reported our initial attempts at extending knowledge within this area of study. Our hope is that this programme of research stimulates discussion and encourages others to identify the important constraints that impact upon recognition performance and anticipation skill in sport.

REFERENCES

Abernethy, B., Baker, J., and Cote, J. (2005). Transfer of pattern recall skills may contribute to the development of sport expertise. *Applied Cognitive Psychology*, *19*, 705-718.

Abernethy, B., Neal, R.J., and Koning, P. (1994). Visual-perceptual and cognitive differences between expert, intermediate, and novice snooker players. *Applied Cognitive Psychology*, *8*, 185-211.

Carling, C., Reilly, T., and Williams, A.M. (2008). *Assessment of Performance in Field Sports*. London: Taylor and Francis.

Chase, W.G. and Simon, A.S. (1973). Perception in chess. *Cognitive Psychology*, *4*, 55-81.

Didierjean, A., and Marmeche, E. (2005). Anticipatory representation of visual basketball scenes by novice and expert players. *Visual Cognition*, *12*, 265-283.

Dittrich, W. H. (1999). Seeing biological motion: Is there a role for cognitive strategies? In A. Braffort, R. Gherbi, S. Gibet, J. Richardson, and D. Teil (Eds.), *Gesture-Based Communication in Human-Computer Interaction* (pp. 3-22). Berlin, Heidelberg: Springer-Verlag.

Ericsson, K.A., and Kintsch, W. (1995). Long-term working memory. *Psychological Review, 102,* 211–245.

Ericsson, K.A., and Lehmann, A.C. (1996). Expert and exceptional performance: Evidence on maximal adaptations on task constraints. *Annual Review of Psychology, 47*, 273-305.

Ericsson, K.A., Patel, V., and Kintsch, W. (2000). How experts' adaptations to representative task demands account for the expertise effect in memory recall: Comment on Vicente and Wang (1998). *Psychological Review, 107*, 578-592.

Ericsson, K.A., and Smith, J. (1991). *Toward a General Theory of Expertise: Prospects and Limits.* Cambridge: Cambridge University Press.

Ericsson, K.A., and Williams, A.M. (2007). Capturing naturally occurring superior performance in the laboratory: Translational research on expert performance. *Journal of Experimental Psychology: Applied, 13*, 115-123.

Gentner, D., and Markman, A.B. (1998). Structure mapping in analogy and similarity. In, P. Thagard (Ed.). *Mind Readings* (pp. 127-156). Cambridge, MA: MIT Press.

Gobet, F., and Simon, H.A. (1996). Templates in chess memory: A mechanism for recalling several boards. *Cognitive Psychology, 31*, 1-40.

Goldin, S.E. (1978). Effects of orienting tasks on recognition of chess positions. *American Journal of Psychology, 91*, 659-671.

Kirchner, H., and Thorpe, S.J. (2006). Ultra—rapid detection with saccadic eye movements: Visual processing speed revisited. *Vision Research, 46*, 1762-1776.

North, J.S., and Williams, A.M. (2007). The processes underpinning skilled recognition and anticipation in soccer. In P. Beek, and R. van de Langenberg (Eds.), *The European Workshop on Movement Science 2007* (p. 42). Koln: Sportverlag Strauss.

North, J.S., and Williams, A.M. (2008). The critical time period for information extraction when identifying patterns of play in soccer. *Research Quarterly for Exercise and Sport, 79*, 2, 268-273.

North, J.S., Williams, A.M, Hodges, N.J., Ward, P., and Ericsson, K.A. (2006). Perceiving patterns in dynamic action sequences: Identifying the critical information underlying anticipation skill in soccer. In H. Hoppeler, T. Reilly, E. Tsolakidis, L. Gfeller, and Klossner, S. (Eds.), *Proceedings of 11th Annual Congress of the European College of Sport Science* (p. 168). Cologne: Sportverlag Strauss 2006.

Savelsbergh, G.J.P., Van der Kamp, J., Williams, A.M., and Ward, P. (2002). Visual search, anticipation and expertise in soccer goalkeepers. *Journal of Sports Sciences, 20*, 279-287.

Savelsbergh, G.J.P, Van der Kamp, J., Williams, A.M. and Ward, P. (2005). Anticipation and visual search behaviour in expert soccer goalkeepers. *Ergonomics, 48*, 1686-97.

Smeeton, N., Ward, P., and Williams, A.M. (2004). Transfer of perceptual skill in sport. *Journal of Sports Sciences, 19*, 2, 3-9.

Stratton, G., Reilly, T., Williams, A.M., and Richardson, D.R. (2005). *Science of Youth Soccer*. London: Taylor and Francis.

Ward, P., Hancock P., and Williams, A.M. (2006). Simulation for performance and training. In K.A. Ericsson, P. Hoffman, N. Charness, and P. Feltovich (Eds.), *Handbook of*

Expertise and Expert Performance (pp. 243-262). Cambridge: Cambridge University Press.

Ward, P., Hodges, N.J., Starkes, J.L., and Williams, A.M. (2007). The road to excellence: deliberate practice and the development of expertise. *High Ability Studies, 18,* 119-153.

Ward, P., and Williams, A.M. (2003). Perceptual and cognitive skill development in soccer: the multidimensional nature of expert performance. *Journal of Sport and Exercise Psychology, 25,* 1, 93-111.

Williams, A.M., and Davids, K. (1995). Declarative knowledge in sport: A byproduct of experience or characteristic of expertise? *Journal of Sport and Exercise Psychology, 17,* 259-275.

Williams, A.M., and Davids, K. (1998). Visual search strategy, selective attention, and expertise in soccer. *Research Quarterly for Exercise and Sport, 69,* 111-128.

Williams, A.M., Davids, K., Burwitz, L., and Williams, J.G. (1994). Visual search strategies in experienced and inexperienced soccer players. *Research Quarterly for Exercise and Sport, 65,* 127-135.

Williams, A.M., Davids, K., and Williams, J.G. (1999). *Visual Perception and Action in Sport.* London: E. and F.N. Spon.

Williams, A.M., and Ericsson, K.A. (2005). Some considerations when applying the expert performance approach in sport. *Human Movement Science,* 24, 283-307.

Williams, A.M., Hodges, N.J., North, J.S., and Barton, G. (2006). Perceiving patterns of play in dynamic sport tasks: Identifying the essential information underlying skilled performance. *Perception, 35,* 317-332.

Williams, A.M., and Reilly, T.P. (2000). Talent identification and development in soccer. *Journal of Sports Sciences, 18,* 657-667.

Williams, A.M., and Ward, P. (2003). Perceptual expertise: development in sport. In J. L. Starkes, and A. Ericsson (Eds), *Expert performance in sport: Recent advances in research on sport expertise* (pp. 219-247). Champaign, IL, Human Kinetics.

Williams, A.M., and Ward, P. (2007) Perceptual-cognitive expertise in sport: Exploring new horizons. In G. Tenenbaum, and R. Eklund (Eds.), *Handbook of Sport Psychology 3rd ed.* (pp. 203-223). New York: John Wiley and Sons.

Williams, A.M., Ward, P., Knowles, J.M., and Smeeton, N.J. (2002). Perceptual skill in a real-world task: Training, instruction, and transfer in tennis. *Journal of Experimental Psychology: Applied, 8,* 4, 259-270.

In: Perspectives on Cognition and Action in Sport
Editors: D. Araújo, H. Ripoll and M. Raab

ISBN: 978-1-60692-390-0
© 2009 Nova Science Publishers, Inc.

Chapter 9

KNOWLEDGE OF ATHLETES AS CUES FOR SIMPLE CHOICES

Jörn Köppen and Markus Raab

Institute of Psychology, German Sport University Cologne, Cologne, Germany

ABSTRACT

Decision making is a central process in sports that is influenced by an athlete's limited knowledge. Because of this constraint, decisions cannot be optimal—but they may be good enough. Bounded rationality describes how humans can make decisions despite limitations in time, information, and cognitive capacity to achieve their goals in a satisficing way. One form of bounded rationality is called simple heuristics. These simple decision strategies consist of rules that govern searching for information (cues), stopping search, and making a decision. In the context of sports, the cues can be the knowledge of the athletes. In Study 1 we analyzed the environment in which allocation decisions take place for volleyball and basketball and found that the base rates of players and their current performance are mostly used for allocation decisions. Further, we demonstrated in Study 2 that these cues are useful for allocation decisions of playmakers, but it is not guaranteed that this information can be perceived sensitively. Therefore, we showed in Study 3 that volleyball players are sensitive to the base rates of players and their changes. In Study 4 we tested the adaptive behavior of players in an experimental setting. The results support evidence of the widespread hot hand belief in sports that seems to be not always correctly labeled as a fallacy. Comparisons to other approaches are drawn; conclusions from the perspective of knowledge-as-cues in simple choices are presented and extended to a broader picture.

INTRODUCTION

In sports, a small decision—for example, passing to a teammate—can lead to a major consequence: the team's win or loss of the game. In every match an athlete has to make myriad decisions and do so with only limited time, limited (imperfect) knowledge, and limited cognitive resources.

The question we want to answer in this chapter is how knowledge influences choices of athletes when making these decisions under time pressure. The answer is simple: Athletes use only a limited amount of knowledge and make fast choices that are not optimal, but good enough. Athletes build simple heuristics, or rules of thumb, that work in very specific situations that regularly occur in the game environment.

KNOWLEDGE DEFINED IN SIMPLE HEURISTICS

Recently Sony presented humanoid robots that play soccer—or more accurately—try to play it. In the future programmers may try developing an electronic clone of Beckham (let's call him eBeckham) and they need to consider a number of sources of perceptual information, such as orientation of eBeckham in space, position and position changes of opponent players and team members, speed and direction of the ball, context such as distance to an outside line or goal, among others. Needless to say, information that can change in a fraction of a second can alter the available response choices, and time is needed for motor implementation as well. Is it possible for eBeckham to consider all this information? Even in the simpler environment of chess, IBM's Deep Blue does not use all of its knowledge or calculate all possible moves, because the problem is intractable.

To be ideal, fully rational decision makers, Beckhams or eBeckhams or computerized chess masters would need to consider their full memory base and calculate all consequences of possible outcomes, but this requires unlimited cognitive capabilities and more time than is available. Because human cognitive capability is limited (as are computers designed to mimic it), the decision-making process cannot conform to the ideal. Therefore humans are believed not to be omnipotent but rather bounded or constrained. The term bounded rationality describes how humans can make decisions despite limitations in time, information, and cognitive capacity to achieve their goals in a complex world. Bounded rationality is neither an inferior form of rationality nor irrational.

A prominent model of bounded rationality consists of simple step-by-step rules, or heuristics, that people use to achieve their goals (Gigerenzer and Selten, 2001). These so-called simple heuristics consist of three building blocks: rules for guiding the search for information (cues), stopping the search, and making a decision. In the context of sports these cues can be the knowledge of athletes. For instance, in soccer, knowledge about a penalty shooter's preferred shooting direction is used by the goalie to decide in which corner to jump before the shot is actually taken. What cue is considered in a given situation depends on its validity. Cue validity is acquired through experience: validity can be estimated from the relative frequency with which the cues predict the criterion. If the cue "preferred corner" is more valid than another cue, such as the "penalty shooter's glance to one of the corners," then this cue is the first or only one used in such situations. The order of cues is independent of neither situation (e.g., a player's direction of glance may help in other situations, such as where he or she will allocate the ball next), nor person (e.g., beginners in penalty shooting may shoot more to the corner they fixate on). Given that even for simple situations, such as a penalty shot, there are a number of cues available, heuristics define the rules for how to search for the important cues, how to stop this search, and how to decide based on the cues considered. In sports, execution rules are added because it is necessary to describe what to choose and to describe how this choice is implemented in complex movements.

Therefore the process of decision making in sports can be divided into the following four simple building blocks (see figure 1).

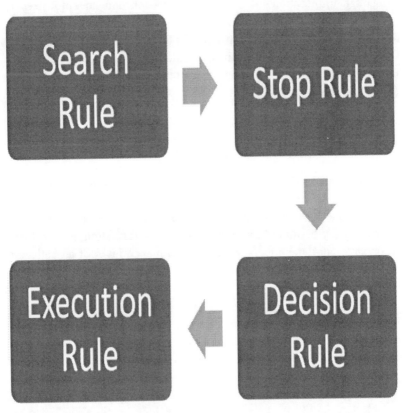

Figure 1. Building blocks of decision making in sports as search, stop, decision and execution rule.

Simple Search Rules

A search rule describes what cues or pieces of information are used and in what order. Cues can come from the environment or from memory. For instance in memory, the allocation decision of a playmaker may depend not only on the information of recent performance of the teammates currently in the game, but also on the coach's instructions in the last time-out. We will focus on knowledge as cues in the experimental studies of this chapter. A search rule describes in what order these cues are taken into account when making a decision such that for instance coach's instructions to play a specific strategy will be used first and then recent performance of players will be considered to make allocation decisions. Another example for a search rule is catching a ball with different information. The cues, such as the direction and acceleration of the ball, may be used in early stages of the catching procedure, for example by outfielders in baseball, as well as shortly before time to contact information (about changes from the retinal display of the ball size) is used to estimate the closing movement of the hand (Raab and Gigerenzer, 2005).

Simple Stopping Rules

A stop rule describes the point after which no further information is used. That can mean on the one hand that there are no other cues available or on the other hand that the playmaker already has enough information for making his decision and does not need to search any more. The above playmaker may use, for instance, only the direct coach instruction ignoring further information about recent performance of players, because this information is enough to allocate the next ball. This stop is defined by knowledge (e.g., instruction of the coach), or in dynamic situations often by the behavior of teammates and opponents that require fast decisions (Raab and Johnson, 2007).

Simple Decision Rules

The decision rule describes what option to choose given the specific knowledge acquired. Various principles can be applied. The playmaker can choose between several options and he has to judge which one is the most satisfying concerning the available cues. For instance, the coach's instruction may be more important than other information, such as the efficiency of the last two or three goal attempts or general performance level of an athlete, and therefore the ball is allocated to the player that is indicated by the coach (Johnson and Raab, 2003).

Simple Execution Rules

The execution rule describes how a chosen option is dynamically executed. For instance, in table tennis the selection of an option (a what decision) and the execution (a how decision) can be described in the form of heuristics. Precisely, the arm movement of the opponent towards the ball is a valid cue from which a decision can be made early from a neutral position of the bat for a forehand or backhand topspin (what decision) using a flat movement trajectory towards the ball (how decision). Concerning heuristics the bat-flat heuristic describes that the angle of the bat toward the ball is constant during the approach of the bat to the ball. The reason for that execution rule is the uncertainty of the correct estimation of ball-bat contact given research showing that motor variability exists and also perceptual variability (e.g. Tresilian, 1994). This execution rule was described as the default description of movements by different levels of expertise (Raab, Masters, and Maxwell, 2005).

Knowledge Used in Changing Environments

We have argued so far that knowledge can be described as cues that are positively correlated with an expected outcome. These cues are used in simple heuristics that consist of a search in order of cue validities rule, a stopping rule that defines when the search is sufficient, and decision and execution rules that define what and how to decide in a given situation. Simple heuristics can be classified as bounded rationality because they make different kinds of decisions despite "bounds" in knowledge and time. In addition they are adaptive to changes in the environment such as let us say that Michael Jordan or his eJordan clone is known to make his shots (hit) more than his teammates. A human playmaker would not deterministically allocate all balls to Michael Jordan because of changes in the defensive pressure. Redefining the importance of knowledge in a changing environment that results in adaptations to those changes is called ecological rationality (Gigerenzer and Selten, 2001). Understanding how knowledge influences athletes' behavior requires us to consider both bounded rationality and ecological rationality.

A TYPICAL EXAMPLE OF ATHLETES' KNOWLEDGE DEFINED IN SIMPLE HEURISTICS

With regard to the statements above we developed a series of four studies to examine closely a typical sports situation, playmaker allocation, with the aim to explore how specific knowledge of a playmaker can result in adaptive behavior in changing situations.

Study 1

First, we wanted to know what knowledge is important when deciding to whom to pass the ball. We asked 121 players, coaches, and spectators in an open questionnaire what kind of information they use to make effective allocation decisions (e.g., to pass the ball to a teammate or to keep the ball and score) in volleyball and basketball. Previous research demonstrated that people believe in the hot hand of players such that they believe that players have a greater chance of scoring if they just hit the last two or three attempts compared to a situation in which they just missed the last two or three attempts. In sum about 79% of participants believed in the "hot hand" of players and 67% reported that playmakers use the current performance of players as well as the base rate to make allocation decisions. We therefore used the base rate of players and their current performance in terms of a hot hand as cues for further experiments.

Research considering both cues in different domains has resulted in heterogeneous conclusions; people may use knowledge about base rate and the hot hand to different degrees and more or less adaptively. More specifically, there is a large body of research showing that people both neglect base rates and consider them in their judgments (Koehler, 1996). Furthermore, it has been shown that coaches, athletes, and spectators believe in the hot hand even if the conditional probabilities of hitting the next ball are about the same in situations where the same player missed or hit his last two or three balls (Gilovich, Vallone, and Tversky, 1985). However, there are some arguments and studies showing that it is adaptive to believe in the hot hand (Gula and Raab, 2004) and even others suggesting that the hot hand really does exist (Bar-Eli, Avugos, and Raab, 2006). For the playmaker allocation situation considered here no such experiments exist, so we conducted one ourselves (Study 2) to see if specific cues such as base rate or a hot hand have validity in real sport situations.

Study 2

We analyzed a TopScorer Database in German First Division Volleyball consisting of 226 games with 36,000 rows of effective (hit) or non-effective (miss) spikes (attacks in volleyball) of individual players. In a selection of 26 randomly selected male players in playoffs we found for roughly half of the players that the conditional probability of scoring after one or two hits (effective spike) was significantly higher than after one or two misses (non-effective spike). For the rest of the players the conditional probabilities are the same. An autocorrelational analysis was conducted revealing for half of the players' hits and misses a significant dependency on what preceded them. The other players had an autocorrelation value around zero (± 0.1). The results of Study 2 revealed the variations in base rates and hot hand information in real games and also validated that these cues are useful for allocation decisions of playmakers. More than half of the players showed a high range of variability for both within and between games. However, showing that this information exists does not guarantee that it can be perceived sensitively or is being used by athletes. These questions were addressed in the next two studies. We used the hit/miss sequences of two players and their base rates for Studies 3 and 4, providing an as ecologically valid environment for the allocation decisions of playmakers as possible.

Study 3

We presented on a computer screen video clips from the Top Scorer Database of 176 attacks that closely matched real performance of attack players (see Study 2) to 20 volleyball players. Two players were shown who either hit or missed in an attack. The number of attacks of the same player was between 1 and 4 and hits and misses were viewed in a random order; both players had the same base rate over all 176 clips but varied within sets. After each 22 attacks (11 from Player A and 11 from Player B) we asked the participants to make allocation decisions for the next 10 balls (How many to Player A, how many to Player B?) as well as to estimate the performances of Player A and Player B (How many hits did Player A/B have?).

Results of this study indicate that participants were able to estimate the correct number of hits quite sensitively (mean difference from real performance was 1.2) and did use the current performance to make allocation decisions for the next 10 allocations based on probability matching that distributed the allocations according to their estimates of the actual performance. We know now that volleyball players in this environment are sensitive to base rates of players and to changes in these base rates. But do they use this information adaptively? Study 4 attempted to answer this question.

Study 4

We used the same clips as in Study 3 but presented sequences of Player A and Player B, varying base rate and hot hand independently. Participants were instructed to make allocation decisions to either Player A (left side of the screen) or Player B (right side of the screen) of their own team. When they clicked on the player they want to allocate the ball to, they saw a clip of a hit or a miss. After seeing the hit or miss of Player A or B, they were asked to make the next allocation decision. As in Study 3 we asked participants after each block of 22 spikes to make allocation decisions for the next 10 attacks as well as to estimate the performance of Player A and Player B. Using a counterbalanced design, we presented participants with four different sets. For example, in Set 1 a participant received random sequences of hits and misses (no hot hand), but a base rate difference of players of up to five points (first half: two points, second half five points). In Set 2 we presented the same base rate of 50% hits (first half) or 64% hits (second half) for Players A and B, but either Player A (first half) or Player B had a hot hand, that is, twice spiked 3 hits in a row. In Set 3 we presented allocation information in favor of one player such that Player A (first half) or Player B (second half) had both a higher base rate and a hot hand. In Set 4 we presented conflicting information; that is, in the first half Player A had a higher base rate but Player B had a hot hand, and vice versa for the second half.

Results of this study indicate that participants did use base rate and hot hand independently (Set 1 and Set 2) to make allocation decisions that mainly mirrored probability matching. They also used hot hand in addition if both informational cues were positively associated with the same player (Set 3). In the case of conflicting information (Set 4), they used hot hand more often than base rate for their allocations.

CONCLUSION: WHAT WE HAVE LEARNED SO FAR

Based on the results of Studies 1–4 we are confident in reporting that base rate and hot hand are used as knowledge (here cues) to make allocation decisions (Study 1) that are valid in real situations (Study 2) and also sensitively picked up in a laboratory experiment (Study 3). These results suggest that the hot hand belief in sports is quite manifested (see Bar-Eli et al., 2006, for an overview) and may not always be correctly labeled as a fallacy (see Gula and Raab, 2004, for a discussion). Most importantly, we demonstrated that the hot hand belief can be used independently from base rate information, which would inform models that assume an indirect use of base rate through the belief in the hot hand (Burns, 2004).

Furthermore, we propose based on our data that using hot hand information is neutral in situations where players have the same base rates but adaptive if hot hand and base rate information correlate positively. In cases in which hot hand and base rate are negatively correlated (e.g., Study 4, Set 4) using hot hand information over base rate is maladaptive; however, we believe that these incidents are very rare in real-life situations. How does this approach differ from or conform to others in this field on how knowledge of athletes is used in behavior? In the following we will concentrate on the perspectives of Araújo (Araújo, Davids, and Hristovski, 2006; Araújo et al., Chapter 10), Beek (Beek, Peper, and Stegeman, 1995), Williams (Williams and Ward, 2007; Williams and North, Chapter 8) and Raab (Raab and Gigerenzer, 2005; Köppen and Raab, this Chapter).

What the approaches have in common is that they are all dynamic models, in the sense that they describe processes, not pure outcome of motor or cognitive behavior in sports. Of course this does not mean that deterministic aspects of the processes are not considered (e.g., van Mourik, Daffertshofer, and Beek, 2006). A further line of comparison of these models is based on the link between cognition and environment. Araújo et al. (2006) and Beek et al. (1995) emphasized a much more direct link between these than Williams and Ward (2007) and Raab and Gigerenzer (2005). Another notable difference lies in the levels of description used. For instance, mathematical description figures prominently in Beek et al. (1995) but is used to a lesser extent by Araújo et al. (2006) and Williams and Ward (2007). Use of such description was just beginning to be explored in Raab and Johnson (2004). Neurophysiological correlates are still absent in most of the approaches and our own approach is still limited mainly to cognitive tasks (Volz, Schooler, Schubotz, Raab, Gigerenzer, and von Cramon, 2006). In addition, Beek et al. (1995) focused on that descriptive level as well.

However, the ability of these approaches to describe how "movement knowledge" controls *how* to act (Beek et al., 1995) versus *what* to select (Araújo et al., 2006; Williams and Ward, 2007) differs. A combined approach that integrates the processes is still needed (Raab et al., 2005).

We hope to begin to understand how knowledge—here defined as cues—that correlates positively with a criterion (e.g., hits) is used in choices in sports. We believe that a bounded rationality approach serves as a good starting point to study the present hot hand phenomenon or other phenomena in sports, because (a) it captures through the description of heuristics how cues and decisions are linked by search, stop, decision, and execution rules; (b) it provides a formal description of information use that can be simulated and described on a mathematical level; (c) it is neurophysiologically plausible to assume such heuristics do exist (Volz et al., 2006), and the processes that determine when to use them and when not go beyond pure direct perception-action or representational approaches; and finally (d), it allows researchers to model both the person and the structure of the environment and follow the old but still valid advice of Nobel Laureate Herbert Simon (1987): Study both environment and cognitive structure of humans to understand when a process is adaptive and when not.

REFERENCES

Araújo, D., Davids, K., and Hristovski, R. (2006). The ecological dynamics of decision making in sport. *Psychology of Sport and Exercise, 7,* 653–676.

Bar-Eli, M., Avugos, S., and Raab, M. (2006). Twenty years of "hot hand" research. The hot hand phenomenon: Review and critique. *Psychology, Sport and Exercise, 7,* 525–553.

Beek, P.J., Peper, C.E., and Stegeman, D.F. (1995). Dynamical models of movement coordination. *Human Movement Science, 14,* 573–608.

Burns, B.D. (2004). Heuristics as beliefs and as behaviors: The adaptiveness of the "hot hand." *Cognitive Psychology, 48,* 295–331.

Gigerenzer, G., and Selten, R. (Eds.). (2001). *Bounded rationality: The adaptive toolbox.* Cambridge, MA: MIT Press.

Gilovich, T., Vallone, R., and Tversky, A. (1985). The hot hand in basketball: On the misperception of random sequences. *Cognitive Psychology, 17,* 295–314.

Gula, B., and Raab, M. (2004). Hot hand belief and hot hand behavior: A comment on Koehler and Conley. *Journal of Sport and Exercise Psychology, 26,* 167–170.

Johnson, J.G., and Raab, M. (2003). Take the first: Option generation and resulting choices. *Organizational Behavior and Human Decision Processes, 91,* 215–229.

Koehler, J.J. (1996). The base rate fallacy reconsidered: Descriptive, normative, and methodological challenges. *Behavioral and Brain Sciences, 19*, 1–53.

Raab, M., and Gigerenzer, G. (2005). Intelligence as smart heuristics. In. R. J. Sternberg, J. Davidson and J. Pretz (Eds.), *Cognition and intelligence* (pp. 188–207). Cambridge: Cambridge University Press.

Raab, M., and Johnson, J.G. (2004). Individual differences of action-orientation for risk taking in sports. *Research Quarterly and Exercise Sport, 75*, 326–336.

Raab, M., and Johnson, J.G. (2007). Implicit learning as a means to intuitive decision making in sports. In H. Plessner, T. Betsch, and C. Betsch (Eds.), *A new look on intuition in judgment and decision making* (pp. 119–133). Mahwah, NJ: Lawrence Erlbaum.

Raab, M., Masters, R., and Maxwell, J. (2005). Improving the how and what decisions of table tennis elite players. *Human Movement Science, 24,* 326–344.

Simon, H.A. (1987). Rational decision making in business organizations. In L. Green and J.H. Nagel (Eds.), *Advances in behavioral economics* (Vol. 1, pp. 18-47). Norwood, NJ: Ablex.

Tresilian, J.R. (1994). Approximate information sources and perceptual variables in interceptive timing. *Journal of Experimental Psychology, Human Perception and Performance, 20*, 154-173.

van Mourik, A.M., Daffertshofer, A., and Beek, P.J. (2006). Deterministic and stochastic features of rhythmic human movement. *Biological Cybernetics, 94,* 233–244.

Volz, K.G., Schooler, L., Schubotz, R., Raab, M., Gigerenzer, G., and von Cramon, D.Y. (2006). Why you think Milan is larger than Modena: Neural correlates of the recognition heuristic. *Journal of Cognitive Neuroscience, 18*, 1924–1936.

Williams, A.M., and Ward, P. (2007). Anticipation and decision-making: Exploring new horizons. In G. Tenenbaum and R. Eklund (Eds.), *Handbook of sport psychology* (pp. 203–223). New York: Wiley.

In: Perspectives on Cognition and Action in Sport
Editors: D. Araújo, H. Ripoll and M. Raab

ISBN: 978-1-60692-390-0
© 2009 Nova Science Publishers, Inc.

Chapter 10

HOW DOES KNOWLEDGE CONSTRAIN SPORT PERFORMANCE? AN ECOLOGICAL PERSPECTIVE

Duarte Araújo [1], *Keith Davids* [2], *Rita Cordovil* [1,3],
João Ribeiro [1] *and Orlando Fernandes* [4]

[1] Faculty of Human Kinetics, Technical University of Lisbon, Portugal
[2] Queensland University of Technology, Australia
[3] Lusófona University of Humanities and Technologies, Portugal
[4] University of Évora, Portugal

ABSTRACT

From an ecological perspective knowledge signifies the degree of fitness of a performer and his/her environment. From this viewpoint, the role of training is to enhance this degree of fit between a specific athlete and the performance environment, instead of the enrichment of memory in the performer. In this regard, ecological psychology distinguishes between perceptual knowledge or "knowledge of" the environment and symbolic knowledge or "knowledge about" the environment. This distinction elucidates how knowing how to act (knowing of) as well as knowing how to verbalize memorial representations (e.g., a verbal description of performance) (knowing about) are both rooted in perception. In this chapter we demonstrate these types of knowledge in decision-making behaviour and exemplify how they can be presented in 1 v 1 practice task constraints in basketball.

INTRODUCTION

This chapter addresses the question of how knowledge constrains (i.e., channels) athlete behaviour in sport performance and training. Different perspectives exist on how this may occur, including enrichment theories and ecological theories (Michaels and Carello, 1981). Enrichment theories hold, for instance, that skilled athletes outperform novices because of the knowledge they have added to their memories during the process of learning. It is proposed that the enrichment of memory allows skilled performers to make more accurate inferences for action from information available in the performance or training environment (examples in sport include McPherson and Kernodle, 2003, see also the other chapters in this section by Köppen and Raab, Chapter 9, Laurent and Ripoll, Chapter 11, and Williams and North, Chapter 8). Ecological theories, in contrast, hold that learning entails changes in properties of the environment to which perceptual systems become sensitive (Jacobs and Michaels, 2007, see Savelsbergh et al., 2004 for an example in sport). In the ecological view, the sophistication of expert performance derives from the improved fits of experts to their environments, rather than from an increased complexity of computational and memorial processes (see Shaw, 2003 for a detailed discussion about the differences between these views).

The ecological approach calls for a complete understanding of the informational aspects of the constraints of performance, as well as the behavioural consequences of such information. In this way, information closes the putative gap between perception and knowledge, with one process continuous with the other (Gibson, 1979). The traditional view that seeing something is quite unlike knowing something emerged from the old doctrine that the process of *seeing* involves a series of temporary sensations during each moment of time. *Knowing* has been proposed as storing permanent concepts in memory. However, perceptual *seeing* involves an awareness of persisting structure (Lee et al., 1982). Human knowledge emerges from experience of the affordances available to be picked up in performance and training environments. This process is based on perception but it enables humans to develop patterns of thought that go well beyond perception. *Knowing* is a process which resides neither wholly within the individual as an effect or response, nor wholly within the world as a cause or stimulus; rather, as an ecological concept, *knowing* stands astride the physical and psychological domains (Turvey and Shaw, 1995, 1999). Thus, to say that expert players "know" what needs to be done in a match, means that the player is sensitive to the events that convey information for his/her aims at any instance of the game (e.g., they understand how to find a path through opponents towards the basket or how to get a shot off despite the close attention of a defender). Through training, the player does not have to rely on constructing special mental representations about the game, but he/she has to learn how to use his/her body to adapt to the sources of information that will help make him/her successful. The development of this sensitivity to the competitive context occurs before the season, for example, through practice and training, and by schematically planning coordinated actions of the team for certain games. These schematic plans may represent the game but representations are not mentally constructed.

Important to this discussion is Gibson's (1966) distinction between knowledge of the environment (perception based on information to control action, which constrains actual action, "what do I do to achieve a certain goal when I'm acting on a task" – exemplified by tactical decision-making) and knowledge about the environment (perception mediated by language, pictures and other symbols, which constrains future action "what can I do to achieve a certain goal before I can act on it" – exemplified by strategic decision-making). We move now to discuss further this notion.

GIBSON'S CONCEPTION OF KNOWLEDGE

Gibson (1966, 1979) argued that virtually all theories of perception had assumed that the objects of which we are immediately aware are based on sensations. These subjective objects give us knowledge about the external world, but only after a complex process of inference, association and interpretation is applied to them. In other words, most theorists held that what are directly perceived are mental symbols or representations, and it is only indirectly, through the mediation of these representations, that we perceive the external world (e.g., Fodor and Pylyshyn, 1981).

Gibson's theory that the perception of environmental objects, places, and events is based on ecologically available information challenged this widespread consensus. Gibson noted that his theory was a form of direct realism, in that it maintained that the surrounding environment could be perceived directly, on the basis of information, and not indirectly, on the basis of sensations and mental representations. Importantly, Gibson never argued that indirect (mediated) perception (or awareness) was impossible, but he made a strong distinction between perception based on information and perception based on language, pictures and other symbols. In 1966 (p. 91) he wrote: "In this book, a distinction will be made between perceptual cognition, or knowledge of the environment, and symbolic cognition, or knowledge *about* the environment. The former is a direct response to things based on stimulus information; the latter is an indirect response to things based on stimulus sources produced by another human individual".

For Gibson the process of detecting information is carried out by a functional system distributed throughout an individual's nervous system. Adjustments of peripheral organs, such as turning the eyes and head, play as significant a role in direct perception as the activity of the higher brain centres. Awareness of the environment is based on the adjustment of the performer's entire perceptual system to the information surrounding it. This adjustment includes a range of processes, all of which may be described as the simultaneous extraction of persisting and changing properties of stimulation, invariants despite disturbances of the array of information (Gibson, 1979). Performers can perceive themselves, their environments, and the changing relationship between themselves and their surroundings.

Gibson introduced the notion of affordance, a term that simultaneously captures and couples objects and events of the world with an individual's behaviour (Turvey and Shaw, 1995). An affordance is a combination of invariant properties in the environment, taken with reference to an organism that specifies an opportunity for action (Turvey, 1992). Consistent with Gibson's (1979) ecological notion of perception-action, affordances are properties of the environment whose actualization requires an individual with reciprocal effectivities; an effectivity is the dynamic actualization of an ability by the individual taken with respect to a particular opportunity for action (Shaw and Turvey, 1981). For an affordance to be a successful goal of an action there must be an affordance-effectivity fit of organism and environment. For example, an unmarked team mate located near the basket opens a passing line as an affordance for the player with the ball. But for the pass to be successful, the player in possession of the ball must have the reciprocal effectivity, i.e., the conjunction of strength (fitness) and accuracy (skill) to move the ball rapidly from the hands to the team mate.

The fundamental hypothesis of Gibson's ecological approach to perception and action is that where specific information about environmental objects, places, events and people is available and picked up, performers will perceive these entities to support their actions. This is what Gibson meant by the term direct perception, or "knowledge *of*" the environment. This type of knowledge is not formulated in pictures or words, because it is the knowledge that makes the formulation of pictures and words possible. However, even though it is tacit, this knowledge of the environment obtained through direct perception is not personal, subjective or private. Information is available in the environment, and it can be picked up by many observers. On the other hand, according to Gibson (1979) these "images, pictures, and written-on surfaces afford a special kind of knowledge that I call *mediated* or *indirect*, knowledge at second hand" (Gibson, 1979, p. 42). This kind of knowledge is intrinsically shared, because it involves the displaying of information to others. In all these cases the information on which direct perception can be based is selectively adapted and modified in a display, exemplified here by a schematic presentation of the disposition of two teams in basketball. The value of these pictures with selected samples of information lies not in the displays themselves, but in what they refer to or *represent*. These mediators are representations; they do not have affordances as objects do, but rather have 'referential meaning' (Reed, 1991). They consolidate gains of perception by converting tacit knowledge into explicit knowledge (Reed, 1991). The role of explicit knowledge, and the processes that make knowledge explicit, is not to create knowledge out of merely potentially meaningful input, nor even to select meanings to assign to inputs. The role of indirect forms of cognition is to make others aware and to share knowledge.

From an ecological point of view, knowledge should be understood in direct and deep connection with dynamic principles (Turvey and Shaw, 1995). From this ecological perspective, characteristic cognitive capabilities are what they are by virtue of laws and general principles. Within this approach, dynamics (involving laws of motion and change) and dynamical systems (involving time evolution of observable quantities according to law) can help us to understand knowledge in sport in line with the work initiated by Kugler, Kelso and Turvey (e.g., 1980, 1982; see also Araújo et al., 2006, for a development of these ideas in sport). The link between the ecological approach to perception and the dynamical systems approach to action is expressed in its most developed state to date in the work of Warren (e.g., 2006). He characterized the agent and environment as a pair of dynamical systems, coupled by both mechanical forces and informational flow fields. The behaviour that emerges from this interaction is referred to as *behavioural dynamics*. Briefly, functional behaviour can often be described by changes in a few key variables. Observed behaviour corresponds to trajectories in the state space of behavioral variables (i.e., the hypothetical totality of all the possible states of order which are achievable by a system). Goals correspond to attractors or regions in state space toward which trajectories converge. Conversely, states to be avoided correspond to repellers, regions from which trajectories diverge. Sudden changes in the number or type of these fixed points are known as bifurcations, which correspond to qualitative transitions in behaviour. In other words, they express decisions. A central theme of Warren's framework is that behaviour is not commanded by a central controller. Rather, the agent learns mappings from information in (e.g., optic) flow to movement that bring about desired states (i.e., goals). Knowing what patterns of flow can and cannot be brought about allows the agent to perceive affordances. Next, we present an illustration of these types of knowledge in the team sport context of basketball.

EVIDENCE FOR THE DISTINCTION BETWEEN KNOWLEDGE OF AND KNOWLEDGE ABOUT IN THE SAME TASK (1VS1 IN BASKETBALL)

In dynamic environments such as a basketball game there is typically not one stimulus to trigger a reaction in a player (such as when a sprinter reacts to the starter's gun), but a constant flux of stimulation available to be picked up from the environment in support of action (Reed, 1996; Whiting, 1991). Therefore, although possible, an explanation for a particular aspect of a complex interaction in an attacker-defender dyad, such as a response to a fake move by one player, cannot easily be explained by relationships like Hick's law (the relation between the number of stimulus-response alternatives and reaction time), stimulus-response compatibility, or the psychological refractory period (although see Schmidt and Lee, 2005). Also, the fact that both players in the dyad are linked by information indicates that one player is not merely responding to the other, but that there is a coupling effect as an emergent property, as predicted by the ecological dynamics systems approach (Davids et al., 2006). An ecological dynamics analysis of the coupling and decoupling of the players in a basketball dyad needs to begin with a measure of order in the stable interpersonal pattern formed by the position of the attacker and defender with respect to the ball and the basket.

Analysis of coaching literature reveals that an order parameter (i.e., a collective variable that synthesizes the relevant coordinated parts of the system as a whole) to describe the organization of an attacker-defender system could be the distance between the basket and the dyad (i.e., medium point of the distance between the attacker and defender) during a 1 v 1 sub-phase of the game (e.g., Bain et al., 1978). Araújo et al. (2002; 2004; Davids et al., 2006) examined whether the distance from the attacker-defender dyad to the basket would become less stable (i.e., not maintaining a similar distance from the dyad to the basket) until some critical value of interpersonal distance was reached. This was even more evident when we decomposed the order parameter (distance between the medium point of the dyad to the basket) showing each player's distance to the basket (see figure 1 for illustration of this decomposition). This investigation considered whether changes in interpersonal distance were associated with dribbling success by attackers. By tracing in the horizontal plane trajectory the mass centre of each player in the dyad, and then computing the values of the described order parameter, we observed that during the initial part of the dyadic entrainment there is a stable state of the order parameter, meaning that the players are coupled. This state was followed by an abrupt change in the system due to an attacker's success in de-stabilizing the dyad and de-coupling the players (see arrows in figure 1). In the case of success by the attacker, the attacker-defender system exhibited initial coupling, which was broken during transition to a new state at a critical value of the control parameter. In other words, the attacker was trying to dribble past the defender, but the defender was attempting to maintain the initial steady state of the dyad. The attacker increased the variability of dribbling actions (deciding what to do) in order to force the emergence of a system transition (deciding when to move past the defender). Suddenly (when dyad was broken), the decision emerged in the 'intending-perceiving-acting cycle' (Kugler and Turvey, 1987), suggesting that it is possible to interpret the dynamics of player interactions in dribbling as emergent properties under constraints.

Similar results were obtained by Ribeiro and Araújo (2005), with top national junior players, where besides analysing the ecological dynamics of the basketball dyad, concorrent verbal protocols were applied. These verbal protocols were carried out immediately after the attacker had finished competing in the 1vs 1 practice task, since it was almost impossible to apply these protocols concomitantly in such a fast moving task (timescale of 1 to 5 seconds) (Ericsson and Simon, 1993). Ericsson and Simon (1993) proposed that there are many types of behaviour where participants spontaneously report concurrent and retrospective thoughts. They suggested that when appropriate verbal reporting procedures are used, participants can report on the information they were attending without changing the structure of the underlying processes. They argued that researchers have now accepted that participants provide valid concurrent verbal reports on their cognitive processes matching other evidence for the associated performance and process-trace data. Interestingly, the ecological psychologist Reed (1996) argued that verbalization is a relevant means of selecting and making information available to others, and that "it refers not to inner representations but to environmental situations and states of affairs" (p. 156). Thus, there is clear support for the circumscribed use of verbal protocol analysis techniques by sport psychologists within different theoretical frameworks in studying cognition, perception, and action.

The categorization of verbalizations in Ribeiro and Araújo's (2005) study was made including three broad topics: i) verbalizations without reference to the context ("I went to the right because is my best side"), ii) verbalization with reference to the context (referring to what the defender did – perturbations promoted by the defender, and action opportunities detected in the situation – perturbations promoted by the attacker), iii) and verbalizations concerning the goal of the attacker in that 1vs 1 situation (i.e., about the shot or the result). Then the number of elements of each protocol was counted, i.e. the number of categories verbalized sequentially by the performer. The researcher used probes such as "what happened in this situation that you just performed?", and then "could you be more detailed?".

The results clearly showed that what the player stated about his actions clearly differed, although it was complementary to what he really did during the task (figure 1).

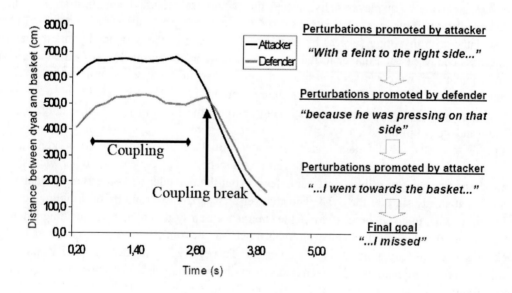

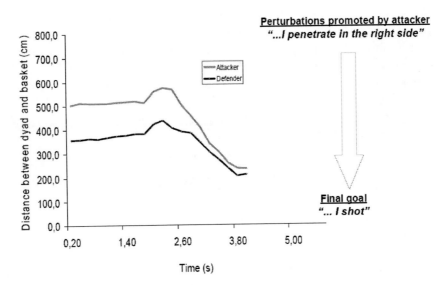

Figure 1. Expressions of player's knowledge in 1vs 1 situations in basketball. Right and left graphs illustrate the two types of knowledge (*knowledge of*, *knowledge about*).

More compelling was the fact that in the top graph of figure 1, the retrospective verbalizations that described the player's *knowledge about* the situation was more detailed than in the bottom graph of figure 1, but their *knowledge of* the situation was equally detailed in both situations. Importantly, the examples in figure 1 were selected since they involved two players playing at the highest national junior level, in similar positions in the attacking system of the team. Their performances ended with a similar result (both shots touched the ring but the ball did not go through the basket), however their expressions of *knowledge about* their performance were quite different.

These results showing individual differences in 'knowledge about' the practice task can be interpreted with reference to Gibson's (e.g., 1979) theorizing. Indeed, Gibson (1979) did not deny the existence of physical objects or individual differences in terms of perceptions of the world; rather, he conceptualized how they could be coupled. Postulating this 'knower-known' coupling, and the importance of grounding it within the context in which the knowing occurs, Gibson avoided a 'knower-known' dualism. Through experience with various environments and their nested affordances, the individual becomes apprised of what changes and what remains the same. In this way, it is possible to account for individual perceptions of change (variance) and permanence (invariance) without the postulation of further mental processes. Subsequent interactions are not dictated by the individual or environment; they emerge out of the dynamics of the interaction itself – an affordance-effectivity fit (Barab et al., 1999). From this view, meaning is not solely in the environment or solely in the individual but in the relation between them.

As participation couples knower and known, it takes on and imbues meaning, within context, through the function it serves. As the goal is met, the function served flows back on the action, imbuing it with contextualized meaning. This notion places meaning within context-embedded experience, where practice takes place in the context of meaningful relations (Barab et al., 1999). The particular meaningful relations that emerge are, in a very real sense, dependent on the performer-context relation in which particular constraints make certain meanings more functional, indeed more probable, than others; that is, context places boundary conditions on the particular meanings that emerge.

In order to further test these ideas we conducted research in which we manipulated perceptual knowledge and symbolic knowledge (Araújo, 2006; Cordovil et al., 2006; Cordovil et al., in press). For this purpose, we studied effects of task and individual constraints on decision-making processes in experienced basketball players.

CHANGES IN PLAYERS' BEHAVIOUR DURING 1VS1 DUE TO MANIPULATION OF KNOWLEDGE CONSTRAINTS

In order to manipulate symbolic/verbal knowledge or *knowledge about*, specific instructions (neutral, risk taking or conservative) were manipulated to observe effects on emergent behaviour of the dyadic system. Instructions were: i) Risk - the game will finish in 10s, the team is losing by 1 point and the player should risk possession to change the scoreline; and ii), Conservative - the game will finish in 20s, the team is winning by 1 point and the player should be conservative to prevent the opposition from changing the scoreline. In order to manipulate perceptual knowledge, or *knowledge of* the environment, body-scaling of participants was systematically altered by creating player dyads with different height and arm span relations. The anthropometric manipulation of dyads (height) was: i) Attacker much taller than defender (difference ranging between 6.7% - 15.4%); and ii) Attacker much shorter that defender (difference ranging between 6.7%- 15.4%). In the control group players had similar height levels (differences ranging between 0.2% - 2.7%) and received neutral instructions (try to score within the rules of basketball).

Data showed how decision-making behaviour could be differentially influenced by *knowledge of* and *knowledge about* the environment. The group with risky instructions and the group with shorter attackers were characterized by greater speed in crossing the mid-court line ($p \leq .001$), and by less variability in the path of the dyad towards the basket, over time ($p \leq .001$). However, the attackers with risky instructions also tended to lose possession of the ball more often. The group with taller attackers was characterized by a lack of coupling breaking ($p \leq .006$). Finally, the group with conservative instructions was slower in crossing the mid-court line ($p \leq .001$), and showed greater variability in the path of the dyad towards the basket, over time ($p \leq .001$), and greater variability in the attacker's trajectory on court ($p \leq .001$). Data showed that the manipulation of these kinds of knowledge created boundary conditions on the particular behaviours that emerged.

In figure 2, it can be observed that, during the initial part of the dyadic entrainment there was a stable state of the collective variables, followed by an abrupt change (de-coupling) in the state of the system due to an attacker's success in de-stabilizing the dyad. These dynamical properties were clarified with the use of statistics. The running correlation curve RC(t) is the time course of correlation coefficients obtained from a sliding rectangular window of waveform data centred at t. The correlation coefficient at each instant is the normalized sample covariance of the windowed waveforms $x'(t)$ e $y'(t)$: RC(t) = $<(x'-m_x)(y'-m_{y'})>/(s_{x'}s_{y'})$ where m and s are the amplitude mean and standard deviation across the duration of each windowed waveform (see Corbetta and Thelen, 1996; Meador et al., 2002). The running correlation RC(t) provides a measure of the degree of coupling of the players in the dyad. Each value of r represents the degree of coupling at each moment of the interactions. Interestingly, this coupling can be inverse (see the "conservative" graph), meaning that the players are not moving both to the same side at the same time, but that each player is moving to a different side at the same time.

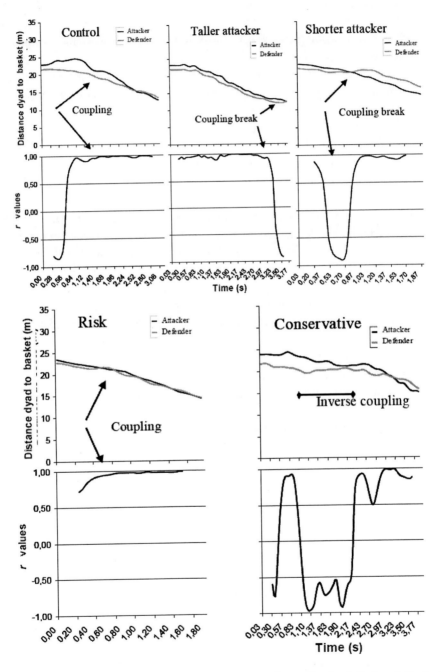

Figure 2. Example of five organizational states of the system formed by the "attacker-defender-basket" in a 1vs 1 situation (Control, Taller attacker, Shorter attacker, Risk and Conservative). The graphs on the top of each of the two ensembles indicate the distance run by the players from the starting point to the basket. The bottom graphs show the corresponding running correlation function.

In figure 2, it can be observed that all the graphs, except the one involving the group given conservative instructions, showed a symmetric coordination pattern between the players. It is clear that typically both players in a dyad approached each other or moved apart almost simultaneously, with the correlation function displaying high positive values. The two graphs with two examples of system dynamics constrained by conservative task instructions, showed that after starting uncoupled, the players formed a system which exhibited symmetry (coupling with $r > .80$) , with changes to uncorrelated states, and with anti-symmetric states (inverse coupling with $r < -.80$).

The example of a situation with risky instructions revealed several zero-crossings (symmetry-breaking occurrences) but maintained a high degree of coupling during the whole trial. The graphs depicting the control group, as well as the example with the taller attackers showed a similar pattern of coordination, with the moment of transition to the antisymmetric state distinguishing most situations.

Note that in the example of the group with shorter attackers, the system changed from symmetry to antisymmetry and returned to symmetry, in synchronization with the zero crossing shown on the upper graph (the distance of the players to the basket).

Symmetry states were broken when correlations between players in a dyad stopped. At that point a zero crossing tended to occur, with the positioning of the players being inverted, but the positive correlation persisted. But in the antisymmetric states, due to its instability, this attractor was visited only when the system transited between symmetries, an infrequent event, perhaps due to the greater amounts of metabolic energy that the players needed to use to maintain this kind of coordination (in comparison to the conservative instruction group in figure 2). It is interesting to note that only the trials of the control group and the conservative instruction group exhibited non-correlated states of interaction. In sum, this macro perspective (compared to perspectives that merely analysed cognitions based on organismic constraints, such as preferences, desires, eye movements) of the coordination states of the dyadic system influence by different constraints showed unique properties, which cannot be observed at other levels of analysis. These observations strengthen the argument that cognition and knowledge of performers in sport should be analysed at the ecological scale.

CONCLUSION

In this chapter, we have used the context of basketball to show how cognition and knowledge can be explained in terms of the relations between performers and the properties of specific environments in sport. In sport, as in other specific performance settings, knowledge is described as fundamentally situated, emerging in context (Barab et al., 1999). It becomes impossible to separate the performer, the task to be performed or the material to be learned, and the context in which training and competition occurs. From this perspective, "knowing of" and "knowing about" are no longer conceived of as static structures residing in an individual's head; instead, knowing of/about refers to an activity that is distributed across the knower, the environment in which knowing occurs, and the task which the performer is attempting to perform - a dynamic unfolding of the perception-action cycle. *Knowing of* as well as *knowing about* are deeply embedded in active participation within the social/material world. Skill development is therefore context dependent, and there is a relation between knowing of/about the world and the world that is being known. Is it possible to scientifically identify a world-class basketball player outside of a basketball context? The answer is clearly no (but confront with Ripoll, Chapter 7).

A full account of cognitive activity in team sports like basketball (as opposed to a static conceptualisation of cognition), knowing about (as opposed to static knowledge), and meaningful relations (as opposed to a collection of symbols in a representation) must include an account of ongoing change, and of the emergence of new order. Emergence is a key aspect of cognition and learning that has not been handled well by information-processing theories.

One implication of these ideas for practice in sports such as basketball is that knowledge transmitted by coaches to performers is at best second hand, since instead of having to be extracted by the performer from the environment, this knowledge is typically communicated in verbal descriptions to the performer. This indirect knowledge transmission process relies on the coach's skill in verbalising concepts and ideas in basketball and on the player's ability to interpret verbal instructions to become more aware of the information in the performance environment. This is not an impossible task. But it is much more challenging than the process of selecting and manipulating task constraints in order to help the performer increase direct awareness of key information sources to obtain knowledge about specific performance circumstances (Davids et al., 2008). To conclude, both direct and indirect cognition constrain performance, but the *expression* of a player's *knowledge of* the environment is perhaps the main purpose of competition (and training).

REFERENCES

Araújo, D. (2006). *Tomada de decisão no desporto* [Decision-making in sport]. Cruz Quebrada: Edições FMH.

Araújo, D., Davids, K., Bennett, S., Button, C., and Chapman, G. (2004). Emergence of Sport Skills under Constraints. In A.M. Williams and N.J. Hodges (Ed.), *Skill Acquisition in Sport: Research, Theory and Practice* (pp. 409-433). London: Routledge, Taylor and Francis.

Araújo, D., Davids, K., and Hristovski, R. (2006). The ecological dynamics of decision making in sport. *Psychology of Sport and Exercise, 7*, 653-676.

Araújo, D., Davids, K., Sainhas, J. and Fernandes, O. (2002). Emergent decision-making in sport: a constraints-led approach. In L. Toussaint and P. Boulinguez (Ed.), *International Congress "Movement, Attention and Perception"* (pp. 77). Poitiers, France: Université de Poitiers.

Bain, B., Hayes, D., and Quance, A. (1978). *Coaching Certification Manual* - Level two. Canada: J.Seaman, Basketball Canada.

Barab, S., Cherkes-Julkowski, M., Swenson, R., Garrett, S., Shaw, R., and Young, M. (1999). Principles of self-organization: Ecologizing the learner-facilitator system. *The Journal of the Learning Sciences, 8*(3 and 4), 349-390.

Corbetta, D., and Thelen, E. (1996). The development origins of bimanual coordination: a dynamic perspective. *Journal of Experimental Psychology: Human Perception and Performance, 22*, 502-522.

Cordovil, R., Araújo, D., Davids, K., Gouveia, L., Barreiros, J., Fernandes, O., and Serpa, S. (2006). The influence of instructions and bodyscaling as constraints on decision-making processes. *Book of Abstracts of the 3rd European Network of Young Specialists in Sport Psychology (ENYSP) Workshop*, Lisbon.

Cordovil, R., Araújo, D., Davids, K., Gouveia, L., Barreiros, J., Fernandes, O., and Serpa, S. (in press). The influence of instructions and bodyscaling as constraints on decision-making processes in team sports. *European Journal of Sport Science*

Davids, K., Button, C. Araújo, D., Renshaw, I., and Hristovski, R. (2006). Movement models from sports provide representative task constraints for studying adaptive behavior in human motor systems. *Adaptive Behavior, 14*,73-95.

Davids, K., Button, C., and Bennett, S. (2008). *Dynamics of Skill acquisition. A constraints-led approach*. Champaign, IL: Human Kinetics.

Ericsson, K., and Simon, H. (1993). *Protocol analysis: Verbal reports as data* (Rev. Ed.). Massachusetts: MIT press.

Fodor, J and Z. Pylyshyn (1981) "How direct is visual perception? Some reflection on Gibson's 'ecological approach". *Cognition, 9*, 139-196.

Gibson, J.J. (1966). *The senses considered as perceptual systems*. Boston: Houghton Mifflin.

Gibson, J.J. (1979). *The ecological approach to visual perception*. Hillsdale, New Jersey: Lawrence Erlbaum Associates.

Jacobs, D., and Michaels, C. (2007). Direct learning. *Ecological Psychology, 19*, 321-349.

Kugler, P.N., Kelso, J.A.S., and Turvey, M.T. (1980). On the concept of coordinated structures as dissipative structures. I : Theoretical lines of convergence. In G. Stelmach and J. Requin (Ed.), *Tutorials in Motor Behavior*. (pp. 3-45). Amsterdam: North Holland.

Kugler, P., Kelso, J.S., and Turvey, M. (1982). On the control and co-ordination of naturally developing systems. In J.S. Kelso and J. Clark (Eds.), The development of movement control and co-ordination (pp. 5-78). New York: Wiley.

Kugler, P.N., and Turvey, M.T. (1987). Information, natural law, and the self-assembly of rhythmic movement. Hillsdale, New Jersey: Lawrence Erlbaum Associates.

Lee, D.N., Lishman, J.R., and Thomson, J.A. (1982). Regulation of gait in long jumping. *Journal of Experimental Psychology: Human Perception and Performance, 8*, 448-458.

McPherson, S., and Kernodle, M. (2003). Tactics, the neglected attribute of expertise: problem representations and performance skills in tennis. In J.L. Starkes and K.A. Ericsson (Eds.), *Expert Performance in Sports: Advances in research on sport expertise* (pp. 137-167). Champaign, IL: Human Kinetics.

Meador, K., Ray, P., Echauz, J., Loring, D., and Vachtsevanos, G. (2002). Gamma coherence and conscious perception. *Neurology, 59*, 847-854.

Michaels, C.F., and Carello, C. (1981). *Direct Perception*. Englewood Cliffs, NJ: Prentice-Hall.

Reed, E.S. (1991). James Gibson's ecological appraoch to cognition. In: A. Still and A. Costall (Eds.), *Against cognitivism: alternative foundations for cognitive psychology*. New York: Harvester Wheatsheaf.

Reed, E.S. (1996). *Encountering the world: Toward an ecological psychology*. Oxford: Oxford University Press.

Ribeiro, J., and Araújo, D. (2005). A dinâmica da tomada de decisão na relação um-contra-um no basquetebol. In D. Araújo (Ed.), *O Contexto da decisão: a acção táctica no desporto* (pp. 109-125). Lisboa: Edições Visão e Contextos.

Savelsbergh, G., van der Kamp, J., Oudejans, R., and Scott, M. (2004). Perceptual learning is mastering perceptual degrees of freedom. In A.M. Williams, and N.J. Hodges (Eds.), *Skill Acquisition in Sport: Research, Theory and Practice* (pp. 374-389). London: Routledge, Taylor and Francis.

Schmidt, R.A., and Lee, T. (2005). *Motor control and learning* (4th ed.). Champaign, Ill: Human Kinetics.

Shaw, R. (2003). The agent-environment interface: Simon's indirect or Gibson's direct coupling. *Ecological Psychology, 15*(1), 37-106.

Shaw, R., and Turvey, M.T. (1981). Coalitions as models for Ecosystems: A Realist Perspective on Perceptual Organization. In M. Kubovy and J. Pomerantz (Eds.), *Perceptual Organization* (pp. 343 - 415). Hillsdale, NJ: Lawrence Erlbaum Associates.

Turvey, M.T. (1992). Affordances and prospective control: an outline of the ontology. *Ecological Psychology, 4*(3), 173-187.

Turvey, M.T., and Shaw, R.E. (1995). Toward an ecological physics and a physical psychology. In R.L. Solso and D.W. Massaro (Ed.), *The Science of the Mind: 2001 and Beyond* (pp. 144-169). New York: Oxford University Press.

Turvey, M.T., and Shaw, R. (1999). Ecological foundations of cognition I: Symmetry and specificity of animal-environment systems. *Journal of Counsciousness Studies, 6*(11-12), 95-110.

Warren, W. (2006). The dynamics of perception and action. *Psychological Review, 113*, 358-389.

Whiting, H.T.A. (1991). Action is not reaction! A reply to McLeod and Jenkins. *International Journal of Sport Psychology, 22*, 296-303.

In: Perspectives on Cognition and Action in Sport
Editors: D. Araújo, H. Ripoll and M. Raab

ISBN: 978-1-60692-390-0
© 2009 Nova Science Publishers, Inc.

Chapter 11

EXTENDING THE RATHER UNNOTICED GIBSONIAN VIEW THAT 'PERCEPTION IS COGNITIVE': DEVELOPMENT OF THE ENACTIVE APPROACH TO PERCEPTUAL-COGNITIVE EXPERTISE

Eric Laurent [1] and Hubert Ripoll [2]

[1] Laboratory of Psychology, University of Franche Comté, France
[2] Information and System Science Laboratory & Sport Sciences Faculty,
Aix-Marseille Universities, France

ABSTRACT

In this chapter, we present the foundations of an enactive approach to cognitive expertise. We first discuss the dichotomy between classical cognitive approaches to expertise and ecological approaches to motor behaviour. The limits of classical cognitive approaches are related to the empirical study of experts on very derived tasks based on the study of memory in laboratory and to the symbols storing problem in continuous and uncertain environments. The limit of the ecological approach is related to the reduction of human complexity to the two-dimensional perception-action system. We propose an alternate framework in which basic cognitive functions such as categorization are taken into account in their links to visual search processes. We report some published experimental data which tend to show that visual perception embody higher-level demands. This shall involves redefining the role of cognition as a teleological constraint for perceptive systems rather than as a mere enrichment process of a poor stimulation, and redefining the ecology of perception as a multiform (i.e., biological, cognitive, physical) and demanding environment rather than as mere array of external light.

INTRODUCTION

"Often nowadays when I talk to an audience about the ecological approach to perception, I am asked whether this approach has anything to say about cognition, or whether there must be a firm line drawn between perception and cognition with different

principles applying. The first answer to this question is that perception *is* cognitive. Cognition has to do with knowing. The number one definition of cognition in my favorite dictionary (Random House) is 'The act or process of knowing: perception'."
E. J. Gibson, 1991 (p. 493)

"I feel that perception relies on very fine clues that do not appear to everybody, and there is something automatic that virtually reacts at our own place". Bruno Martini (French handball goalkeeper, twice world champion)
In Ripoll, 2008 (p. 80)

The above (second) statement, relying on empirical experience of an expert player highlights the theoretical need for characterising clues that are critical for reducing uncertainty and for regulating one's own behaviour. For about three decades, research in psychology has brought evidence for the existence and use of such critical clues in memory and perception. However, the above statement also supports research endeavours directed towards the building of a theory of automatic and invasive processes in expert perception. The latter aspect is rather poorly understood and little is known about the ability of experts to spontaneously 'couple' to those predictive clues, especially under time pressure. On what basis do they select picked up information? In the present chapter, we advocate for the development of an enactive approach to expertise that should account for both perceptual sensitisation to predictive stimuli *and its relations to usual task goals*. In the course of our development we should contribute to fill in the gap found in the literature between mnemonic and perceptual adaptations. Both processes have been envisaged as a system, which allows linking perceptual behaviour to task demands on the basis of a memory trace which is embodied in the coupling between the variables.

Our approach builds on recent experimental evidence, which demonstrates that: 1) expert visual search behaviours are rather global in nature thereby reflecting and embodying the nature of their *global-and-structural* domain-specific cognition, 2) categorization is a basic phenomenon in expert enhanced perceptual performance, 3) perceptual expertise relies on tight coupling between perception and categorization.

From the 70's, research on expertise has developed in sport and other contexts such as chess, medical diagnosis or music. Chess was certainly the most influential domain with seminal works of de Groot (1946/1978) and Chase and Simon (1973) having dramatic impact on the definition of research protocols on memory, which were imported in sport psychology. Globally, these studies showed that experts are better than novices at recalling familiar material pertaining to chess game. Moreover, Chase and Simon, in 1973, showed that this advantage is mediated by a chunking process by which experts recall sequences of multiple pieces, whereas novices organize information in a more elementary way. From the first moments of experimental research on cognitive expertise, memory and perception were considered together. What we propose here is *to strengthen the fruitful study of the links between perception and cognition*.

In sport, since the 80's, a first trend of research involved a series of authors who proposed laboratory protocols, building on chess literature or memory tasks derived from cognitive psychology (Abernethy, Neal, and Koning, 1994; Allard, Graham, and Paarsalu, 1980; Chiesi, Spilich, and Voss, 1979; Deakin and Allard, 1991; Didierjean and Marmèche, 2005; Garland and Barry, 1991; Starkes, 1987; Werner and Thies, 2000; Williams, Davids, Burwitz, and Williams, 1993). This research corpus demonstrated: i) enhanced recall and recognition skills, ii) decreased change blindness for 'semantic' changes, iii) increased automatic anticipatory abilities for extrapolating future scenarios (even from static displays), iv) the specificity of the expert advantage, the latter rising when the material used is coherently organized, that is structured according to the rules of the game, and according to adaptive principles of players' organisation. The research trend, relying on classical concepts of cognitive psychology, has contributed to the importation of the information processing approach in sport psychology. This participated in revealing cognitive characteristics of expert adaptation in sports while emphasising the role of memory in performance. During the same period, several authors reported research on perceptual aspects of expertise in sport (Abernethy, 1987; Bard and Fleury, 1976; Helsen and Pauwels, 1993; Ripoll, 1988; 1991; Ripoll, Kerlirzin, Stein, and Reine, 1995; Williams, Davids, Burwitz, and Williams, 1994). Visual parameters have been studied mainly either in relation to motor control or in relation to decision making in uncertain environments, though, on the field, both aspects of visual function (i.e., 'sensorimotor', 'semantic') interact (see Ripoll, 1991, for examples of studies of the interaction between both functions). The synthesis of the results is not fairly easy because of the diversity of the protocols employed by authors. Fixation duration and number during visual search were sometimes taken as discriminating between expert and novice populations. In several studies, fixation duration was longer and number of fixations was less important in experts than in novices (Helsen and Pauwels, 1993; Ripoll, 1988). However contradictory results were obtained, with experts having more and shorter fixations (Williams et al., 1994). More recently, Martell and Vickers (2004) provided evidence that both behaviours could occur during the same task. For instance, in a live defensive zone task, the visual strategy consisted in elite ice-hockey players of both early and rapid fixations followed by a late fixation of long duration prior to the final execution. Actually, it appears that there is no such thing as a basic change of visual search that would be independent from task nature/progress or cognitive constraints. We believe that understanding perceptual expertise implies giving an account for the multiple coupling between perception, action, cognition and diverse task variables. This is motivated by the will of describing the dynamics of expertise and not only mnemonic performance obtained on very derived tasks. In that, we are sympathetic with the "expert performance approach" – initiated by Ericsson and colleagues (Ericsson and Williams, 2007; Williams and Ericsson, 2005) – which may contribute to "capture" exceptional performance and mediating psychological processes. However, we stress the need to know about the inner nature of the psychological processes involved rather than stressing the need for simulating 'more and more' actual performance. What we propose here is to focus on cognition-perception couplings. We think that capturing the inner psychological constraints also involves understanding the basic relationships between psychological processes, beyond describing patterns of differences in accuracy performance in more and more realistic experimental protocols. In the end, we aim at exemplifying a theoretical-driven approach to expertise, in which perceptual expertise can be conceived as an emergent property of the coupling between usual cognitive tasks encountered on a daily basis (e.g., linguistic labelling of game scenes in expert basketball players when they are working on game systems and tactics with their coach) and visual search parameters (e.g., oculomotor behaviours). This will imply to briefly recall basic principles of the ecological approach to visual perception and to extend its systemic framework to higher-level processes.

It is nowadays traditional and convenient to present an opposition between 'ecological' approaches to perception and action and 'cognitive' approaches to motor control or decision making. In the first framework (J. J. Gibson, 1979), a two-dimensional system is conceived, in which action is specified by perception and perceptual events are created by action (figure 1). It excludes representational concepts because of the 'knowing character' of senses.

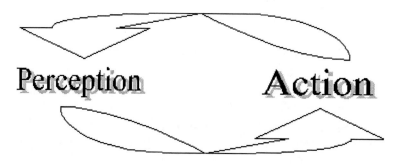

Figure 1. The perception-action cycle in the ecological approach to perception.

Information is significant: there is no need to produce mental representation in order to enrich and interpret incoming stimulation. The approach has been applied with success in 'movement science' for explaining a series of motor behaviours like catching a ball or driving a car, and more generally for explaining the direct perception and the use of optical variables like time-to-collision or vertical optical acceleration (Bootsma and Oudejans, 1993; Lee, 1976; McLeod and Dienes, 1996; McLeod, Reed, and Dienes, 2002). From the other side, there is no such thing as an intelligible 'system' that would account for the determinants of expert performance. Building on both the ecological approach to visual perception (J. J. Gibson, 1979) and the theoretical trend of enaction (Varela, Thomson, and Rosch, 1991), we will be considering cognitive constraints as 'ecological constraints' of perception. In contrast with the usual role attributed to cognition by sport scientists, which would restrict to a support system in charge of the enrichment of initial stimulation, we see cognition as a 'teleological constraint' that weighs on perceptual systems. By 'teleological', we understand the *final* dimension of a process. That is, in a systemic theory, perception and eye movements are seen as embodying higher level cognitive *demands,* which are largely dependent on both the cognitive task at hand and expertise. The perceptual systems are constrained by their ecology, which is not only the external and 'visible' environment – as in the Gibsonian theory –, but also a *dynamic psychological environment.* Behavioural constraints such as categorisation or diverse verbal descriptions of the game imply that search for information is in relation with cognition, not for its symbolic enrichment function, but rather because of its 'output', teleological status. As a consequence, cognition as conceived here may be one term of a two-dimensional coupling with perception. *Cognition, in our chapter is not conceived as an interpretation tool, but rather as a directional force that drives search towards information that has 'historically' or ontogenetically been found to be diagnostic for the satisfaction of cognitive-like outputs.* Moreover, the effect of cognition on perception will be considered as a rather straightforward influence which can let perception embody the teleological dimension of usual cognitive outputs (e.g., labelling the category of a defensive organisation in basketball) (figure 2). This does not imply that *symbolic* structures 'pilot' perception or that perception is 'indirect' as suggested by Rock and others (see Rock, 1996).

Note that in our proposal, symbolic structures are not required for getting influence from higher-level functions on perception-action cycles. For example, it is because a given part within a visual scene usually affords a player a given categorisation that he or she will become sensitized to the parts diagnostic of the categorisation. In the remaining part of the present chapter we gather data collected both in the general psychology literature and in our laboratories, which tend to give support for the embodiment view of high-level processes in perceptual systems.

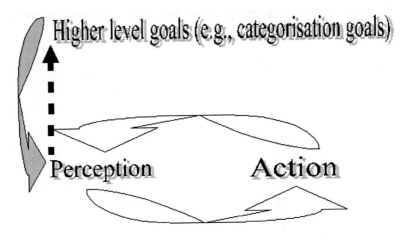

Figure 2. The perception-action cycle and the embodiment of psychological constraints in perception.

THE EMBODIMENT OF CATEGORISATION IN PERCEPTION AS A DIMENSION OF THE PSYCHOLOGICAL ECOLOGY OF PERCEPTION

We first suggest bringing together the domain of perceptual-cognitive expertise in sport and a recent paradigmatic trend in psychology that deals with the interaction between perceptual and conceptual processes (Goldstone, 1994; 2001; Goldstone and Barsalou, 1998; Goldstone, Steyvers, and Larimer, 1996; Harnad, 1987; Laurent, 2002; Livingston, Andrews, and Harnad, 1998). Though it is recent, the systematic study of conceptual learning influences on perception has strong experimental and theoretical bases in an earlier "New Look" psychology initiated during the 1940's. The role of 'complexity' in perceptual judgment might date back to those times when Jerome S. Bruner and Cecile C. Goodman published their very amazing data on the organizing role of value and need in perception (1947). In their paper (p. 33), the authors themselves quote Thurstone (1944): "For, as Professor Thurstone has put it, 'In these days when we insist so frequently on the interdependence of all aspects of personality, it would be difficult to maintain that any of these functions, such as perception, is isolated from the rest of the dynamical system that constitutes the person". We think that the fashion of the 'non-cognitive' approach to motor behaviour has conducted to a new reductionism in sport science[1], which paradoxically, in the same time, is associated to a noisy defence of models of 'complexity'. The perception-action couple is a system, but can not afford *alone* satisfactory explanations for other factors than strictly motor ones. Nevertheless, an individual engaged in a sport task is submitted to constraints that do not restrict to the

---

[1] Sometimes non-arbitrarily called 'human movement science'

'realm' of coordination between body segments or to the catching of mobiles. We argue here that sport context is not only a field for the application of psychological concepts but also an ideal field to help building a real theory of complexity. Because on the field players are submitted to a wide variety of constraints (i.e., decisional, emotional, motor, physiological) and because sport science is an 'interdisciplinary field', reducing a theory of behaviour to the motor dimension would be especially misleading and uninspired. In our laboratories, we have developed an experimental program to work on the interaction between perceptual performance and higher-level cognition, such as categorisation.

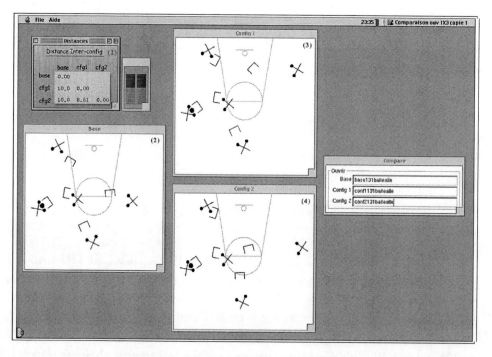

Figure 3. Procedure used for controlling and equating the physical distortion index in both 'between-category' and 'within-category' conditions (adapted from the cluster encoding method validated by Courricu, 2001, first method). On the left (box 1), a matrix affords the numerical coding of physical distances between the three configurations. In this example, the source (box 2) belongs to the '1-3-1' category. On the right, the between-category configuration (box 3) belongs to the '1-2-2' category. The 'within-category' configuration (box 4) belongs to the '1-3-1' category, like the source. Offensive players are represented by crosses and defensive players are represented by half squares.

We have been working with expert basketball players which have been known to use schematic diagrams – such as those that are presented on figure 3 – on a daily basis. We hypothesised that expert perception could be sensitised to critical visual features on the basis of their conceptual activity which consists in describing game situations, for example in order to subsequently reproduce an offensive or a defensive plan on the real field. This type of routines has been thought to promote an attunement of search process to visual features that are critical to a given categorisation. Therefore, we set up a series of experiments in which expert and novice basketball players had to discriminate between schematic basketball configurations under severe time pressure (Laurent, 2003a; Laurent and Ripoll, 2002). In a 'same-different' judgment task, two coherent basketball configurations were presented sequentially, each during 1200 ms, the first on the left part and the second on the right part of a screen and were projected by a video beamer. Given both the complexity of the scenes, and time constraints, the task was very challenging for the participants. The configurations could be identical or different. When different, they varied either physically, within the same defensive category, or both physically and categorically. That is to say that a physical change could produce or not a categorical change (see figure 3 for an overview of the procedure used for creating stimuli).

After the 1200 ms presentation time period of the second configuration, participants had 1000 ms more, during which they still could give their answer. During this last period, a grid mask was presented on the screen and served as a signal since participants were informed that if their response was not given before the mask had vanished, then their answer would be recorded as "incorrect". Responses were given by pressing two keys of a computer keyboard corresponding to "identical" and "different" responses. Analysis of variance and subsequent post-hoc (all $p < .05$) showed that experts were better than novices at discriminating patterns of game only when a category boundary was straddled between the base and the target (figure 4).

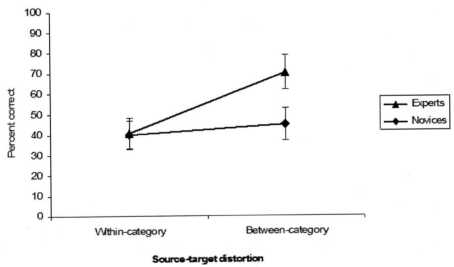

Figure 4. Response accuracy as a function of source-target distortion (within-category, between-category).

In the present study, it is shown that experts can be as weak as novices for discriminating two coherently organised patterns of play. In the literature it has been commonly admitted, since the first studies in sport in the 80's, that coherence was the critical factor for predicting expert performance in laboratory tasks. In our speeded perceptual task, what are critical are the categorical relationships that are established between both configurations. For a similar amount of physical distortion in both "within-category" and "between-category" distortion conditions, expert perceptual abilities are differentiated. The differentiated pattern is due to the sensitivity of the perceptual system to visual features that are diagnostic of the categorisation. Several arguments tend to favour an early access to categorical features in vision: i) no within-category compression effect was found; it is likely that if a verbal labelling process mediated expert response, then they would have considered different members of the same category as being 'identical'; however experts were not found to be weaker than novices in finding within-category differences; ii) given the complexity of the scenes and the comparison to do, the task placed strong temporal constraints on the psychological mechanisms, which make us privilege a low-level perceptual hypothesis rather than a double perceptual and linguistic labelling process; iii) none of the experts reported to be aware of such a mechanism during the debriefing of the experiment; at most they reported to be aware of some pieces of game organisation. Then, it seems that conceptual categorisation can influence perception, but this influence might not require a conceptual representation to be elaborated during such perceptual tasks. We can conceive that extended practice constrains search and sensitise perceptual systems to visual features that are usually diagnostic of task success. Those features generally afford the player to be successful, so that it becomes highly adaptive for players to search for them when they are dealing with such stimuli. Perceptual discrimination abilities in expert basketball players are dependent on the sensitisation of vision that occurs as a result of a daily coupling between vision and conceptual outputs. In the enactive framework proposed here, we can say that visual expertise is the embodied history of couplings between different organism search components (e.g., vision) and the behavioural or cognitive outputs of the action in which the individual is engaged on a daily basis (e.g., production of categorical labels denoting game configurations).

THE RELIANCE OF PERCEPTUAL EXPERTISE ON PERCEPTION-ACTION CYCLES: EMBODIMENT OF COGNITIVE CONSTRAINTS

The perception-action cycles play a major role in ecological approaches to perception (J. J. Gibson, 1966; 1979). These cycles allow the individual to modify his or her relationship to the world by the regulation of behaviour as a function of perceptual information. Traditionally, the reliance on such cycles is evoked in the framework of motor coordination. In order to get evidence of the embodiment of *cognitive* constraints on perceptual-motor processes, we (Laurent, Ward, Williams and Ripoll, 2006) analysed eye movements of experts and novices in a discrimination task. Basketball experts and novices had to judge whether two configurations were the same or different. The configurations were presented subsequently in the following sequence: first configuration (during 4 seconds) – mask (during 2 seconds) – second configuration (until the answer). The number of elements displaced between the first one and the second one was varied (i.e., 0, 1, 2, and 3). Results mainly indicated that during the perception of the second configuration, novices had their number of eye fixations varied linearly as a function of the number of displaced elements. The greater the number of elements displaced, the fewer the number of eye fixations. This relation was well described by a linear equation of the type $y = -.5236x + 6.8613$ ($p < .05$, $R^2 = .89$). In contrast, experts had their number of eye fixations unchanged across discrepant similarity conditions (figure 5). We have interpreted this as evidence for the embodiment of teleological constraints of cognition in perception and action. The object and the dynamics of visual search are dependent upon the history of couplings between the stimulation (i.e., game scenes) and usual cognitive demands (i.e., verbally describing schematic patterns of games). As far as novices are concerned, they have got no historic coupling between their search process, schematic basketball configurations, and conceptual outputs. It seems then that the information picked up by them involves entities of the visual display; the greater the number of figured entities manipulated, the greater the likelihood to find quickly a local distortion of the display. On the opposite, experts have coupled for years the invariants concerning alignments of players (provided by visual stimulation) with conceptual labels (see the preceding section for examples of labels). Therefore, their search is not sensitive to local manipulation of the display. Their eye movement number is rather constant in this experiment (figure 5).

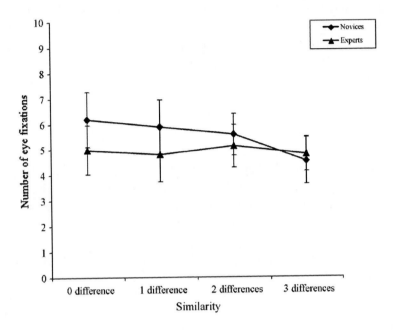

Figure 5. Mean number of fixations (and standard deviations) in experts and novices in the various source-target similarity conditions [reproduced with permission of the Psychology Press, Taylor and Francis Group (http://www.informaworld.com), from Laurent *et al.*, 2006, Experiment 1].

Together with our results obtained when categorical relations between displays were manipulated, this indicates that expertise penetrates vision ability and search, as soon as the eye movement stage, but *most important*, the perceptual sensitization is dependent upon teleological constraints relative to higher-order cognitive goals. A daily conceptual behaviour relying on relational invariants of the visual array generates a search for information that is embodied in specific motor patterns of the eyes.

CONCLUSION

In the theory and experiments discussed in the chapter, perception and discrimination abilities were conceived as: i) being dependent upon the manipulation of categorical features of the visual display, ii) relying on eye movements that embody the task goals usually associated to the processing of such stimuli (i.e., the production of a conceptual response). It is then possible to see cognitive expertise (including sport expertise) as a process that penetrates perceptual systems. A good candidate for explaining the acquisition of a skill subject to give rise to such a pattern of result is "learned differentiation" of visual stimulation (Gibson and Gibson, 1955). Actually, we do not think that symbolic models that have been developed for chess expertise can be applied directly to sport expertise. Some earlier studies in chess reported that experts could decrease the number of their eye fixations, fixate between related pieces, and increase their perceptual span (Reingold and Charness, 2005). This might be interpreted in the mainstream expertise framework. Since the pioneering work of Chase and Simon (1973), it is proposed that experts distinguish from less skilled people in the way they "chunk" visual stimulation in their domain of expertise. These pieces of encoded visual stimulation have been variably estimated in chess (see Reingold and Charness, 2005) to be between 10 000-100 000 (Simon and Gilmartin, 1973), 50 000 (Simon and Chase, 1973) or 300 000 (Gobet and Simon, 2000). However, as Varela and colleagues (1991) put it, chess is like a "crystalline" world. There are particular positions, with a finite number of possible moves. Sport scientists have been tempted by the importation of chunking models in sport, envisaging for example, the programming of eye movements on the basis of abstract knowledge bases (see Williams, Davids and Williams, 1999): "Traditionally, it has been assumed that visual search strategies are determined by task-specific knowledge structures stored symbolically in long-term memory. It is argued that through learning a performer builds up an immense knowledge base of experience which can be used to interpret events encountered in circumstances similar to those previously experienced. These knowledge structures direct the performer's visual search strategy towards more important areas of the display based on past experience and contextual information" (p. 153). However, if symbolic knowledge bases are made of such a huge amount of chunks and higher-level knowledge like templates (Gobet and Simon, 1996), and that such a modelling is *ad-hoc* for sport, how many chunks and other symbols do experts should *store* whereas their environment of expertise is not "crystalline"? If their environment does not include discrete spaces but rather continuous spaces (e.g., a basketball field)? Since any given situation is not strictly the same as another, would an expert have an infinite number of chunks to elaborate? A computational explosion could then occur! We think that perceptual sensitisation to relevant parts of stimuli (such as perceptual zones corresponding to empty parts, between entities) occurs but we do not envisage symbolic storing of "chunks" in memory. We showed earlier that categorisation could be put forward in order to account for perceptual expertise while taking into consideration the bounded character of human resources, and that perceptual systems are themselves constrained to select invariants relevant to usual task goals. In that, we join to the declaration of E. J. Gibson (1991, p. 493): *"Many psychologists think of cognition exclusively as problem solving, reasoning, remembering, and so on, however. I like to point out that these processes begin with and depend on knowledge that is obtained through perception, which extracts information through arrays of stimulation that specify the events, layout, and objects of the world. The ecological approach holds that this process is a direct one, in that the information is picked up without the intermediary of secondary sources, like inference from past experience or from premises that are somehow inherited"* (E. J. Gibson, p. 493). We do not state here that mental representations do not exist or that they are not useful, but their functional role can be questioned and might be even limited to a mental simulation of affordances (see Laurent, 2003b, for such a proposal), giving rise to conscious experience. That is, mental representations can be thought of as subjective, emergent, and synthetic end products and serve as a cognitive basis for the conscious experience of the state of subject-environment relationships. Though we cannot formally exclude symbolic computational models of expertise from our empirical results, we show that we need to understand both categorization-perceptual abilities and cognition-eye movements couplings as cases of coordinative structures within a larger psychological system. Furthermore, our conception based on dynamic couplings is more parsimonious in terms of constraints that weigh on the storage of information. Instead of postulating the existence of an infinite number of symbolic chunks (or at least a great number of "classes of chunks", and/or schemas or templates) in memory, we define an enactment process by which the *coordination* – such as the ones evoked in the empirical studies reported in this chapter – allows the pick-up process and potentially, as a non-mandatory consequence, the emergence of a mental representation.

On the other hand, the Gibsonian approach has not been very powerful in describing how expertise emerges. The non-specific concept of "attention" (a disembodied one) has been repeatedly used by the Gibsonian tenants for explaining the psychological adaptation underlying expertise. Alternatively, authors have employed an "ecological approach" to expertise in order to model the progressive attunement of experts to task constraints (Vicente and Wang, 1998). Our approach is slightly different and complementary, in that we try to focus on a new type of ecology: the ecology of psychological processes, at a microscopic scale, can be made of other psychological, physiological or behavioural processes themselves, and the attunement can concern the dynamic coupling *between* these processes in addition to the coupling between the subject and the environmental structure, at the macroscopic scale. We would like to extend the "ecological" frame of perception to other contexts than strictly motor ones. In our enactive view, we defend the idea that historic couplings between perception and cognition can actively modulate the detection of invariants that are predictive of adaptive behaviour. Indeed, beyond the 'realm' of motor production, the adaptive behavioural output of experts can be 'cognitive-like' (e.g., concept production describing the game). Furthermore, each teleological dimension that has got an adaptive value for the human being, including physiological factors (e.g., thirst, see Changizi and Hall, 2001, for an illustration of basic needs effects on perception), can weighs on the attunement of the perceptual system to some invariants in order to get information that specify the state of subject-environment relations with regards to the adaptive needs. These multiple needs have been embodied possibly at different periods of phylogenesis and certainly at different moments of the ontogenesis and at different time scales (from learning during the first months of childhood to the present of physiological variations, and from the macrodynamic scale of learning to the microdynamic scale of physiological changes). This is the reason why sport behaviour, with its composite characteristics, including a wide panel of active determinants (i.e., biochemical, biomechanical, neurological, psychological, etc.), might be a privileged field for the development of this paradigm of enaction, which should prove to be fruitful for people 'truly' interested by complexity. By 'complexity' we understand multiple components that potentially can interact and assemble in different coordinative patterns within a system. Hence we do not state that disembodied symbolic functions such as hypothetic schemas, templates or chunks 'pilot' an enslaved embodied sensorimotor system. Neither do we hypothesize that sensorimotor loops are sufficient to give an account for expertise, as if all adaptive behaviours could be restricted to the range of movement and to perception-action coupling. We suggest adopting the enactive perspective for improving our knowledge of interactions between cognitive and sensorimotor dynamics, as well as in order to better understand the multiple factors underlying expert behaviour in the framework of a single theoretical system.

REFERENCES

Abernethy, B. (1987). Selective attention in fast ball sports II: Expert-novice differences. *Australian Journal of Science and Medicine in Sport, 19*, 7-16.

Abernethy, B., Neal, R.J., and Koning, P. (1994). Visual-perceptual and cognitive differences between expert, intermediate, and novice snooker players. *Applied Cognitive Psychology, 8*, 185-211.

Allard, F., Graham, S., and Paarsalu, M.E. (1980). Perception in sport: Basketball. *Journal of Sport Psychology, 2*, 14-21.

Bard, C., and Fleury, M. (1976). Analysis of visual search activity during sport problem situations. *Journal of Human Movement Studies, 2*, 214-222.

Bootsma, R.J., and Oudejans, R.R. (1993). Visual information about time-to-collision between two objects. *Journal of Experimental Psychology: Human Perception and Performance, 19*, 1041-1052.

Bruner, J.S., and Goodman, C.C. (1947). Value and need as organizing factors in perception. *The Journal of Abnormal and Social Psychology, 42*, 33-44.

Changizi, M.A., and Hall, W.G. (2001). Thirst modulates a perception. *Perception, 30* 1489-1497.

Chase, W.G., and Simon, H.A. (1973). Perception in chess. *Cognitive Psychology, 4*, 55-81.

Chiesi, H.L., Spilich, G.J., and Voss, J.F. (1979). Acquisition of domain-related information in relation to high and low domain knowledge. *Journal of Verbal Learning and Verbal Behavior, 18*, 257-273.

Courrieu, P. (2001). Two methods for encoding clusters. *Neural Networks, 14*(2), 175-183.

De Groot, A.D. (1946/1978). *Thought and Choice in Chess*. The Hague: Mouton. (Original work published in 1946).

Deakin, J.M., and Allard, F. (1991). Skilled memory in expert figure skaters. *Memory and Cognition, 19*, 79-86.

Didierjean, A., and Marmèche, E. (2005). Anticipatory representation of visual basketball scenes by novice and expert players. *Visual Cognition, 12*, 265-283.

Ericsson, K.A., and Williams, A.M. (2007). Capturing naturally occurring superior performance in the laboratory: Translational research on expert performance. *Journal of Experimental Psychology: Applied, 13*, 115-123.

Garland, D.J., and Barry, J.R. (1991). Cognitive advantage in sport: The nature of perceptual structures. *American Journal of Psychology, 104*, 211-228.

Gibson, E.J. (1991). Reading in retrospect: Perception, cognition, or both? In E. J. Gibson (Ed.), *An Odyssey in Learning and Perception* (pp. 493-495). Cambridge, MA: MIT Press.

Gibson, J.J. (1966). *The Senses Considered as Perceptual Systems*. Boston: Houghton Mifflin.

Gibson, J.J. (1979). *The Ecological Approach to Visual Perception*. Boston, MA: Houghton-Mifflin.

Gibson, J.J., and Gibson, E.J. (1955). Perceptual learning: differentiation or enrichment? *Psychological Review, 62*, 32-41.

Gobet, F., and Simon, H.A. (1996). Templates in chess memory: A mechanism for recalling several boards. *Cognitive Psychology, 31*, 1-40.

Gobet, F., and Simon, H.A. (2000). Five seconds or sixty? Presentation time in expert memory. *Cognitive Science, 24,* 651-682.

Goldstone, R.L. (1994). Influences of categorization on perceptual discrimination. *Journal of Experimental Psychology: General, 123,* 178-200.

Goldstone, R.L. (2001). The sensitization and differentiation of dimensions during category learning. *Journal of Experimental Psychology: General, 130,* 116-139.

Goldstone, R.L., and Barsalou, L. (1998). Reuniting perception and conception. *Cognition, 65,* 231-262.

Goldstone, R.L., Steyvers, M., and Larimer, K. (1996). Categorical perception of novel dimensions. *Proceedings of the Eighteenth Annual Conference of the Cognitive Science Society* (pp. 243-248). Hillsdale, NJ: Lawrence Erlbaum Associates.

Harnad, S. (Ed.) (1987). *Categorical Perception: The Groundwork of Cognition.* New York: Cambridge University Press.

Helsen, W., and Pauwels, J.M. (1993). A cognitive approach to visual search in sport. In D. Brogan, A. Gale and K. Carr (Eds.), *Visual Search,* (Vol. 2, pp. 379-388). London: Taylor and Francis.

Laurent, E. (2002). From Piaget's assimilating mind to Navon's clockland: Towards a categorical account of mirror vision. *Psycoloquy, 13*(005). Retrieved online from http://psycprints.ecs.soton.ac.uk/archive/00000197/

Laurent, E. (2003a). *Une Approche Écologique de l'Expertise Cognitive* [An Ecological Approach to Cognitive Expertise]. Unpublished doctoral dissertation. University of the Mediterranean, France.

Laurent, E. (2003b). *Mental* representations as simulated affordances: not intrinsic, not *so much* functional, but intentionally-driven. *Intellectica, 36-37,* 185-187.

Laurent, E., and Ripoll, H. (2002). Categorical perception occurs in expert basketball players. In M. Koskolou, N. Geladas and V. Klissouras (Eds.), *Proceedings of the 7th Annual Congress of the European College of Sport Science,* Athens, Greece, 24-28th July, Vol. 2, (p. 609). Athens: Pashalidis Medical Publisher.

Laurent, E., Ward, P., Williams, A.M., and Ripoll, H. (2006). Expertise in basketball modifies perceptual discrimination abilities, underlying cognitive processes and visual behaviours. *Visual Cognition, 13,* 247-271.

Lee, D.N. (1976). A theory of visual control of braking based on information about time-to-collision. *Perception, 5,* 437-459.

Livingston, K.R., Andrews, J.K., and Harnad, S. (1998). Categorical perception effects induced by category learning. *Journal of Experimental Psychology: Learning, Memory and Cognition, 24,* 732-753.

Martell, S.G., and Vickers, J.N. (2004). Gaze characteristics of elite and near-elite athletes in ice hockey defensive tactics. *Human Movement Science, 22,* 689-712.

McLeod, P. and Dienes, Z. (1996). Do fielders know where to go to catch the ball or only how to get there? *Journal of Experimental Psychology: Human Perception and Performance, 22,* 531-543.

McLeod, P., Reed, N., and Dienes, Z. (2002). The optic trajectory is not a lot of use if you want to catch the ball. *Journal of Experimental Psychology: Human Perception and Performance, 28,* 1499-1501.

Reingold, E.M and Charness, N. (2005). *Perception in chess: Evidence from eye movements.* In G. Underwood (Ed.), *Cognitive Processes in Eye Guidance* (pp. 325-354). Oxford: Oxford University Press.

Ripoll, H. (1988). Analysis of visual scanning patterns of volleyball players in a problem solving task. *International Journal of Sport Psychology, 19,* 9-25.

Ripoll, H. (1991). The understanding-acting process in sport: The relationship between the semantic and the sensorimotor visual function. *International Journal of Sport Psychology, 22,* 221-243.

Ripoll, H. (2008). *Le Mental des Champions* [The Mental of Champions]. Paris: Payot.

Ripoll, H., Kerlirzin, Y., Stein, J.-F., and Reine, B. (1995). Analysis of information processing, decision making, and visual strategies in complex problem solving sport situations. *Human Movement Science, 14,* 325-349.

Rock, I. (Ed.) (1996). *Indirect Perception.* Cambridge, MA: MIT Press.

Simon, H.A., and Chase, W.G. (1973). Skill in chess. *American Scientist, 61,* 394-403.

Simon, H.A., and Gilmartin, K. (1973). A simulation of memory for chess positions. *Cognitive Psychology, 5,* 29-46.

Starkes, J.L. (1987). Skill in field hockey: The nature of the cognitive advantage. *Journal of Sport Psychology, 9,* 146-160.

Thurstone, L. L. (1944). A factorial study of perception. Chicago: University of Chicago Press.

Varela, F.J., Thomson, E.T., and Rosch, E. (1991). *The Embodied Mind: Cognitive Science and Human Experience.* Cambridge, MA: MIT Press.

Vicente, K.J., and Wang, J.H. (1998). An ecological theory of expertise effects in memory recall. *Psychological Review, 105,* 33–57.

Werner, S., and Thies, B. (2000). Is "Change Blindness" Attenuated by Domain-specific Expertise? An Expert-Novices Comparison of Change Detection in Football Image. *Visual Cognition, 7,* 163-173.

Williams, A.M., and Davids, K. (1998). Visual search strategy, selective attention and expertise in soccer. *Research Quarterly for Exercise and Sport, 69,* 111-129.

Williams, A.M., Davids, K., Burwitz, L., and Williams, J.G. (1993). Cognitive knowledge and soccer performance. *Perceptual and motor Skills, 76,* 579-593.

Williams, A.M., Davids, K., Burwitz, L., and Williams, J.G. (1994). Visual search strategies in experienced and inexperienced soccer players. *Research Quarterly for Sport and Exercise, 65,* 127-135.

Williams, A.M., Davids, K., and Williams, J.G. (1999). *Visual Perception and Action in Sport.* London: E and FN SPON.

Williams, A.M., and Ericsson, K.A. (2005). Perceptual-cognitive expertise in sport: Some considerations when applying the expert performance approach. *Human Movement Science, 24,* 283–307.

SECTION 3. JUDGMENT AND DECISION MAKING IN SPORT AND EXERCISE

In: Perspectives on Cognition and Action in Sport
Editors: D. Araújo, H. Ripoll and M. Raab

ISBN: 978-1-60692-390-0
© 2009 Nova Science Publishers, Inc.

Chapter 12

JUDGMENT AND DECISION MAKING IN SPORT AND EXERCISE: A CONCISE HISTORY AND PRESENT AND FUTURE PERSPECTIVES

Michael Bar-Eli [1,2] *and Markus Raab* [3]

[1] School of Management, Ben-Gurion University of the Negev, Beer Sheva, Israel
[2] Zinman College of Physical Education and Sport Sciences, Wingate Institute, Israel
[3] Institute of Psychology, German Sport University Cologne, Cologne, Germany

ABSTRACT

This chapter provides an overview of judgment and decision-making (JDM) research to date and predicts future developments in the domain of sports and exercise. Historically, JDM research has described normative theories and their development in economics and psychology. Applications in sports psychology have been investigated only relatively recently. These applications are summarized here and a taxonomy is presented that orders the different theoretical approaches along two dimensions. We describe how the chapters in the JDM section of this book fit into this taxonomy. Finally we analyze current developments and predict that future research will focus more on dynamic and probabilistic approaches. In addition, we describe findings on different levels, including the neuropsychological level, formalize models mathematically, and integrate theory and applied research to a greater extent than has been done previously.

INTRODUCTION

When engaged in choosing from among several alternative courses of action, individuals in sport and exercise settings are involved in judgment and decision making (JDM). It is generally assumed that an understanding of how JDM processes work—be they related to spontaneous decisions or deliberative ones, and if they are made under conditions of certainty, risk, or uncertainty (March and Simon, 1958; Simon, 1960)—can increase the efficiency and effectiveness of the decisions (Slack and Parent, 2006).

Some leading (management) scholars have used the terms "judgment" and "decision making" quite interchangeably; for example, Drucker (1966, p. 143) viewed a decision as "a judgment…a choice between alternatives." However, it is currently agreed that the two terms apply to different concepts: Judgments are generally thought to refer to "a set of evaluative and inferential processes that people have at their disposal and can draw on in the process of making decisions" (Koehler and Harvey, 2004, p. xv). This process is separate from the consequences of the decision itself. Decision making (DM) refers to the process of making a choice from a set of options, with the consequences of that choice being crucial. This broad distinction between "J" and "DM" is essential for mapping the history as well as current and future trends in research on judgment and decision making in sport and exercise (Bar-Eli and Raab, 2006a). These issues will be concisely discussed in this introductory chapter.

HISTORY

Since the late 1940s, when the first JDM studies were published, this topic has been researched by scholars from many disciplines, with three major, quite independent approaches emerging: decision and game theoretical, psychological, and social-psychological/sociological. Researchers investigating JDM processes have been especially attuned to the interrelated, yet distinctive facets of the normative and descriptive characterizations of such processes (Over, 2004).

Normative theories are concerned with prescribing human JDM and are based on postulates that enable a person's optimal gain maximization and loss minimization (Baron, 2004). Despite the inherent logic of the systematic approach outlined in such models, humans are rarely this thorough and precise in their actual JDM behavior—a fact that was first identified by Nobel laureate Herbert Simon (1955, 1960). Simon suggested that human JDM was bounded by limited cognitive information-processing ability, by factors such as imperfect information and time constraints, and last but not least—by emotions.

Since the introduction of this "bounded rationality" concept by Simon as well as Meehl's (1954) seminal study on the differences between statistical and clinical prediction, the area of JDM has been heavily "psychologized," turning its major focus on the descriptive characteristics of real human JDM behavior. JDM psychology has concentrated on the gaps between the ideal and real (i.e., between normative and descriptive) aspects of JDM, repeatedly demonstrating—in an attempt to understand the sources of such gaps—that actual JDM departs substantially from norms and prescriptions. As the different approaches to JDM demonstrate (see, for example, Koehler and Harvey, 2004), JDM is currently regarded to a large degree as part of social and/or cognitive psychology and is very often conceived in terms of human information processing.

As noted recently, almost none of the above has been reflected in either the sport psychology (Bar-Eli and Raab, 2006a) or the sport management (Slack and Parent, 2006) literature. The first seminal work on cognitive sport psychology was Straub and Williams' (1984) collection of theoretical and applied book chapters, in which Gilovich (1984) stated that the world of sport—being a potential laboratory for the study of cognitive processes associated with humans—was most appropriate for JDM research. In 1991, Ripoll edited a special issue on information processing and decision making in the *International Journal of Sport Psychology*. Ripoll (1991) stated that the mechanisms dealt with in the publication were

> "specifically concerned with the processes which intervene between the intake of information and the behavioral response, that is to say, between the input and the output. These processes concern the underlying logic of the system, which corresponds to the "software." (p. 187)

This means mainly (experiments related to) cognitive psychophysiology, priming, attention orientation, timing accuracy and decision time, anticipation and control in visually guided locomotion, semantic and sensorimotor visual function, and visual search.

In line with this approach, Tenenbaum and Bar-Eli (1993) discussed cognitive processes such as sensation and memory, short-term store, visual search, attention and concentration, anticipation, field dependence/independence, sport intelligence, problem solving, and expertise in a chapter on DM in sport included in Singer, Murphy, and Tennant's (1993) landmark *Handbook of Research on Sport Psychology*. However, Tenenbaum and Bar-Eli were also among the first to discuss the possible distortions and disturbances in competitive DM, proposing that Bayes's theorem (see Baron, 2004) be used as a normative model for coping with such inefficient decision processes. Later, Tenenbaum and Bar-Eli (1995) presented the Bayesian approach as a novel device to advance sport psychology research, and conducted a series of investigations using this approach to establish a crisis-related aid for decisions made during sport competitions (for a review, see Bar-Eli, 1997).

Later publications on JDM in sports primarily addressed the subject as more or less a derivative of a particular framework, within specific contexts. Tenenbaum (2003), for example, focused on the performance of highly skilled athletes, using the cognitive approach and emphasizing the information-processing stages underlying JDM. He proposed a conceptual scheme of accessing DM in open-skill sports and described different DM topics and their corresponding cognitive components. More recently, Tenenbaum and Lidor (2005) focused on the way in which mechanisms determining JDM quality are acquired and modified through expertise development and deliberate practice. These authors emphasized—from an applied perspective—the major role visual attention plays in affecting anticipation and the interactive collaboration between working memory and knowledge structure. They elaborated on the efficacy of cognitive strategies such as attentional control, pre-performance routines, and simulating training in improving JDM quality in sports. Along these lines, Williams and Ward (2007) recently discussed DM as a derivative of anticipation processes.

It seems that except for what has elsewhere (see Bar-Eli and Raab, 2006a) been called "the Ripoll–Tenenbaum research tradition" (e.g., Ripoll, 1991; Tenenbaum, 2003), the study of JDM in sport has substantially lagged behind its potential. This state of affairs is quite surprising, since in 1985 one of the most provocative studies in the history of JDM was published, namely, Gilovich, Vallone, and Tversky's (1985) investigation of the misperception of the "hot hand" in basketball. This study was a part of the famous research program on heuristics and biases (see, for review, Gilovich, Griffin, and Kahneman, 2002), which culminated in the Nobel Prize being awarded in 2002 to Daniel Kahneman for his work conducted jointly with the late Amos Tversky. Gilovich et al. (1985) demonstrated how the use of the representativeness heuristic (Tversky and Kahneman, 1982) led to deficient perceptions of random occurances during top-level athletic events, such as NBA basketball games. From a more general perspective, they were interested in showing how deeply rooted misconceptions—that is, beliefs that are incompatible with the real physical world or with normative considerations based on paradigmatic reasoning models—can dominate human JDM behavior (for a review, see Bar-Eli, Avugos, and Raab, 2006).

Despite the great theoretical and practical potential for advancing understanding in sport and exercise psychology, these findings were to a large degree disregarded in that discipline's literature. This state of affairs is evident, for example, from the history of the seminal project of the International Society of Sport Psychology (ISSP), namely, the Handbook of (research on) sport psychology (Singer, Hausenblas, and Janelle, 2001; Singer et al., 1993; Tenenbaum and Eklund, 2007). In the first edition, one DM chapter (Tenenbaum and Bar-Eli, 1993) was published, whereas the second edition (Singer et al., 2001) did not address JDM at all. The third edition included a chapter that addressed DM (Williams and Ward, 2007), but its discussion was focused mainly on anticipation rather than on DM as such. Similarly, other important handbooks and/or popular introductory textbooks in sport and exercise psychology (e.g., Anshel, 2003; Horn, 2002; Weinberg and Gould, 2003) treated JDM negligibly—if at all—with the "J" component as good as nonexistent. Despite the fact that DM was explicitly discussed from time to time in this field (for example, by Bakker, Whiting and van der Brug, 1990), it can be safely concluded that in general, minor attention was paid to these issues in the sport/exercise psychology literature until the middle of the present decade.

PRESENT AND FUTURE PERSPECTIVES

To rectify this present state of affairs and to stimulate new theories, research, and application in this area, Bar-Eli and Raab (2006b) edited a special issue of *Psychology and Exercise* in which they introduced to the readership different approaches to JDM that had not been sufficiently covered in sport/exercise psychology up to that time. This thematic issue included eight articles—three in the "J" and five in the "DM" category. The articles on judgment were classified (a) by a theoretical approach, that is, as either economics- or (social) psychology-based, and (b) by application, that is, whether the subject were judges and referees, or other participants in the sport scene, such as athletes, spectators, coaches, managers, and bettors. The taxonomy of DM articles in the special issue was in fact an extended version of a matrix originally proposed by Townsend and Busemeyer (1995); DM articles were classified according to their (a) nature: deterministic (i.e., given a set of options, the one with the highest product of utility and expected success is always chosen), probabilistic (i.e., in most cases the option with the highest utility is chosen), or deterministic/probabilistic; and (b) characterization: static (i.e., all options compared at one time), dynamic (i.e., where there is an interdependency of decisions or actions over time, with the time of their occurrence being crucial) or static/dynamic.

In the "J" category, Bar-Eli et al.'s (2006) review of the "hot hand" phenomenon fell into the economics theoretical background, with a main application focus on bettors, spectators, and players. Plessner and Haar's (2006) review of the ways in which social cognition may explain biased sports performance judgments and Boen, Van den Auweele, Claes, Feys, and De Cuyper's (2006) article on how open feedback changes conformity among judges in rope skipping both fell into the (social) psychology theoretical background and applied to judges and referees.

In the "DM" category, Kibele's (2006) two-stage process, which explains how primed motor reactions rely on earlier learning experience in acquisition and execution, thereby demonstrating how cognitive processes can be utilized for the selection of fast motor responses, was classified as deterministic and static. Bennis and Pachur (2006) presented "fast and frugal" heuristics in sports, an approach identified as deterministic and dynamic, and Johnson's (2006) description of how sequential information is sampled based on "decision field theory" applied to the choices of athletes and was classified as probabilistic and dynamic. Araújo, Davids, and Hristovski (2006) discussed the ecological dynamics of DM in sport—an approach that incorporates a dynamic characterization with components that are either of a deterministic or a probabilistic nature. Poolton, Masters, and Maxwell (2006)—who argued that implicit motor learning is stable when DM is processed concurrently during movement execution—presented an approach that was static/dynamic and deterministic/probabilistic.

Bar-Eli and Raab (2006a) suggested that the taxonomical model used in the special issue (Bar-Eli and Raab, 2006b) could be a useful approach stimulating further JDM theory, research, and application in sport and exercise. In the present volume, one chapter can be assigned to the judgment area of JDM: Brand, Plessner, and Schweizer (Brand, Plessner, and Schweizer, Chapter 15) use a dynamic and probabilistic approach to examine multi-cue learning in soccer referees. Their main accomplishment is the development of an online training and diagnostic tool which promotes learning and weighting of the major cues required for increasing the probability of correct foul calls in soccer.

The decision-making area is represented by three papers that fit neatly into the DM taxonomy described above. Araújo, Davids, Chow, and Passos (Araújo, Davids, Chow, and Passos, Chapter 13) describe a dynamic and probabilistic approach for athletes using a dynamical system approach. They dedicate the major part of their chapter to the development of the decision-making skill, and advance some important ideas for training. Johnson (Johnson, Chapter 14) takes a computational approach with a formalized model of choices of athletes under various situations and sports. His central argument is that this linear and deterministic approach provides a formalized perspective on differences between athletes or situations in two behavioral variables, choice time and choice quality. Vickers (Vickers, Chapter 16) presents an overview of the "quiet eye" in a dynamical and deterministic approach. Quiet eye describes how gaze can be related to choices and suggests ways to improve choices by training. Finally, Land and Tenenbaum (Land and Tenenbaum, Chapter 17) present a broader approach on how attention and movement variability can be jointly combined for describing skilled performance, giving new insights for selecting movements in line with other JDM perspectives.

A full description of all past and present approaches is not possible in this introductory chapter, but we can point out a number of changes in progress that may be indicators of future research. First, the approaches presented in this section of the book represent the entire range of dimensions described above, and a tendency can be observed that the theories and detailed models derived from them are becoming increasingly dynamical and probabilistic. Second, we have noted a move toward integrating a number of different description levels in current theorizing and modeling. For example, Johnson (Johnson, Chapter 14) presents an approach that formalizes parameters for choices, allowing a decision maker to estimate probabilistic choices and decision times. Third, we have seen a number of theory-led applications of knowledge in the sports arena, and even direct cooperation with people in sports and their organizations. For instance, Brand et al. (Brand, Plessner and Schweizer, Chapter 15) demonstrate how a theory-led diagnostic leads to applications for referees in soccer.

We feel that broader theories of cognition and action are being applied far too slowly in sports. For instance, Klein's recognition-primed decision-making (RPD) model was published in 1989, but the first application in sports was not published until 2004, by Martell and Vickers. Similarly, decision field theory (DFT), published by Busemeyer and Townsend in 1993, was not systematically applied to sports until late 2006, by Johnson. There are some instances in which this time lag is not as pronounced, but it is fair to say that developments in theories of decision-making processes are not quickly adopted by researchers in sports. This is unfortunate; DFT provides predictions about decision times, for example, and the RPD model reveals new solutions for fast priming. Both issues are central to making fast choices in applied settings such as sports.

It is the nature of sports to involve both cognition and action. Therefore, we believe that JDM research, focusing on both what people decide and how they implement their decisions through movements, may come to play an important role in integrating research presented in other sections of this book, such as perception-action and knowledge.

REFERENCES

Anshel, M.H. (2003). *Sport psychology: From theory to practice* (4th ed.). San Francisco: Benjamin Cummings.

Araújo, D., Davids, K., and Hristovski, R. (2006). The ecological dynamics of decision making in sport. *Psychology of Sport and Exercise, 7,* 653-676.

Bakker, F.C., Whiting, H.T., and van der Brug, H. (1990). *Sport psychology: Concepts and applications.* Chichester: John Wiley.

Bar-Eli, M. (1997). Psychological performance crisis in competition, 1984-1996: A review. *European Yearbook of Sport Psychology, 1,* 73-112.

Bar-Eli, M., Avugos, S., and Raab, M. (2006). Twenty years of "hot hand" research: Review and critique. *Psychology of Sport and Exercise, 7,* 525-553.

Bar-Eli, M., and Raab, M. (2006a). Judgment and decision making in sport and exercise: Rediscovery and new visions. *Psychology of Sport and Exercise, 7,* 519-524.

Bar-Eli, M., and Raab, M. (Eds.). (2006b). Judgment and decision making in sport and exercise [Special Issue]. *Psychology of Sport and Exercise, 7*(6).

Baron, J. (2004). Normative models of judgment and decision making. In D.J. Koehler and N. Harvey (Eds.), *Blackwell handbook of judgment and decision making.* (pp. 19-36). Malden, MA: Blackwell.

Bennis, W.M., and Pachur, T. (2006). Fast and frugal heuristics in sports. *Psychology of Sport and Exercise, 7,* 611-629.

Boen, F., Van den Auweele, Y., Clais, E., Feys, J., and De Cuyper, B. (2006). The impact of open feedback on conformity among judges in rope skipping. *Psychology of Sport and Exercise, 7,* 577-590.

Busemeyer, J.R., and Townsend, J.T. (1993). Decision field theory: A dynamic cognition approach to decision making. *Psychological Review, 100,* 432-459.

Drucker, P. (1966). *The effective executive.* New York: Harper and Row.

Gilovich, T. (1984). Judgmental biases in the world of sport. In W.F. Straub and J.M. Williams (Eds.), *Cognitive sport psychology* (pp. 31-41). Lansing, MI: Sport Science.

Gilovich, T., Griffin, D., and Kahneman, D. (2002). *Heuristics and biases.* New York: Cambridge University Press.

Gilovich, T., Vallone, R., and Tversky, A. (1985). The hot hand in basketball: On the misperception of random sequences. *Cognitive Psychology, 17,* 295-314.

Horn, T.S. (Ed.). (2002). *Advances in sport psychology* (2nd ed.). Champaign, IL: Human Kinetics.

Johnson, J.G. (2006). Cognitive modeling of decision making in sports. *Psychology of Sport and Exercise, 7,* 631-652.

Kibele, A. (2006). Non-consciously controlled decision making for fast motor reactions in sports—A priming approach for motor responses to non-consciously perceived movement features. *Psychology of Sport and Exercise, 7,* 591-610.

Klein, G. (1989). Recognition-primed decisions. In W.B. Rouse (Ed.), *Advances in man-machine system research* (Vol. 5, pp. 47–92). Greenwich, CT: JAI.

Koehler, D.J., and Harvey, N. (Eds.). (2004). *Blackwell handbook of judgment and decision making.* Malden, MA: Blackwell.

March, J.G., and Simon, H.A. (1958). *Organizations.* New York: Wiley.

Martell, S.G., and Vickers, J.N. (2004). Gaze characteristics of elite and near-elite athletes in ice-hockey defensive tactics. *Human Movement Science, 22,* 689–712.

Meehl, P.E. (1954). Clinical versus statistical prediction: A theoretical analysis and review of the evidence. Minneapolis, MN: University of Minnesota Press.

Over, D. (2004). Rationality and the normative/descriptive distinction. In D.J. Koehler and N. Harvey (Eds.), *Blackwell handbook of judgment and decision making* (pp. 3-18). Malden, MA: Blackwell.

Plessner, H., and Haar, T. (2006). Sports performance judgments from a social cognitive perspective. *Psychology of Sport and Exercise, 7,* 555-575.

Poolton, J.M., Masters, R.S.W., and Maxwell, J.P. (2006). The influence of analogy learning on decision-making in table tennis: Evidence from behavioral data. *Psychology of Sport and Exercise, 7,* 677-688.

Ripoll, H. (Ed.). (1991). Information processing and decision making in sport [Special Issue]. *International Journal of Sport Psychology, 22*(13), 189-210.

Simon, H.A. (1955). A behavioral model of rational choice. *Quarterly Journal of Economics, 69,* 99-118.

Simon, H.A. (1960). *The new science of management decisions.* Englewood Cliffs, NJ: Prentice Hall.

Singer, R.N., Hausenblas, H.A., and Janelle, C.M. (Eds.). (2001). *Handbook of sport psychology.* New York: Wiley.

Singer, R.N., Murphy, M., and Tennant, L.K. (Eds.). (1993). *Handbook of research on sport psychology.* New York: Macmillan.

Slack, T., and Parent, M.M. (2006). *Understanding sport organizations* (2nd ed.). Champaign, IL: Human Kinetics.

Straub, W.F., and Williams, J.M. (Eds.). (1984). *Cognitive sport psychology*. Lansing, MI: *Sport Science*.

Tenenbaum, G. (2003). Expert athletes: An integrated approach to decision making. In J.L. Starkes and K.A. Ericsson (Eds.), *Expert performance in sports.* (pp. 191-218). Champaign, IL: Human Kinetics.

Tenenbaum, G., and Bar-Eli, M. (1993). Decision making in sport: A cognitive perspective. In R.N. Singer, M. Murphy, and L.K. Tennant (Eds.), *Handbook of research on sport psychology.* (pp. 171-192). New York: Macmillan.

Tenenbaum, G., and Bar-Eli, M. (1995). Contemporary issues in exercise and sport psychology research. In S. J. H. Biddle (Ed.), *European perspectives on sport and exercise psychology* (pp. 292-323). Champaign, IL: Human Kinetics.

Tenenbaum, G., and Eklund, R.C. (Eds.). (2007). *Handbook of sport psychology*. New York: Wiley.

Tenenbaum, G., and Lidor, R. (2005). Research on decision-making and the use of cognitive strategies in sport settings. In D. Hackfort, J.L. Duda, and R. Lidor (Eds.), *Handbook of research in applied sport psychology: International perspectives* (pp. 75-91). Morgantown, WV: Fitness Information Technology.

Townsend, J.T., and Busemeyer, J.R. (1995). Dynamic representation of decision-making. In R.F. Port, and T. van Gelder (Eds.), *Mind as motion: Explorations in the dynamics of cognition* (pp. 101-120). Cambridge, MA: MIT Press.

Tversky, A., and Kahneman, D. (1982). Judgments of and by representativeness. In D. Kahneman, P. Slovic, and A. Tversky (Eds.), *Judgment under uncertainty: Heuristics and biases* (pp. 84-98). New York, NY: Cambridge University Press.

Weinberg, R.S., and Gould, D. (2003). *Foundations of sport and exercise psychology* (3rd ed.). Champaign, Il: Human Kinetics.

Williams, A.M., and Ward, P. (2007). Anticipation and decision making: Exploring new horizons. In G. Tenenbaum and R.C. Eklund (Eds.), *Handbook of sport psychology* (3rd ed., pp. 203-223). New York: Wiley.

In: Perspectives on Cognition and Action in Sport
Editors: D. Araújo, H. Ripoll and M. Raab

ISBN: 978-1-60692-390-0
© 2009 Nova Science Publishers, Inc.

Chapter 13

THE DEVELOPMENT OF DECISION MAKING SKILL IN SPORT: AN ECOLOGICAL DYNAMICS PERSPECTIVE

Duarte Araújo [1], *Keith Davids* [3],
Jia Yi Chow [4] *and Pedro Passos* [1,2]

[1] Faculty of Human Kinetics/Technical University of Lisbon, Portugal
[2] Lusófona University of Humanities and Technologies, Portugal
[3] Queensland University of Technology Australia
[4] National Institute of Education, Nanyang
Technological University, Singapore

ABSTRACT

In this chapter we introduce a theoretical framework for studying decision making in sport: the ecological dynamics approach, which we integrate with key ideas from the literature on learning complex motor skills. Our analysis will include insights from Bernstein (1967) on the coordination of degrees of freedom and Newell's (1985) model of motor learning. We particularly focus on the role of perceptual degrees of freedom advocated in an ecological approach to learning. In introducing this framework to readers we contrast this perspective with more traditional models of decision-making. Finally, we propose some implications to the training of decision-making skill in sport.

INTRODUCTION

Accurate perception, action and decision-making are characteristics of expert performance in sport (Hodges, Starkes and MacMahon, 2006; Starkes and Ericsson, 2003, see Bar-Eli and Raab, Chapter 12, for an overview). Although skill-related differences in these processes have been observed in research, the underlying reasons for these differences are largely unknown (Starkes and Ericsson, 2003). Typical responses for studying skill acquisition include characteristics such as reaction time, and movement rate, amplitude, and duration, rather than the detailed structure of action and the learning process (Newell et al.,

2001, 2003, see also Jacobs and Michaels, 2007). In this paper we discuss the structure of learning processes in developing decision-making skill in a principled way.

In cognitive science it is presumed that decision-making behavior is predicated on the existence of a centralized controller—a schema or mental model that is responsible for its organization and regulation (see Johnson, Chapter 14). However, this suggestion is unsatisfactory, because it merely displaces the original problem of behavioral decision making to a pre-existing internal structure, begging the question why that particular neurobiological organization developed and how that specific structure originated (Turvey et al., 1981). We discuss Gibson's (1979) suggestion that, rather than being localized in an internal structure, control is actually distributed over the agent– environment system.

This different view suggests that the structure and physics of the environment, the biomechanics of each individual's body, perceptual information about informational variables, and specific task demands all serve to constrain behavior as it is expressed (Warren, 2006). Adaptive behavior, rather than being imposed by a pre-existing structure, emerges from this confluence of constraints under the boundary condition of a particular task or goal (Araújo et al., 2004, Davids et al., 2008). From this perspective, the role of information and intentionality in decision making and action can be understood in physical terms (i.e., a law-based understanding of discrete and dynamic aspects of human behavior, see Shaw, 2001; Shaw and Turvey, 1999; see Araújo et al., 2006 for an application in sport).

A major challenge for this ecological dynamics approach is to understand how each individual learns to perceive the surrounding layout of the performance environment in the scale of his/her body and action capabilities (Turvey and Shaw, 1995, 1999). The aim of ecological learning theories is to explain how perceivers take advantage of the informational richness of environmental properties (e.g., E. Gibson and Pick, 2000; Jacobs and Michaels, 2007). The ecological approach to learning originated with the rejection of enrichment theories of learning (J. Gibson and E. Gibson, 1955). In enrichment theories stimulus variables are necessarily ambiguous with respect to the environment; perceivers are said to resolve the ambiguity by enriching information-poor stimuli through processes such as inference or with memories. Enrichment theories portray the emergence of expertise as an increase in the sophistication of the enrichment processes (Jacobs and Michaels, 2007).

Ecological theories, in contrast, hold that learning results in changes in the environmental properties to which perceptual systems are sensitive (Jacobs and Michaels, 2007). The sophistication of expert performance derives from the improved fit of experts to their environments, rather than from an increased complexity of computational and memorial processes (Shaw, 2003). We next elaborate on this ecological framework and discuss how skill in decision making is developed. Later, we discuss some implications for enhancing decision-making skill in sport.

ECOLOGICAL DYNAMICS OF DECISION MAKING

There are two complementary attributes of accurate and functional performance in dynamic environments (Warren, 2006): *stability* and *flexibility*. On the one hand, successful performance is characterized by stable and reproducible low-dimensional patterns, which are functional actions consistently reproducible over time and resistant to perturbation. On the other hand, "behavior is not stereotyped and rigid but flexible and adaptive" (Warren, 2006, pp. 359). Although action patterns exhibit regular morphologies, skilled performers are not locked into rigidly stable solutions (e.g. technical, tactical) but can modulate their behaviors. Successful performers need to adapt their actions to dynamically shifting environments that characterise competitive sport. Such requisite flexibility is tailored to current environmental conditions and task demands, and implicates perceptual control of action (Araújo et al., 2006). In line with this argument, Kelso and Engström (2006) argued that transitions among stable states of organisation occur as a result of dynamic instability, which provides a universal decision-making platform for switching between and selecting among different states order. So, if more functional movement patterns emerge to fit the circumstances and context of a performance setting, fluctuations from dynamic instabilities will help the performer discover and explore them. Importantly, this is not a switch, per se, but a qualitative change that arises due to the intrinsic nonlinearity of the action pattern dynamics.

Moreover, agent–environment interactions give rise to emergent behavior that has a dynamics of its own, which Fajen and Warren (2003) call the *behavioral dynamics*. According to Warren (2006) the core claim is that stable behavioral solutions correspond to attractors in the behavioral dynamics, and transitions between behavioral patterns correspond to bifurcations. Bifurcations provide a selection mechanism, the means to decide when one mode of behaviour is no longer functional and to switch to more functional behavioral solutions (Kelso and Engström, 2006). Such stabilities do not exist a priori in the structure of the performer but are co-determined by the confluence of task and environmental constraints. These ideas are congruent with Gibson's (1979) proposition that control lies in the agent–environment system, and behavior can be understood as *self-organized*, in contrast to organization being imposed from within.

Behavior patterns emerge in the course of learning and development, through a bootstrapping process in which agent–environment interactions give rise to behavioral dynamics, and stabilities in these dynamics in turn capture the behavior of the performer (Warren, 2006). During bootstrapping, the performer actively explores a goal path for a task, both contributing to and locating its stabilities (stable solutions). Reciprocally, attractors in the behavioral dynamics feed back to temporarily fix a performer's action patterns, in a form of circular causality. Thus, rather than a central controller dictating the intended behavior, the agent develops perceptual–motor mappings that tweak the dynamics of the system in which it is embedded so that the desired behavior arises from the entire ensemble. From the performer's viewpoint, the task is to exploit physical (e.g. surface qualities of the grass field in soccer) and informational constraints (e.g. an opponent's running speed approach) to stabilize an intended behavior. The emergent solution may rely more or less upon physical or informational regularities, depending on the nature of the task, and within given constraints there are typically a limited number of stable solutions that can achieve a desired outcome. Note that because cognition is conceived as the ability to use specifying information (i.e., information in the Gibsonian sense) in controlling action, all action involves some amount of awareness, as well as vice versa (Reed, 1997).

In sport, a player's expertise is only revealed in the consequences of movement and perception embedded in actions, as observable properties of the environment-actor system. Decision making, therefore is a complex temporally extended process expressed by actions at the ecological scale (Turvey and Shaw, 1995). This functional analysis of decision making contrasts with traditional approaches in which humans have been modelled as rational decision-makers computing and selecting options from those represented in mental or neural models designed to maximize utility for performance (Mellers et al., 1998). As Klein (2001) argued: "A decision maker who faithfully follows the rules for estimating expected utilities will not necessarily understand the affordances of a situation and will be less prepared than a decision maker who is studying the opportunities and constraints in the situation" (p. 118).

In ecological dynamics the behavior of a performer may intend consequences at some later time and place beyond the context in which the movements were initiated. Actions (construed as goal-directed behaviours), like perceptions, are intentional because their meaning and significance lie elsewhere from their causal origins. Indeed, "actions are inherently forms of true choice behaviour" (Shaw, 2001, p. 283). Intending a behavioral goal (i.e., a final condition) involves the performer selecting an initial condition as a pathway that permits attainment of the final condition under the existing (physical) law domain. Along the goal path, with each step closer to the final outcome, the information sources detected and used to regulate action must become ever more specific. They are used to narrow the possible actions available for the movement system, until ultimately, at the moment of goal accomplishment, the emergent path becomes uniquely defined (Shaw, 2001), i.e., with less degrees of freedom. Given this perspective, decision-making is viewed as a functional and emergent process in which a selection is made among converging paths of actions for an intended goal (see figure 1). Choices are made at bifurcation points where more specific information becomes available, constraining the environment-athlete system to switch to a more attractive path. In sum, to make decisions is to direct a course of personal interactions with the environment towards a goal, and decisions emerge from this cyclical process of searching for information to act and acting to detect more information.

In such an approach, learning to make successful decisions is concerned with the education of intention, attunement, calibration (Fajen et al., 2009; Jacobs and Michaels, 2007) and mastering perceptual-motor degrees of freedom (Newell, 1985; Savelsbergh and Van der Kamp, 2000; Vereijken et al., 1992). In the next section, we discuss how these learning processes contribute to three possible phases of the development of decision making: i) exploration, ii) discovery and stabilization, and iii) exploitation.

THE DEVELOPMENT OF DECISION-MAKING SKILL IN SPORT

For Gibson (1966) the best way to understand how perception regulates action is by detecting informational constraints specific to goal-paths (Shaw and Turvey, 1999). Goal constraints, compared to physical constraints, can be considered extraordinary (Kugler and Turvey, 1987), taking the form of a rule that indicates how to act if a particular outcome is intended. More to the point, the rule asserts that one should act to change current information, non-specific to an intended outcome, into information that is specific (Shaw and Turvey, 1999). This argument implies that the first step for any learning process to occur is the "education of intention" (Jacobs and Michaels, 2002, 2007), which will initiate the process of exploring degrees of freedom.

This means that changing constraints shape emerging behaviour in dynamical movement systems. It is clear that a particular set of interactions of an individual performer, environment, and task over time can produce a particular function of behavioural change.

Newell's (1986) model describes how emergence in movement system occurs, and it was argued that "the relative impact of these three categories of constraint on the pattern of coordination varies according to the specific situation" (p. 354). We can visualise how their relative impact changes with time in figure 1. Here we can see how constraints are channelling the system to define the goal's path.

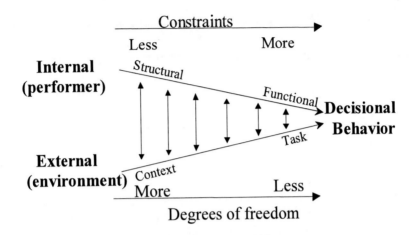

Figure 1. A scheme that shows that to make decisions is to influence - by educating intention, by attunement, and by re-calibration - the interaction of a performer with environment in a goal directed activity. The closer the performer is from actual performance the more she is sensitive to momentary variations, and the more she is constrained by past events.

According to Newell (1986): "Environmental constraints are generally recognised as those constraints that are external to the individual performer. Any constraint on the performer-environment interaction that is not internal to the individual performer can be viewed as an environmental constraint" (p. 350). However, task constraints are a specific set of environmental constraints. Following a similar reasoning we can consider that the functional constraints (like fatigue; as opposed to structural constraints, like height) of the individual performer, since they are more time dependent, are the ones that should be progressively tuned to task goal. As Newell (1986) argued "It is clear that a variety of individual performer constraints converge to *specify* the appropriate pattern of coordination" (p. 348, our emphasis) and that "Environmental constraints reflect the ambient conditions for the task, whereas the focus of task constraints is the goal of the activity and the *specific* constraints imposed" (p. 352, our emphasis). So, the more defined the goal path, the more the functional constraints and the task constraints specify the emergent behaviour. In seeking solutions to behavioural task goals, the performer is attempting to discover the dynamic characteristics of the system, where the system is defined over the individual performer, environment, and task.

To exemplify the ideas in the Figure 1, when a soccer player is at home before the game, environmental constraints will have a dominant impact on the athlete, but when she is at the ground preparing to perform a penalty kick, task constraints are much more influential. The cultural and social constraints are more influential in a long range than the relative position of the ball and the goalkeeper. During the beginning of her career, the structural constraints of the player were very influential in the emergency of control, coordination and skill. But during a competitive game it is her level of fatigue, emotional state, and other functional constraints that will be most influential for achieving the movement goal of scoring the penalty kick.

Exploration: Manipulating Degrees of Freedom

It is clear that many perceptions and actions are possible in any performance situation (see Land and Tenenbaum, Chapter 17). In specific performance situations, certain perceptions and actions are more functional than others and, with experience, individuals improve on choosing the perceptions and actions they intend to actualize. Different intentions are presumed to organize perceptual-motor systems differently. The education of intention might have an important influence on which particular informational variable needs to be perceived by a performer.

Intentions depend on multiple factors, such as needs, expectations or beliefs, and also external influences such as instructions, which make it challenging to study sport. Ecological studies often proceed by choosing situations in which a particular intention can be assumed. In a 1 vs 1 basketball game close to the basket, for instance, it can be assumed that attackers with the ball intend to dribble past the defender and to shoot at the basket in order to score, rather than to simply maintain possession of the ball. Such assumptions are necessary because intentions constrain tasks. For instance assuming a particular intention is required to define and identify what informational variables are relevant at any moment (Jacobs and Michaels, 2007). Given particular intentions, therefore, some variables can be said to be informational and others not.

Bernstein (1967) raised the problem of how to control the many degrees of freedom that characterize motor coordination. He argued that the complex interaction between the different components of the human movement system (e.g., muscles, tendons, joints) make separate control of all these components impossible. Therefore, the large number of individual degrees of freedom to be regulated has to be reduced in order to make control possible. This reduction is a process of "...mastering redundant degrees of freedom of the moving organ, in other words, its conversion to a controllable system" (Bernstein, 1967, p. 127). Bernstein's question, implies that a system with many degrees of freedom can simplify its organisation only if sufficient constraints, or linkages, are established among its components by coupling them into a synergy. The coupling of external, environment-based force fields with internal, performer-based force fields by means of information fields (Kugler and Turvey, 1987) forms the basis of a theory of cognition for goal-directed behavior, and guides the principles for the development of decision-making skill.

When the intention of a performer corresponds to the task goal there is a need to coordinate the redundant degrees of freedom of his/her movement system. There is a need to establish basic relationships with the environment to acquire minimum control over the degrees of freedom, both intrinsic and transactional, to realise the task. Control may be obtained by "freezing" solutions that may facilitate goal achievement (Vereijken et al., 1992;

Savelsbergh and van der Kamp, 2000), or by increasing the variability of the environment-performer system to find a solution that gets the job done (Araújo et al., 2005). It is not surprising that different people may rigidly stabilise different solutions (i.e., acquire movement patterns, and, or, use informational variables) to achieve the same goal. At this stage, movement may be coupled to a certain source of information that works, but it does not mean that it specifies the property of the environment that the performer intended to perceive, i.e., it may be a non-specifying variable. The term "specifying variable" is used only for a variable that specifies the property (i.e., the informational variable) that a perceiver intends to perceive (e.g., the focus of expansion of the ball on a performer's retina), and the term "non-specifying variable" for a variable that does not specify the property that a perceiver intends to perceive (e.g., a player attempting to judge the flight path of a ball from the deceptive movements of an opponent striking it), regardless of whether a so-called non-specifying variable might specify other properties (Jacobs and Michaels, 2007). When performers increase variability in the environment-performer system this is due to the difficulty in discriminating what properties of the environment constitute information and which do not. Exploration of what is available in a performance situation can reveal what environmental properties are informative in relation to a specific intention (Araújo et al., 2005).

Importantly, the appearance of control over abundant degrees of freedom characterizes this first stage through the exploration of the relationship between movement and information. The degrees of freedom that need to be constrained are much more than those necessary to control the performer-environment system to achieve the task goal.

Discovering Solutions and Stabilizing Them

In the next phase, the performer uses these tentative solutions and attempts to reproduce them when performing the task. With the irreducible variability of the initial conditions to perform the task, these movement-information couplings start to become more regular. A way to stabilize a movement solution is to "de-freeze" the previously exaggerated constriction of degrees of freedom. This means that the most relevant degrees of freedom for achieving the task goal are identified, and also that the conditions when an informational variable is useful are also identified and acted upon. Therefore, new action possibilities start to be identified (for example, when an informational variable is not useful). For example, this can occur in sport when a learner in soccer discovers from proprioceptive feedback that stiffening the muscles of the lower limb is not useful for receiving a pass, but can be useful for making a wall-pass to a team-mate.

During this stage, the same intention might lead to the detection of other variables. The process of attending to more useful variables is referred to as the education of attention, or perceptual attunement (Gibson, 1966, 1979). Thus, even if an intention does not change, with experience, perceivers attend to more useful variables. Perceptual attunement is the process of learning which sources of information to attend to in which situations and when to attend to these variables. With practice, performers converge from sources of information that may be only partly useful in one particular situation (i.e. non-specifying) to sources of information that are more useful (i.e. specifying), under a variety of performance circumstances. For example, ball players learn that it is more accurate to perceive the spatial location of a ball rather than to wait for a coach to tell them where a ball is (the latter may be useful only in certain situations).

The stabilization of discovered solutions, as well as the exploration of the limits of these solutions, and consequent search for new, specifying, information-movement couplings, are the dominant characteristics of this phase.

Exploiting Degrees of Freedom

Specifying information sources tend to be regularly used when performing a task and the fluidity of movement (i.e., the mastering of motor degrees of freedom) appears due to the use of external forces, contrasting with previous opposition or elimination of these forces. The exploitation of motor and perceptual degrees of freedom allows adaptation to situational demands and effective goal achievement. An important point at this stage is the manifestation of attunement to wider spatial and temporal variables, and more sensitivity to the contextual consequences of one's actions (Araújo et al., 2005). Although more variability in the action may occur, this variability is constrained and convergent to goal achievement. This process is typically described in the literature as *motor equivalence* (e.g., Hebb, 1949), but here we would like to extend this concept to perception and cognition. Degeneracy or the ability of elements that are structurally different to perform the same function or yield the same output may be a more appropriate conceptualisation of this process (Davids et al., 2006).

A relevant process at this stage is that of calibration, or the scaling of the perceptual-motor system to information. Specifying information can appropriately constrain a perception or an action. Body dimensions and action capabilities are not fixed, but often change across both short and long time scales. For example, in racket sports, implements such as racquets alter a performer's effective body dimensions (reach). Action capabilities change across short time scales as a result of factors such as fatigue and injury, and across longer time scales as a result of development and training. When body dimensions and action capabilities change, actions that were once possible may become impossible (or vice-versa see Fajen et al., 2009). In perception and action, calibration and recalibration are necessary to establish and update the mapping between the units in which the relevant properties of the world are perceived, and the units in which the action is realised. Calibration in practice makes it possible for performers to perceive the world in intrinsic units even after changes in body dimensions and action capabilities. Successful calibration results in judgements that are appropriately scaled to the property to be perceived, independent of which informational variable is used for perception. For a properly calibrated performer, body-scaled and action-scaled affordances can be directly and reliably perceived by simply picking up the relevant sources of information (Fajen et al., 2009). Although recalibration occurs quite rapidly, it is likely that continued experience leads to further improvements in calibration.

Importantly, the development of decision-making is not a normative or homogeneous process, and idiosyncratic manifestations are expected to occur (Newell et al., 2003). Also it is worth mentioning that processes like education of intention, attunement, and calibration can occur in all the three phases. Finally, we would like to acknowledge that, learning may benefit from some kinds of enrichment, as discussed in the introduction to this chapter. This enrichment, however, is not of a symbolic type and does not explain the learning process, enrichment merely facilitates learning. For example, an increase in quadriceps muscle mass with training (enrichment of the organism), at a certain expertise level, may facilitate learning to successfully perform long distance ball passes in soccer. Similarly, the transition from playing bare foot to the use of soccer shoes (enrichment of task conditions) may facilitate the learning of dribbling skills.

IMPLICATIONS FOR TRAINING

According to the ecological dynamics approach, it makes little sense to tell novices how experts make decisions or to ask them to think like experts (see also Klein, 1997). Rather it seems that the training of decision-making should be based on organizing practice conditions that promote the acquisition of expertise, even in non-experts (Araújo, 2007). Without slipping into the predefinition of the nature of expertise, we concur with Klein's (1997) view that a better solution is to teach performers to learn like experts, and to gain expertise autonomously when practicing in training sessions or in competitions. The challenge for the coach is the principled organization of the training session including the intervention in the performer to foster decision-making skills. However, there is not a general "optimal organization", since there is no common answer to all practices. The organization of training practices that are useful (i.e., to develop expertise in decision making) is that which is relevant to improve performance of a certain athlete, or groups of athletes, in a certain context learning a certain task (see Davids, Button and Bennett, 2008).

From this perspective, the coach's task is to identify i) the expertise level of the performer on the task, ii) the functions (goals) to be trained, and iii) the primary constraints (organismic, task and environmental) to be manipulated or taken into account during practice. The next step for the coach is to prescribe a plan about what to do, and when and how to do it, i.e., to organize the practice sessions including the interventions with the performer. We argue that a constraint-led approach may be adopted if one wants to develop decision making in sport (see Davids, Button and Bennett, 2008 for a detailed discussion and representative case studies). Other approaches to the training of decision making in sport are explained by Vickers (Vickers, Chapter 16) and by Brand, Plessner, and Schweizer (Brand et al., Chapter 15).

Manipulation of appropriate constraints can direct performers to explore suitable movement behaviors, culminating in functional decisions undertaken by the performer. The key to assisting performers in acquiring effective decision-making behaviors comes about through presenting the relevant constraints during the three different developmental phases in decision-making as discussed in the earlier sections.

Understandably, coaches are particularly concerned with manipulating task constraints, since they are open to control and provide a direct channel to shape the progression of an athlete. Particularly, a major challenge is to consider the functional representativeness of training exercises (Araújo et al., 2007), i.e., to evaluate the correspondence of a performer's behaviour in training and competition. Rules, instructions and equipment can be manipulated to narrow the search within the perceptual-motor workspace such that effective decisions can be made corresponding to functional coordination of limbs in performance context to achieve the set task goal.

Organismic constraints are obviously important, but they should be intimately related with task constraints. Therefore, interventions may occur by selecting or transforming aspects of the task in order to facilitate a specific impact on an athlete, for example, to select athletes differing in height to play 1vs 1 near the basket in basketball. Also some interventions (e.g., induction of fatigue, changes in emotional state) may be appropriate immediately before certain tasks, in order to facilitate coping skills in the athlete. There is abundant research and examples of this kind of intervention in sport (e.g., Vealey, 2007), specifically in the development of decision-making skills (e.g., Pliske, McCloskey and Klein, 2001). These interventions can almost certainly be functional. But these organismic constraints are only indirectly related to decision-making. They are not directly involved in the process of decision-making during perceptually guided action (see Van der Kamp et al., 2008). For these reasons we argue that interventions out of the representative task are meta-cognitive, or specifically, meta-decisional, being particularly useful for reflective performers, or performers with high verbal skills. Meta-decisional training requires additional training for the transfer of verbal skills to motor skills, otherwise the enhancement of performance may be based on perceptual judgements rather than actual performance.

Finally, environmental constraints cannot be typically manipulated, but they may be taken into account to promote a better adaptation of the performer to the context of the competition. These influences can be social (e.g., Alfermann and Stambulova, 2007) or physical (e.g., Reilly, 2003), and they can be more global (e.g., religion, culture) or more local (e.g., coach's attitudes promoting ego or task involvement of the performers; Roberts et al., 2007).

CONCLUSION

To conclude, we have argued that effective training of decision making should not be characterised as an association between stimulus and responses constrained by 'If-then' rules or verbalizations in the head of the athletes, but rather by a functional organization of practice activities. The focus of practice in sport should be to direct perceptually guided actions of an athlete to the information sources that specify goal achievement. The aim of training is to guide the athlete towards a state where he/she learns like an expert, where he/she can act to discover information to guide action, i.e., by exploring, discovering and exploiting intrinsic and transactional degrees of freedom for successful performance.

REFERENCES

Alfermann, D., and Stambulova, N. (2007). Career transitions and career termination. In G. Tenenbaum and R. Eklund (Eds.), *Handbook of Sport Psychology* (3rd ed., pp. 712-733). Hoboken, NJ: John Wiley.

Araújo, D. (2007). Promoting ecologies where performers exhibit expert interactions. *International Journal of Sport Psychology, 38*, 73-77.

Araújo, D., Davids, K., Bennett, S., Button, C., and Chapman, G. (2004). Emergence of Sport Skills under Constraints. In A.M. Williams and N.J. Hodges (Ed.), *Skill Acquisition in*

Sport: Research, Theory and Practice (pp. 409-433). London: Routledge, Taylor and Francis.

Araújo, D., Davids, K., and Hristovski, R. (2006). The ecological dynamics of decision making in sport. *Psychology of Sport and Exercise, 7*, 653-676.

Araújo, D., Davids, K., and Serpa, S. (2005). An ecological approach to expertise effects in decision-making in a simulated sailing regatta. *Psychology of Sport and Exercise, 6(6)*, 671-692.

Araújo, D., Davids, K., and Passos, P. (2007). Ecological Validity, Representative Design and Correspondence between Experimental Task Constraints and Behavioral Settings. *Ecological Psychology, 19*, 69-78.

Bernstein, N. (1967). *The co-ordination and regulation of movements.* Oxford: Pergamon Press.

Davids, K., Button, C. Araújo, D., Renshaw, I., and Hristovski, R. (2006). Movement models from sports provide representative task constraints for studying adaptive behavior in human motor systems. *Adaptive Behavior, 14*(73-95).

Davids, K., Button, C., and Bennett, S. (2008). *Dynamics of Skill acquisition. A constraints-led approach.* Champaign: Human Kinetics.

Fajen, B., and Warren, W. (2003). Behavioral dynamics of steering, obstacle avoidance, and route selection. *Journal of Experimental Psychology: Human Perception and Performance, 29*, 343-362.

Fajen, B.R., Riley, M.A., and Turvey, M.T. (2009). Information, affordances and the control of action in sport. *International Journal of Sport Psychology, 40*, 79-107.

Gibson, E.J., and Pick, A.D. (2000). *An ecological approach to perceptual learning and development.* New York: Oxford University Press.

Gibson, J. (1966). *The senses considered as perceptual systems.* Boston: Houghton Mifflin.

Gibson, J.J. (1979). *The ecological approach to visual perception.* Hillsdale, New Jersey: Lawrence Erlbaum Associates.

Gibson, J., and Gibson, E. (1955). Perceptual learning: Differentiation or enrichment? *Psychological Research, 62*, 32-41.

Hebb, D. (1949). *The organization of behavior: A neuropsychological theory.* New York: John Wiley.

Hodges, N., Starkes, J.L., and MacMahon, C. (2006). Expert performance in sport: A cognitive perspective. In K.A. Ericsson, N. Charness, P. Feltovich and R. Hoffman (Ed.), *The Cambridge Handbook of Expertise and Expert Performance.* (pp. 471-488). New York: Cambridge University Press.

Jacobs, D.M., and Michaels, C.F. (2002). On the apparent paradox of learning and realism. *Ecological Psychology, 14*, 127-139.

Jacobs, D.M., and Michaels, C.F. (2007). Direct learning. *Ecological Psychology, 19*, 321-349.

Kelso, J., and Engström, D. (2006). *The complementary nature.* Cambridge: The MIT Press.

Klein, G. (1997). Developing expertise in decision making. *Thinking and Reasoning, 3*(4), 337-352.

Klein, G. (2001). The fiction of optimization. In G. Gigerenzer, and R. Stelten (Ed.), *Bounded Rationality. The adaptive toolbox* (pp. 103-121). Massachusetts: MIT.

Kugler, P.N., and Turvey, M.T. (1987). *Information, natural law, and the self-assembly of rhythmic movement.* Hillsdale, New Jersey: Lawrence Erlbaum Associates.

Mellers, B., Schwartz, A., and Cooke, A. (1998). Judgment and decision making. *Annual Review of Psychology, 49*, 447-477.

Newell, K. (1985). Coordination, control, and skill. In D. Goodman, R. Wilberg and I. Franks (Eds.), *Differing perspectives in motor learning, memory and control.* (pp. 295-317). Amsterdam: North-Holland.

Newell, K.M. (1986). Constraints on the development of coordination. In M.G. Wade and H.T.A. Whiting (Eds.), *Motor development in children. Aspects of coordination and control.* (pp. 341-360). Dordrecht, Netherlands: Martinus Nijhoff.

Newell, K.M., Liu, Y.-T., and Mayer-Kress, G. (2001). Time scales in motor learning and development. *Psychological Review, 108*(1), 57-82.

Newell, K., Liu, Y.-T., and Mayer-Kress, G. (2003). A dynamical systems interpertation of epigenetic landscapes for infant motor development. *Infant Behavior and Development, 26*, 449-472.

Pliske, R., McCloskey, M. and Klein, G. (2001). Decision skills training: Facilitating learning from experience. In E. Salas and G. Klein (Ed.), *Linking expertise and naturalistic decision making.* (pp. 37-54). Mahwah, NJ: LEA.

Reed, E.S. (1997). The cognitive revolution from an ecological view. In D.M. Johnson and C.E. Erneling (Eds.), *The future of the cognitive revolution.* (pp. 261-273). New York: Oxford University Press.

Reilly, T. (2003). Environmental Stress. In T. Reilly and M. Williams (Eds.), *Science and Soccer.* (pp. 165-184). New York: Routledge.

Roberts, G., Treasure, D., and Conroy, D. (2007). Understanding the dynamics of motivation in sport and physical activity: an achievement goal interpretation. In G. Tenenbaum and R. Eklund (Ed.), *Handbook of Sport Psychology.* (3rd ed., pp. 3-30). Hoboken, NJ: John Wiley.

Savelsbergh, G., and Van der Kamp, J. (2000). Information in learning to coordinate and control movement: is there a need for specificity of practice? *International Journal of Sport Psychology, 31*, 467-484.

Shaw, R. (2001). Processes, acts, and experiences: Three stances on the problem of intentionality. *Ecological Psychology, 13*(4), 275-314.

Shaw, R. (2003). The agent-environment interface: Simon's indirect or Gibson's direct coupling. *Ecological Psychology, 15*(1), 37-106.

Shaw, R., and Turvey, M. (1999). Ecological foundations of cognition: II. Degrees of freedom and conserved quantities in animal-environment systems. *Journal of Counsciousness Studies, 6*(11-12), 111-123.

Starkes, J., and Ericsson, K.A. (Eds.). (2003). *Expert performance in sport: Recent advances in research on sport expertise.* Champaign, IL: Human Kinetics.

Turvey, M. T., Shaw, R.E. Reed, E.S., and Mace, W.M. (1981). Ecological laws of perceiving and acting: In reply to Fodor and Pylyshyn (1981). *Cognition, 9*, 237-304.

Turvey, M.T., and Shaw, R.E. (1995). Toward an ecological physics and a physical psychology. In R.L. Solso and D.W. Massaro (Eds .), *The Science of the Mind: 2001 and Beyond* (pp. 144-169). New York: Oxford University Press.

Turvey, M.T., and Shaw, R. (1999). Ecological foundations of cognition I: Symmetry and specificity of animal-environment systems. *Journal of Counsciousness Studies, 6*(11-12), 95-110.

Van der Kamp, J., Rivas, F., van Doom, H., and Savelsbergh, G. (2008). Ventral and dorsal contributions in visual anticipation in fast ball sports. *International Journal of Sport Psychology, 39,* 100-130.

Vealey, R. (2007). Mental skills training in sport. In G. Tenenbaum and R. Eklund (Eds.), *Handbook of Sport Psychology* (3rd ed., pp. 287-309). Hoboken, NJ: John Wiley.

Vereijken, B., van Emmerik, R.E., Whiting, H.T., and Newell, K. (1992). Free(z)ing degrees of freedom in skill acquisition. *Journal of Motor Behavior, 24,* 133-142.

Warren, W. (2006). The dynamics of perception and action. *Psychological Review, 113,* 358-389.

In: Perspectives on Cognition and Action in Sport
Editors: D. Araújo, H. Ripoll and M. Raab

ISBN: 978-1-60692-390-0
© 2009 Nova Science Publishers, Inc.

Chapter 14

COGNITIVE MODELS OF ATHLETE DECISION MAKING

Joseph Johnson

Department of Psychology, Miami University, Miami, Florida, USA

ABSTRACT

The purpose of this paper is to provide an introduction to the advantages of applying computational cognitive models to sports decisions. Most research is aimed at identifying relationships between manipulations and observable outcomes, such as how various game characteristics affect athlete behaviors. In contrast, I outline an approach that formally models the cognitive processes that give rise to these behaviors. Specifically, I characterize athletes' decisions as consisting of: information search and selective attention, generation of possible courses of action, deliberation among these possible actions, and selection and implementation of a single option. Theoretical arguments and empirical evidence are provided to support this approach.

INTRODUCTION

Perhaps the most fundamental characteristic of human behavior is our agency—our ability to make and enact decisions. Naturally, the question arises: How do we make decisions? There are a number of different disciplines that examine this question and, indeed, a number of different approaches within each discipline. Those in psychology, economics, marketing, philosophy, political science, and many other domains study why we choose what we do. For the field of sports science, it is not only an academic pursuit to understand why athletes and coaches make the decisions they do, but it can also be used practically for improvement through training as well as to gain competitive advantage.

The current chapter will provide a brief survey regarding one particular framework for studying athlete decision making in real-world contexts (i.e., athletic contests). Consider as an example a basketball point guard who is poised with the basketball in the backcourt and must decide to whom he will pass the ball (or to shoot the ball himself). A traditional, behavioral study might manipulate one or more variables such as time pressure, skill level, defender characteristics, or situational demands, and examine how the choices of the point guard change as a function of these. Alternatively, the current approach examines the intervening processes that lead the point guard to make the decision. In particular, I advocate the use of computational cognitive modeling (CCM) to represent and understand these processes.

When considering the situation facing the point guard, the relevant cognitive processes evolve in a sequence of events. First, he must survey the field and ascertain any relevant information, such as defender positions and the dynamic movements of his teammates. Additional information is attended as well, ranging from relevant information from long-term memory—such as the preferences of his center and forwards in receiving passes and shooting—to immediate context information such as the type of defense (zone or man-to-man) and the time remaining on the shot clock. This attended information is then used to generate possible options—such as a pass to the other guard player, a bounce pass to a forward, a lob pass to the center, a shot, or continued dribbling. As additional information is considered, additional options may come to mind and all of these are constantly reevaluated based on the current information at hand. As this process continues, at some point an overt decision is made which of these options to enact.

Before proceeding with how to analyze these decisions, a few qualifications are in order. Note that these options may not necessarily be explicitly generated and verbalizable at any given moment; that is, the point guard may not be consciously considering these different courses of action. Nevertheless, from among this set of potential options a decision is made, presumably requiring some level of cognitive processing. Perhaps a default decision to dribble is maintained unless another option becomes sufficiently desirable. This could occur through a simple, repeatedly rehearsed "if-then" rule, based on pattern matching, which is almost automatically enacted. For example, the point guard waits for a set play which has been well-practiced by the team to provide a screen, which affords the center an open opportunity towards the basket. In other cases, it could be that a more systematic analysis of the possible options reveals a clear "best choice" and results in a more explicit overt choice. In any case, the framework outlined below appreciates three key cognitive components, regardless of the speed with which they are applied: attention, generation, and deliberation. In essence, the CCM approach simply formalizes the description of the point guard's behaviors provided above, involving a series of integrated processes linking inputs to intended actions.

COMPUTATIONAL COGNITIVE MODELING

The specific CCM framework described here represents athletes' information processing as dynamic, probabilistic models of the cognitive processes that produce decision behaviors. This class of model is preferred on a number of theoretical grounds (see Bar-Eli and Raab, 2006; Busemeyer and Townsend, 1993). Dynamic models are necessary because relevant variables change over the course of a decision, making it impossible to treat these as static entities in models. Defender and teammate positions, the game clock, coach instruction, and crowd noise are just some examples of dynamic variables, which outweigh and outnumber static variables such as game location (home field or away). Furthermore, a decision is not made by an instantaneous evaluation of all possible information, but the accumulation of information over time during a decision situation. The point guard does not instantly and exhaustively process all the information before him, but rather selectively attends to different dimensions over time—perhaps first noting the game situation (score and time remaining), then scanning the defense, then considering teammate abilities in the current situation, etc.

Probabilistic models are superior to deterministic models in the sports domain because athlete behavior is indeed variable. Granted, some advantageous training is based on deterministically mapping specific game characteristics to associated responses (McPherson and Kernodle, 2003), such as "if this situation exists, then you should perform this way." However, this Skinnerian ideal of "if-then" rules is not realistic in practice, where experienced athletes have the flexibility to adapt their behavior. Even when faced with the same game situation on different occasions, an athlete is likely to make different decisions. Practically, this can be beneficial for exploratory purposes in learning how different actions may perform in a single situation, otherwise one would never know whether a different course of action could improve outcomes. Furthermore, it allows unpredictability that is obviously advantageous in competitive sports, without which an opponent could perfectly anticipate and respond to one's actions.

The CCM model subtype that frames the specific examples provided in the remainder of this chapter can be described as a sequential sampling or "horse race" model, because it involves the accumulation of evidence for competing responses until one of the response options "wins the race" and is enacted (Townsend and Ashby, 1983; see Busemeyer and Johnson, 2004, for a general application to decision behaviors and Johnson, 2006, for an overview in the sports domain). Figure 1 provides a visual representation of these concepts. Mathematically, it suggests a dynamic input $I(t)$ that represents the information under consideration at time t. As the point guard's attention shifts to different information over time, $I(t)$ changes accordingly. The momentary input gives rise to some sort of value at time t for each potential course of action i, denoted $V_i(t)$. These momentary inputs are accumulated over time by defining a preference state for each option $P_i(t)$, such that the preference state contains the summed evaluations of all previous $V_i(t' \leq t)$ values. For example, attention to defender distances at one moment in $I(t_1)$ may produce a favorable evaluation of the center player at that moment $V_{center}(t_1)$ if he is not closely guarded when other teammates are. However, attention at the next moment to the information conveyed by a three-point deficit in the waning seconds of regulation time $I(t_2)$ would provide a relatively unfavorable evaluation of the center $V_{center}(t_2)$ because he cannot afford an opportunity to tie or win the game. The overall preference for the center after these two moments would then be represented by $P_{center}(t_2)$; the exact nature of this value depends on the tradeoff between the large defensive cushion and the inability to score the necessary points.

The challenge of the modeling pursuit is defining the relationships among these components; that is, the functions that map current inputs to current perceived value, and that aggregate perceived values to form overall preference. Additionally, one must detail the nature of the informational input and its dynamics, as well as how potential courses of action are generated. The remainder of this chapter will provide a brief summary of advances on these fronts within the sports domain (but see Busemeyer and Johnson, 2004, for a summary in traditional laboratory choice tasks).

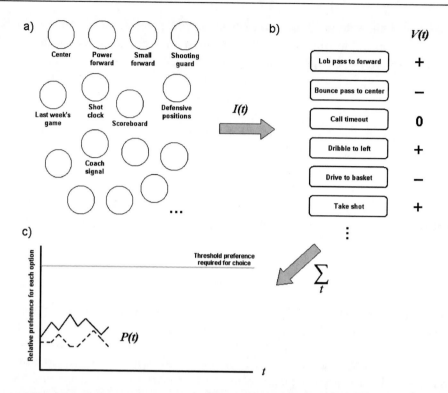

Figure 1. Illustration of CCM to a hypothetical point guard's decision. Attention is assumed to shift over time to various bits of information, shown as circles in (a). At any given moment in time, the attended information $I(t)$ gives rise to momentary evaluations $V(t)$ for each option under consideration. Example options are shown as boxes in (b), and the associated values for the current $V(t)$ are shown as discretely positive, negative, or neutral. Additional options can be generated at any point in time, which would add boxes to those shown. The momentary evaluations for each option are summed over time to produce an overall preference state $P(t)$, which is plotted for each option against time t in (c). Two illustrative plots are shown: the solid line illustrates an option which has gained preference due to a positive evaluation in the current moment, such as "dribble to left;" the broken line illustrates a decrement at the tail end of its preference plot, suggesting an option evaluated negatively in the current moment, such as "drive to basket." The preference plots for each option increase and decrease with shifting attention over time; the first option to reach the threshold level of preference to warrant choice, shown as a gray line in (c), is selected.

INFORMATION SEARCH: SELECTIVE ATTENTION AS AN INPUT TO EVALUATING COURSES OF ACTION

The first cognitive process to be modeled involves attention shifting over time; in figure 1, which circle of information is considered at each moment. Selective attention serves as an information filter guided by both enduring factors such as experience and habit, as well as the immediate game context. The importance of modeling the dynamic stream of attention is that it dramatically affects the subsequent processing of information. That is, without specifying assumptions about the momentary informational input, I(t), it is impossible to understand how the remaining processes evolve. If the midfielder momentarily considers the height advantage and cushion that his center has against the opposing defender, he may be more apt to lob pass to this teammate; whenever he thinks about the score deficit and time remaining, he may be inclined to consider a teammate with better potential to score three points. Thus, attentional flux over time can dramatically shift not only the options that come under consideration, but also the relative preference for each option.

Empirically, there is considerable evidence in sports of differential use of task dimensions, such as the way in which certain dimensions are used or the ranking of different cues by their relative importance (e.g., Abernethy, 1991; McPherson, 1993). The CCM can directly represent these findings by specifying attention shifts differentially across groups (e.g., experts and novices), which then lead to behavioral differences in terms of choices. Other recent work utilizes eye-tracking data to help understand the role of attention in athletes' subsequent cognitive processes, thereby integrating the components of the CCM (Raab and Johnson, 2007). In particular, this methodology uses visual attention as an input to a simple CCM to predict generated options and ultimate choices. Raab and Johnson (2007) found a high degree of correspondence between visual attention and subsequent option generation; in particular, they found a significant relationship between the first visual fixation and the first option generated. This supports the CCM predictions regarding the link between attended information $I(t)$ and the generation of relevant options.

In the CCM framework, shifting attention is also the primary driver for choice variability, and thus it is possible to formally model the link between attention and decision as well. That is, beyond the link between attention and option generation (i.e., determining which boxes exist in figure 1b), there is a hypothetical CCM link between attention and evaluation as well (the values of the boxes' $V(t)$ in figure 1b). Of course, it is presumptive to assume too strong of a correlation between visual attention as measured by eyegaze by Raab and Johnson (2007) and the information attended in working memory. However, a simple CCM can be developed for their task by assuming: (1) direct mapping of $I(t)$ to $V(t)$, such that attention to a region provides positive evidence for options in the region; and (2) weighted summation of evaluations to produce preferences, $P_i(t) = \beta P_i(t-1) + V_i(t)$, where a single parameter β determines whether initial ($\beta>1$) or recent ($\beta<1$) evaluations carry more weight. Appling this CCM to the Raab and Johnson (2007) data correctly predicts 71% of choices (where chance is 33%), simply by fitting the parameter β for each individual. In regards to the role of attention, earlier-attended information seems to play a larger role, because the majority (over 75%) of individual best-fitting β values, as well as the median and mean across individuals, were greater than one.

OPTION GENERATION: DETERMINING WHICH POTENTIAL COURSES OF ACTION ARE EVALUATED

Over the course of a decision, different potential courses of action may develop. That is, one may think of additional solutions to the problem as one ruminates, rather than explicitly cataloging all possible options prior to collecting information. Referring to figure 1b, the boxes are likely to appear sequentially over time, rather than all boxes being immediately and instantly present at the onset of a decision situation. Rather than having a preconceived set of options in mind, the point guard may dynamically generate these options as he scans the court during a play. For example, attention to the baseline area under the basket is likely to lead to generation of a possible option of "pass to center." Maybe subsequent consideration of the center's height advantage over his defender refines this option to "lob pass to center." In this sense, option generation could be formalized as dynamic additions or changes to the choice set during the deliberation process, expressed as the incrementing of i and the creation of new $V_i(t)$. Finally, option generation could in turn affect the patterns of attention, such as by explicitly seeking information to confirm a new option that comes to mind.

This option generation process has also been formalized in a CCM framework (Johnson and Raab, 2003; Raab and Johnson, 2007). This model, in essence, proposes the cascading introduction of options as attention shifts over time, as mentioned above. The model supposes that individuals have a specific strategy to which they explicitly or implicitly adhere, which then dictates how attention progresses and options are generated. As additional options are generated, then this promotes the inclusion of similar options as well. For example, assume that the point guard plays under a coaching system that emphasizes "pounding the paint," or focusing on getting the ball to inside players for easier scoring opportunities. In this case attention will first focus to the baseline area, as described above. Continuing from above, generation of "lob pass to center" is likely to also bring to mind similar options, such as "lob pass to power forward" or "lob pass to small forward" if these players are also in the vicinity.

This model makes specific predictions about the nature of the generated options, such as the diminishing quality of generated options with an increase in serial position (i.e., better options are generated sooner). This prediction arises from the expected correlation between training and experience with options that are successful; unsuccessful options face selection pressures that discourage their continued use. Furthermore, salience largely dictates initial attention, which then determines initial generations, and later generations are mostly generated "merely" by their similarity to previously-generated options, rather than by any merit of their own. Indeed, the option generation component has been shown to predict the number and type of generated options, as well as explaining the degree to which initial "intuitive" options differed from those options ultimately selected after subsequent deliberation (Johnson and Raab, 2003). The option generation component was extended and applied to differing levels of expertise by Raab and Johnson (2007), where it was also able to account for the basic empirical results (number of options generated, decision quality, etc.). More sophisticated paradigms for eliciting generated options could produce further refinements to the CCM. For example, "think-aloud" protocols similar to those used in the cited studies could be collected concurrently with information search to formally model the points in time when new options are added, and task interruption at various intervals could try and determine the resulting relative values of V_i and P_i.

DELIBERATION AND CHOICE:
ACCUMULATING EVALUATIONS AND MAKING A DECISION

The third and most directly relevant process is the selection of an option or course of action from the generated set. That is, once the potential options have been identified, some mechanism must evaluate these options and select a course of action. In the CCM, this corresponds to the aggregation function that produces $P_i(t)$ from the preceding $V_i(t' \leq t)$ values. Psychologically, the choice model assumes that the $V_i(t)$ values represent affective reactions to each option that result from the information input $I(t)$. These are largely based on previous experiences (if available) and/or implicit predictions of potential outcomes. If the point guard considers defender distances, and one teammate is closely guarded, this may produce a negative reaction towards passing to this teammate based on recalled instances of turnovers or the predicted possibility of a turnover. If he considers the fact that his team is down three points with little time remaining, then passing to teammates in three-point scoring position will be evaluated positively. Affective valences such as these are produced for each option, at each moment in time, based on the current informational input. These valences are integrated over time to develop a preference state for each option (the plots in figure 1c). The evolution of preference states proceeds as additional information is considered, and preference states exist for each option that is generated and added to the choice set.

At some point a course of action must be implemented. The choice model contains a threshold, or level at which an option is considered "good enough," to determine choice. As preferences for each relevant option accumulate (figure 1c), the point guard eventually must decide that the preference for one single option is strong enough to deserve action. As alluded to earlier, this could be formulated relative to a default option, such as the point guard retaining possession of the ball and dribbling. Suppose the preference for continuing with the current course of action at any given moment t is represented as $P^*(t)$, shown as the gray line in figure 1c. Then, the decision of action occurs when any option in the choice set exceeds this preference, $P_i(t) > P^*(t)$, for any i, meaning that its plot has crossed the gray line in figure 1. When this occurs, the corresponding option i has "won the race" and is selected; the response time prediction naturally follows by simply noting the time t when this occurs.

These CCM assumptions regarding the nature of deliberation and choice have accounted for a variety of findings that have challenged other decision models in standard laboratory tasks (for example, see Johnson and Busmeyer, 2005; and the references therein). In the sports domain, the model has been used to explain effects such as time pressure and speed-accuracy tradeoffs (Raab, 2001), as well as decisions and response times by basketball playmakers such as the one used in the running example of the current chapter (Raab and Johnson, 2004).

NOVEL PREDICTIONS

Beyond providing an alternative theoretical account for empirical results, CCMs can also deliver novel predictions, such as those regarding response times that are not possible with "outcome-only" predictive theories. Furthermore, one can take advantage of the underlying psychological meaning imputed upon the mathematical parameters in CCMs. This allows one to explore multiple psychological mechanisms that may give rise to similar overt behaviors so that we can identify differences in experimental conditions as well as determine what information processing characteristics may be responsible. This can be done, for example, by comparing best-fitting parameter estimates across predefined groups, or across *post hoc* groups of experimental participants that exhibit similar performance characteristics. In either case, the logic is that for any given (observable, measurable) performance differences, their may be multiple underlying (mental, unobservable) causes. With the assistance of a CCM, it is possible to differentiate between these contributing factors.

As an example of these unique contributions, in the application to decisions by basketball playmakers (Raab and Johnson, 2004), both decisions about to whom to pass as well as the response times to make these decisions were predicted by a CCM. Furthermore, individual differences between participants were incorporated in the model by presetting model parameters based on an independent measurement of the action-orientation of playmakers. Increased action-orientation, an analogue of risk-taking, could be incorporated in the model by either a greater initial preference $P(0)$ for riskier options, increased attention to information favoring these options, or a lower threshold for acting. The CCM allowed for quantitative comparison of these different explanations, which revealed that the initial preference was the most accurate in predicting choices and response times in this application. In a similar vein, Raab and Johnson (2007) were able to explain differences between three different expertise levels by examining differences in the visual search patterns and the strategy driving the option generation in a CCM.

CONCLUSION

This chapter has argued for the utility in using computational models of the processes that give rise to observable behaviors. There are many benefits to using such models to complement empirical investigations of behavior. First and foremost, such models allow one to specify the underlying causes for observable behaviors, rather than simply enumerating behavioral differences. Second, models such as those reviewed here allow for predictions of additional measures such as attentional data (e.g., eye-tracking, see Land and Tenenbaum, Chapter 17) and response times. Third, the free parameters of these models can be interpreted psychologically, and provide additional meaning to observed differences. These models can be applied to many different sports situations where the information processing attributes can be specified.

Many open questions remain not only for the CCM approach in general, but for application to any sport or situation in particular. Exactly what information is considered in a given situation, and in what manner—what are the relevant circles in figure 1 for a particular sport situation, and how is the momentary $I(t)$ selected from among these? What is the precise nature of evaluating different options—how are the generic pluses and minuses in figure 1 quantified for a specific task? How are these momentary evaluations integrated over time? For example, is the primacy effect reported earlier consistent beyond the handball task of Raab and Johnson (2007)? How are the dynamics of not just the cognitive processes, but also the game environment itself, best appreciated in the CCM context (cf. Araújo et al., Chapter 10; Araújo, Davids, and Hristovski, 2006)?

The CCM framework can intersect with other approaches to athlete decision making, especially those with cognitive emphasis. Tenenbaum and Bar-Eli (1993) provide a comprehensive survey of how cognitive factors, including those explicitly included in the CCMs of this chapter, can influence athlete decision making. It would be interesting to extend the CCMs with even more cognitive components such as those, and thereby progress towards answering the questions posed above. It is very likely that athlete decisions in real game contexts are not made by computation of some optimal action, as the dominant theories in the broader decision research would suggest (see, e.g., Luce, 2000). In fact, many sports decisions are probably made very efficiently by very basic strategies or heuristics (Bennis and Pachur, 2006). It is interesting to note how the current CCM framework could incorporate these simpler assumptions. For example, a strict ordering of informational inputs and a low threshold for acting would allow the sequential sampling CCM to mimic many heuristic processes (Lee and Cummins, 2004).

The CCM approach, as outlined here, exhibits considerable potential for the formal modeling of athlete decisions. Furthermore, this could then contribute to training paradigms that are able to focus on specific component processes to improve decision making, such as the training programs posited in other chapters in this volume (i.e. Araújo et al., Chapter 13; Brand et al., Chapter 15). The CCM approach is stringent enough to formulate testable predictions, yet flexible enough to incorporate many important elements. Ideally, this approach would be used across different sports and different game situations, as well as across athletes with different characteristics (e.g. skill level, playing style). In this manner, a "critical mass" would be achieved that could very well make this framework the standard for developing new representations of the processes that give rise to athlete behavior.

REFERENCES

Abernethy, B. (1991). Visual search strategies and decision-making in sport. *International Journal of Sport Psychology, 22(3–4)*, 189–210.

Araújo, D., Davids, K., and Hristovski, R. (2006). The ecological dynamics of decision making in sport. *Psychology of Sport and Exercise, 7*, 653-676.

Bar-Eli, M. and Raab, M. (2006). Judgment and decision making in sport and exercise: Rediscovery and new visions. *Psychology of Sport and Exercise, 7*, 519-524.

Bennis, W.M., and Pachur, T. (2006). Fast and frugal heuristics in sports. *Psychology of Sport and Exercise, 7*, 611-629.

Busemeyer, J.R., and Johnson, J.G. (2004). Computational models of decision making. In D. Koehler and N. Harvey (Eds.), *Blackwell Handbook of Judgment and Decision Making* (pp. 133–154). Oxford, UK: Blackwell Publishing Co.

Busemeyer, J.R., and Townsend, J.T. (1993). Decision field theory: a dynamic-cognitive approach to decision making in an uncertain environment. *Psychological Review, 100*, 432–459.

Johnson, J.G. (2006). Cognitive modeling of decision making in sports. *Psychology of Sport and Exercise, 7*, 631-652.

Johnson, J.G., and Busemeyer, J.R. (2005). A dynamic, stochastic, computational model of preference reversal phenomena. *Psychological Review, 122*, 841–861.

Johnson, J.G., and Raab, M. (2003). Take the first: Option generation and resulting choices. *Organizational Behavior and Human Decision Processes, 91*(2), 215–229.

Lee, M.D., and Cummins, T.D.R. (2004). Evidence accumulation in decision making: Unifying the "take the best" and "rational" models. *Psychonomic Bulletin and Review, 11*, 343–352.

Luce, R.D. (2000). *Utility of gains and losses*. Philadelphia, PA: Lawrence Erlbaum Associates.

McPherson, S.L. (1993). The influence of player experience on problem solving during batting preparation in baseball. *Journal of Sport and Exercise Psychology, 15*(3), 304–325.

McPherson, S.L., and Kernodle, M.W. (2003). Tactics, the neglected attribute of expertise: Problem representations and performance skills in tennis. In J.L. Starkes and K.A. Ericsson (Eds.), *Expert performance in sports: Advances in research on sport expertise* (pp. 137–168). Champaign, IL: Human Kinetics.

Raab, M. (2001). T-ECHO: Model of decision making to explain behavior in experiments and simulations under time pressure. *Psychology of Sport and Exercise, 3,* 151–171.

Raab, M., and Johnson, J.G. (2004). Individual differences of action-orientation for risk-taking in sports. *Research Quarterly for Exercise and Sport, 75*(3), 326–336.

Raab, M. and Johnson, J.G. (2007). Expertise-based differences in search and option-generation strategies. *Journal of Experimental Psychology: Applied, 13*(3), 158-170.

Tenenbaum, G., and Bar-Eli, M. (1993). Decision making in sport: A cognitive perspective. In R.N. Singer, M. Murphy and L.K. Tennant (Eds.), *Handbook of research on sport psychology* (pp. 171–192). New York: Macmillan.

Townsend, J.T., and Ashby, F.G. (1983). *Stochastic modeling of elementary psychological processes*. New York: Cambridge University Press.

In: Perspectives on Cognition and Action in Sport
Editors: D. Araújo, H. Ripoll and M. Raab

ISBN: 978-1-60692-390-0
© 2009 Nova Science Publishers, Inc.

Chapter 15

CONCEPTUAL CONSIDERATIONS ABOUT THE DEVELOPMENT OF A DECISION-MAKING TRAINING METHOD FOR EXPERT SOCCER REFEREES

Ralf Brand[1], Henning Plessner[2] and Geoffrey Schweizer[1]

[1] University of Potsdam, Germany
[2] University of Leipzig, Germany

ABSTRACT

This chapter explains the underlying conceptual considerations (i.e. the pragmatic modeling) that led to the development of a decision-making training tool for expert soccer referees. Considerations are inferred from research on social cognition and social judgments, namely social judgment theory and multi-cue probabilistic learning. The resulting SET-tool (SET is a German acronym for *"Schiedsrichter-Entscheidungs-Training"*, i.e. "referee decision-making training method) consists of a database for storing video training items and an online interface, therefore providing the possibility of conducting online training sessions for participants, as well as for online training administration. It is briefly described how the tool can be used for conducting empirical investigations. The main point of this chapter, however, is to illustrate the concept of pragmatic modeling as a strategy in applied (i.e. technological) sport psychological research on judgment and decision-making.

INTRODUCTION

During the final tournament of the "UEFA Euro 2000" soccer championship, referees made an average of 137 observable decisions per match (Helsen and Bultynck, 2004). It is difficult to quantify unobservable decisions (e.g. a referee's decision not to call a foul), but it is likely that there were about 200 situations per game at least, in which referees had to decide whether to blow their whistle or not. Other analyses from various studies on offside decisions in soccer let us suppose that the absolute rate of expert soccer referees' misjudgments per game are as high or low as 25% (Helsen, Gilis and Weston, 2006; Oudejans, Verheijen, Bakker, Gerrits, Steinbrückner and Beek, 2000). Most authors would agree that such empirically attestable imperfection of referees' decision-making is largely due to the nature of their physically and psychologically extremely demanding task (Mascarenhas, O'Hare and Plessner, 2006), and that mistakes will forever be "part of the game". But as long as one incorrect penalty decision can decide a game – or even a world championship – there should be some "natural" interest in reducing error rates to a minimum.

What can referees do to improve their decision-making skills? Referees can – and surely they do – elaborate their knowledge on the game's rules continuously (MacMahon and Plessner, 2007): they watch and analyze videotaped games at home, meet several times per season and discuss situations, and they receive instruction as to why one situation has to be considered foul play and another situation not. However, from a sport psychological point of view, such training methods are suboptimal in at least one important aspect: they may lay a necessary foundation of relevant knowledge on *how* situations should be judged. But none of them includes actually *making* decisions.

The basic idea of our work is that decision-making itself should be trained, and that it is not enough to just know the reasons why a decision is correct or incorrect. Therefore, our goal is to design an effective training method to be used by expert referees in order to systematically improve their decision-making skills.

This chapter aims at illustrating how our decision-making training method has been developed. It concentrates on what we call *pragmatic modeling*, i.e. the work steps from problem definition, to the assortment of a theoretical framework, to the design of a training-tool prototype. Certainly, there are various areas of research that could provide theoretical bases for creating decision-making training methods (for example from the motor learning domain, where video-based training settings for athletes are already used successfully, e.g. Guadagnoli and Lee, 2004). However, we chose to focus on concepts from research on social cognition and multiple-cue probability learning.

PRAGMATIC MODELING OF REFEREE DECISIONS IN SPORT GAMES

The first step toward the development of such a training method is to answer two questions: What should be trained, and which psychological mechanisms contribute to the process of decision-making? It is important to note that it is not our goal here to fully explain the basic psychological mechanisms underlying decision-making processes in sport, but to design a pragmatic model that allows us to "get a grip" on the problem as to how to train complex decision-making skills with referees.

Accurate-Plus-Adequate Decisions

Theoretical as well as recent empirical research on the task of officiating sport games suggests, that the decisions of sport game referees can be motivated by either of the two goals Enforcement of the Laws of the Game (i.e. to be accurate; Plessner and Betsch, 2001, 2002) or Game Management (to ensure the flow of the game, to be/appear unbiased; Brand and Neß, 2004; Brand, Schneeloch and Schmidt, 2006; Mascarenhas, Collins and Mortimer, 2002; Rains, 1984; Unkelbach and Memmert, 2008). Furthermore it is easy to find evidence that there are numerous situations, in which even groups of expert referees disagree on the decision to be made in a possible foul situation (Brand, et al., 2006; Nevill, Balmer and Williams, 2002).

Expert soccer referees' anecdotal reports suggest that most of these ambiguous contact situations could be resolved when video recordings from different viewing angles and slow motion pictures would be consulted. But the point is that the referee on the field has to decide within fractions of a second. Sometimes viewing-angles are suboptimal and a large amount of situations exist in which referees are challenged to instantly weigh up whether a call is necessary to control the game (e.g. when emotions go high after a tackle and regulations have to be applied rigorously; Snyder and Purdy, 1987) or whether a call would be termed as a small-minded decision of a rule expert (e.g. when teams and players accept or demand a certain style of play, for example in high-level international games, when the referee has to develop some "feeling for the game"; Brand and Neß, 2004). These thoughts, which are mainly inspired by the practice of officiating sport games, lead us to believe that referees' decisions should be theoretically captured within an accurate-plus-adequate paradigm.

Being accurate in one's decision-making is a necessary condition for high quality refereeing. Accuracy refers to the referee's ability to categorize an incident as foul or no foul according to the written laws of the game. But beyond matters of accuracy, sport game officials' decisions can be considered as being more or less adequate (it is important to note that a decision can only be regarded as adequate if the referee was also able to categorize the incident accurately). The concept of adequacy is at the heart of the idea of what is meant with the term game management. Besides being accurate, referees should use the whistle only when the "consequences for not doing so may adversely affect the tempo or temper of the game" (Mascarenhas et al., 2002, p. 330). In order to manage games, referees should adjust their interpretation of single contacts (foul or no foul) to the concrete context of the ongoing situation.

This idea of accurate-plus-adequate decisions in the practice of sport game refereeing is crucial for subsequent considerations about the field of application of the decision training tool presented in this chapter: It solely aims at improving the *accuracy* of expert soccer referees' decisions. However, as has been said, we consider accuracy as a necessary requirement for making adequate decisions.

A Social-Cognition Framework

It is a widely held assumption that the decisions of sport game referees are prone to systematic, cognitive biases of which they are at least partly unaware. It is possible that some misjudgments may be products of strategic deliberation. However, we assume that in most of the cases – at least in the moment of their decision – referees are convinced that their decision is accurate and adequate. Sport psychologists have demonstrated that referees are biased by a home crowd's noise (Nevill, et al., 2002), by players' reputations (Jones, Paul and Erskine, 2002), by a team's origin (Messner and Schmid, 2007), and even by their own prior decisions (Brand, et al., 2006; Plessner and Betsch, 2001). In order to design the training program, it is necessary to know *why* these biases occur.

It has been argued that many decision situations of referees resemble typical social judgment situations and, thus, can be analyzed on the basis of a social cognition framework (Plessner, 2005; Plessner and Haar, 2006). Among other things, this means that it would be useful, at least for pragmatic reasons, to differentiate between several subtasks of information processing (i.e., perception, categorization, memory processes, information integration; Bless, Fiedler and Strack, 2004, see figure 1). These processes lead from the actual performance (e.g., a player's tackling) to a referee's decision (e.g., sending a player off the field).

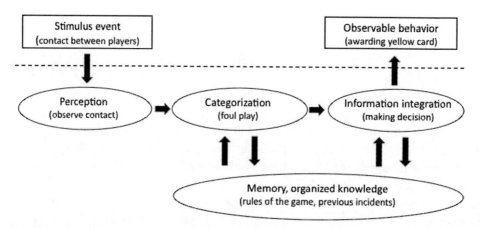

Figure 1. The sequence of social information processing applied to the example of a soccer referee's decision task (Plessner and Haar, 2006, p. 558; figure mod.).

An interesting social-cognition explanation for the home-crowd effect is that the bias is due to heuristic judgment processes in which a salient, yet insignificant stimulus (the biased response of the home crowd) is more or less deliberately – used as an additional decision *cue*.

A Multi-Cue Probabilistic Learning Framework

The idea of cue-based judgments goes back to classic social judgment theory (Goldstein, 2004, for an overview). The so-called *lens model* approach presented by Brunswik (1943, 1952) can be used to illustrate that social judgments on distal events are based on (typically) sets of proximal cues. Within the framework of the lens model, the terms distal and proximal do not refer to space, but to the type of access judges have to a variable: Proximal variables are directly observable, while distal ones are not and thus need to be inferred. Cognitive strategies are needed to infer from this proximal information, and the ecological validity of single cues can vary (figure 2).

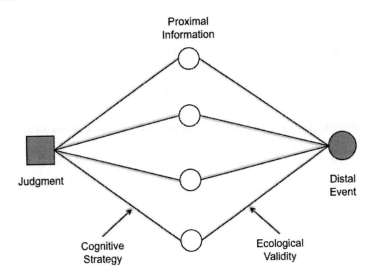

Figure 2. The lens model of social judgment (Brunswik, 1952).

It is reasonable to apply this basic idea to situations in which referees have to judge whether a contact between players is legal or illegal: Referees should have the ability to identify (and then to infer solely from) *relevant cues* in order to decide accurately (see Bisantz, Kirlik, Gay, Phipps, Walker and Fisk, 2000, for another application of this idea).

In respect to the conceivable dissimilarity of specific contact situations in soccer, thus, one has to answer the question as to how anybody should decide which cues (or prototypical situations) are "worth" being integrated into the training program. Imagine a situation in which the referee has difficulties to exactly see whether a defender's tackling hits an opponent's leg instead of the ball or whether the ball is played legally. The opponent's tumbling is a more than ambiguous sign or cue to trigger the referee's foul call. It is the only one the referee has though. There may be numerous situations in "real life soccer" where no *deterministic relation* between a relevant cue (here: 'tumbling of the player') and the referee's decision (here 'call the foul' or 'not call the foul') exists.

In fact, there is a paradigmatic framework in cognitive psychology that deals with a comparable problem, i.e. when people should learn from repeated exposure to probabilistic information. It is best illustrated with one of its prototypical, experimental set-ups called the weather prediction task (Lagnado, Newell, Kahan and Shanks, 2006, p. 162). Here, people learn to predict a binary outcome (rainy or nice weather) on the basis of four cues (four distinct tarot cards). Each card is associated with the outcome at a different probability, and these probabilities combine to determine the over-all probability of the outcome for any particular pattern of cards. On each learning trial, participants see a specific pattern of cards, predict the weather, and receive feedback as to the correct outcome. This enables them to gradually learn the cue-outcome relations and thus improve the accuracy of their predictions. And what is important to note is that learning rates in probabilistic, multi-cue learning seem to be essentially independent of a learner's insight into the underlying regularities or decision rules (e.g. Bisantz et al., 2000).

In our setup, we apply this concept of *probabilistic multiple-cue learning* to the problem of designing a training method (i.e. training tool) for improving the quality of referees' decision-making. Thus, contact situations in soccer can be seen as containing a set of cues (as proximal information) with each of them being more or less significant for the accurate judgment. Imagine the situation when an offending player passes the ball and shortly afterwards a second player violently pulls his shirt. As a result, the offending player falls to the ground. In this situation, a referee's decision has to account for the tackling player's grasp of the offending player's shirt (cue 1) as well as for the fact that the ball has already been successfully passed (cue 2) and for the offending players fall (cue 3).

In some situations, when the team against which the offence has been committed benefits from the referee's decision not to stop the game (Law 5 in the Official Laws of the Game of Soccer), cue 2 would be a sufficient criterion for a referee not to call a foul. Under other circumstances, for example when the contact is rude and there is the danger of injury, cue 2 (ball has been passed successfully) may not have the necessary significance to "outweigh" cue 3 (offender is falling) and cue 1 (grasping of the shirt). In such situations, calling the foul may be the accurate decision.

THE SET TRAINING TOOL:
AN ONLINE MULTIMEDIA TRAINING ENVIRONMENT

During the year 2007 our project group's focus was on the conception, design, and programming of a computer-based online training device for decision-making, based on the above-described pragmatic modeling. The tool that has resulted, *SET* (SET is an acronym for German "*Schiedsrichter-Entscheidungs-Training*", i.e. "referee decision training-method"), is an interactive, online multimedia learning-environment. It has a high-capacity database in its background and it is especially optimized for storing and presenting video training items. Uploaded scenes can be annotated at any time with whatever information considered as being important (for example the sequence's origin, the type of foul shown, or the accurate decision as rated by the German Football Association's Referee Board). The information stored can be used to assemble training sessions, for example on selected types of contact situations (e.g. pushing, holding). Referees participating in the program can access the training environment via personalized logins on the SET project homepage. Referees attend training sessions at fixed time intervals.

The SET prototype focuses on the judgment of contact situations. During a typical training routine, referees are presented several videos showing contact situations (figure 3). Videos are stopped immediately after the contact and referees indicate their decision by clicking the mouse. Time pressure is imposed upon participants to resemble real life conditions.

In a first step, they can choose between the options "foul" versus "no foul". If they choose "foul", in a second step they are given the possibility to award a personal sanction (yellow or red card). After their decision, referees are informed about the accuracy of their decision via online feedback. Feedback content (correct answer only vs. correct answer plus explanations) as well as feedback latency (immediately vs. delayed) and feedback accumulation (feedback for single decisions vs. feedback for several decisions at a time) can be manipulated by training administrators. Administration of SET is designed most flexibly. Training sessions can be varied systematically (by a few mouse-clicks) between single training sessions, as well as for different groups of participants. Referees' decisions, as well as other relevant data (e.g., referees' reaction times), are stored in the database for research purposes. Training success can thus be evaluated by comparing proportion of correct decisions between pre- and post-training tests for various training scenarios.

Figure 3. SET-training session screenshot.

During the year 2008 our research group has focused on conducting empirical studies in order to validate assumptions on the optimal design of training sessions. These assumptions were based on findings from multiple-cue probability learning and insight on the role of feedback for learning processes (e.g. Hogarth, 2001, 2008). Preliminary results (research in progress) indicate that immediate feedback (right or wrong, as classified by the DFB Referees's Board, without explanation of reasons) after each decision most effectively ameliorates learning rates.

The SET training environment offers a highly flexible online tool that can be used as a training device, as well as for research purposes. Researchers interested in SET-Base can find a project homepage, supplemented with additional information and including a demo-training scenario, in the Internet (*www.sethome.de*).

CONCLUSION

This book aims to introduce readers to some new perspectives on cognition and action in sport. The goal of Section three (Judgment and decision-making) of the book was to present divergent theoretical approaches, applied to various domains within the sport context. In his chapter Joseph G. Johnson (Johnson, Chapter 14) has provided an introduction into the advantages of applying formal models of cognitive computations that produce decision behaviors. Choosing an attentional approach William Land and Gershon Tenenbaum (Chapter, 17) have elaborated on the idea that task-related decision-making (in the form of attention) develops as a function of age and skill level. Joan N. Vickers (Chapter, 16) has presented her perception-action approach and has given ideas on how vision-in-action differences change athletes' choices. The ecological approach presented by Duarte Araújo and colleagues (Chapter 13) have taught us that the modeling of ecological dynamics of the environment helps to predict decisions in concrete decision-making settings (sport game situations among others). Now, what is the special aspect we sought to highlight with the work presented in our chapter?

Most of the answer lies in the formal *structure of the knowledge* we seek to gain. In terms of fundamental methodological considerations (Herrmann, 1994) the work presented here is clearly of a *technological* nature. This means that we seek to develop a technological rule (or a set of rules; Bunge, 1983) following the formal structure "to resolve the practical problem *x*, do *y*", rather than to establish nomological ("if *x*, then *y*"; e.g. Araújo et al., Chapter 13; Johnson, Chapter 14; Land and Tenenbaum, Chapter 17) or nomopragmatic knowledge ("if *x* is done, then *y* will happen"; e.g. Vickers, Chapter 16), that would be necessary for establishing and testing theories to explain the decision-making process itself. As a consequence the first step in our empirical testing is optimized for yielding results on the *efficacy* of the training method (in order to show *that* it works), and not on the validation of the nomological theory behind the conceptual framework (explaining *how* the training method works; though this step may follow at a later stage of the research process).

The core of our research strategy is to develop a sound paradigm (social cognition, social judgment theory, probabilistic multi-cue learning) to be *applied* to a practical problem (training of decision-making skills of soccer referees), so that forthcoming empirical results can be interpreted in a theoretically informed manner. We hope that the work presented here has the potential to foster further foundational research on human decision-making in ambiguous situations and therefore add a complementary perspective to the psychology of cognition and action in sport.

ACKNOWLEDGMENTS

The work reported here is part of the SET-Project, which is funded by the Federal German Sports Institute (BISp IIA1-071017/06-08) and the Referee Board of the German Football Association (DFB). Special thanks go to our partners from InsertEffect GbR (Nürnberg, Germany) who have programmed and implemented the *SET* online multimedia tool.

REFERENCES

Bless, H., Fiedler, K., and Strack, F. (2004). *Social cognition – How individuals construct social reality*. New York: Psychology Press.

Bisantz, A. M., Kirlik, A., Gay, P., Phipps, D.A., Walker, N., and Fisk, A.D. (2000). Modeling and analysis of a dynamic judgment task using a lens model approach. *IEEE Transactions on Systems, Man, and Cybernetics – Part A: Systems and Humans, 30*, 605-616.

Brand, R., and Neß, W. (2004). Regelanwendung und Game-Management. Qualifizierende Merkmale von Schiedsrichtern in Sportspielen [Rule administration and game management. Qualifying characteristics of referees in sport games]. *Zeitschrift für Sportpsychologie, 11*, 127-136.

Brand, R., Schmidt, G., and Schneeloch, Y. (2006). Sequential effects in elite basketball referees' foul decisions: An experimental study on the concept of game management. *Journal of Sport and Exercise Psychology, 28*, 93-99.

Brunswik, E. (1943). Organismic achievement and environmental probability. *Psychological Review, 50*, 255–272.

Brunswik, E. (1952). *The Conceptual Framework of Psychology*. Chicago: Chicago University Press.

Bunge, M. (1983). *Treatise on basic philosophy* (Vol. 6, Epistemiology and methodology II: Understanding the world). Dordrecht and Boston: D. Reidel Publishing Compagny.

Goldstein, W.M. (2004). Social judgment theory: Applying and extending Brunswik's probabilistic functionalism. In D.J. Koehler and N. Harvey (Eds.), *Blackwell handbook of judgment and decision-making* (pp. 37-61). Malden, MA: Blackwell Publishing.

Guadagnoli, M.A., and Lee, T.D. (2004) Challenge point: A framework for conceptualizing the effects of various practice conditions in motor learning. Journal of Motor Behavior, 36, 212-224.

Herrmann, T. (1994). Forschungsprogramme [Research programs]. In T. Herrman and W.H. Tack (Eds.), *Methodologische Grundlagen der Psychologie [Methodological Bases of Psychology]* (Enzyklopädie der Psychologie [The Encyclopedia of Psychology], Themenbereich B, Serie I, Band 1, pp. 251-294). Göttingen: Hogrefe.

Helsen, W., and Bultynck, J.B. (2004). Physical and perceptual-cognitive demands of top-class refereeing in association football. *Journal of Sports Sciences, 22*, 179-189.

Helsen, W., Gilis, B., and Weston, M. (2006). Errors in judging "offside" in football: Test of the optical error versus the perceptual flash-lag hypothesis. *Journal of Sports Sciences, 24*, 512-528.

Hogarth, R. (2001). *Educating intuition*. Chicago, IL: University of Chicago Press.

Hogarth, R. (2008). On the learning of intuition. In H. Plessner, C. Betsch and T. Betsch (Eds.), *Intuition in Judgment and Decision Making* (pp. 91-105). Mahwah, NJ: Lawrence Erlbaum Associates.

Jones, M.V., Paull, G.C., and Erskine, J. (2002). The impact of a team's aggressive reputation on the decisions of association football referees. *Journal of Sports Sciences, 20*, 991-1000.

Lagnado, D.A., Newell, B.R., Kahan, S., and Shanks, D.R. (2006). Insight and strategy in multiple-cue learning. Journal of *Experimental Psychology, 135*, 162-183.

MacMahon, C., and Plessner, H. (2007). The sports official in research and practice. In D. Farrow, J. Baker and C. MacMahon (Eds.), *Developing elite sports performers: Lessons from theory and practice* (pp. 172-188). London: Routledge.

Mascarenhas, D.R.D., Collins, D., and Mortimer, P. (2002). The art of reason versus the exactness of science in elite refereeing: Comments on Plessner and Betsch (2001). *Journal of Sport and Exercise Psychology, 24,* 328-333.

Mascarenhas, D.R.D., O'Hare, D., and Plessner, H. (2006). The psychological and performance demands of association football refereeing. *International Journal of Sport Psychology, 37,* 99-120.

Messner, C., and Schmid, B. (2007). Über die Schwierigkeit, unparteiische Entscheidungen zu fällen: Schiedsrichter bevorzugen Fußballteams ihrer Kultur [About the difficulty to make impartial decisions: Referees favor culturally familiar football teams]. *Zeitschrift für Sozialpsychologie, 38,* 105-110.

Nevill, A.M., Balmer, N.J., and Williams, A.M. (2002). The influence of crowd noise and experience upon referring decisions in football. *Psychology of Sport and Exercise, 3,* 261-272.

Oudejans, R.R.D., Verheijen, R., Bakker, F.C., Gerrits, J.C., Steinbrückner, M., and Beek, P. J. (2000). Errors in judging 'offside' in football. *Nature, 404*(6773), 33.

Plessner, H. (2005). Positive and negative effects of prior knowledge on referee decisions in sports. In T. Betsch and S. Haberstroh (Eds.), *The routines of decision-making* (pp. 311-324). Hillsdale: Lawrence Erlbaum.

Plessner, H., and Betsch, T. (2001). Sequential effects in important referee decisions: The case of penalties in soccer. *Journal of Sport and Exercise Psychology, 23,* 254-259.

Plessner, H., and Betsch, T.(2002). Refereeing in sports is supposed to be a craft, not an art. Response to Mascarenhas, Collins, and Mortimer (2002). *Journal of Sport and Exercise Psychology, 24,* 334-337.

Plessner, H., and Haar, T. (2006). Sports performance judgments from a social cognitive perspective. *Psychology of Sport and Exercise, 7,* 555-575.

Rains, P. (1984). The production of fairness: Officiating in the national hockey league. *Sociology of Sport Journal, 1,* 150-162.

Snydcr, E. and Purdy, D.A. (1987). Social control in sport. An analysis of basketball officiating. *Sociology of Sport Journal, 4,* 394-402.

Unkelbach, C. and Memmert, D. (2008). Game-Management, Context-Effects, and Calibration: The case of yellow cards in soccer. *Journal of Sport and Exercise Psychology, 30,* 95-109.

In: Perspectives on Cognition and Action in Sport
Editors: D. Araújo, H. Ripoll and M. Raab

ISBN: 978-1-60692-390-0
© 2009 Nova Science Publishers, Inc.

Chapter 16

THE QUIET EYE AS A FACTOR IN DECISION MAKING IN MOTOR PERFORMANCE

Joan N. Vickers

Faculty of Kinesiology, University of Calgary, Canada

ABSTRACT

The quiet eye is defined within a unique gaze control framework derived from current research in sport. Rather than each motor task having unique gaze characteristics, research shows that the gaze is controlled in distinct ways within large three categories of motor tasks (targeting, interceptive timing, and tactical tasks). Within each of these categories (and their sub-categories) four factors affect the control of the gaze: the number of visuomotor workspaces over which the gaze must be controlled; the number and type of locations and objects that exist in the visuo-motor workspace; the spotlight of attention; and perception- action coupling, or the optimal timing of the gaze with the phases of the action. The quiet eye represents a moment of optimal perception-action coupling associated with higher levels of motor performance. The relationship of the quiet eye to attention, decision-making and the effectiveness of training is discussed. In the final part of the chapter a number of interpretations are presented that have been used to explain the quiet eye phenomenon along with some controversies and future directions.

INTRODUCTION: GAZE CONTROL IN MOTOR PERFORMANCE

During the performance of a motor task visual information is acquired through shifts of gaze that bring information onto the retina where neural processing begins. The retina converts light into energy that results in neural activation. The retina is lined with two types of visual receptors, called rods and cones. Cones are located within the fovea and are responsible for the detection of color and light and for resolving detail. The proportion of rods increases in the periphery of the retina, which is specialized for detecting low light and motion. The line of sight must be aligned with the fovea in order for an object or other location in space to be viewed clearly, with full acuity.

Due to the small area of the fovea, the area over which a performer is able to see with full acuity is actually very small, about 2 - 3° of visual angle (Coren, Ward, and Enns, 2004; Goldstein, 2007), or about the size of your thumb held out in front of you at arm's length. The visual angle indicates the size of the image on the retina, and it is determined by extending lines from the edges of the object or location as viewed in space through the lens to the fovea. Both the size of the object and its distance affects the visual angle, so an image seen at a distance will subtend a smaller visual angle on the fovea than one viewed from a shorter distance. Most athletes are surprised that they are only able to see clearly over such a small area. They must move their gaze purposely in order to see the different aspects of a scene with full acuity.

The total amount of light that stimulates from the eyes at any moment in time is called the visual field (Coren, Ward, and Enns, 2004). A line of gaze originates from each eye and passes through the right and left visual fields, intersecting in front in a line of gaze. The line of gaze is defined as "the absolute position of the eyes in space and depends on both eye position in orbit and head position in space" (Schmid and Zambarbieri, 1991, p. 229). Gaze control is defined as the process of directing the gaze to objects or events within a scene in real time and in the service of the ongoing perceptual, cognitive, and behavioral activity (Henderson, 2003). Visual discrimination begins immediately and is maintained steadily on the target or other locations even though the head is moving. This is achieved through the vestibular ocular reflex (VOR), which induces a movement of the eyes in the opposite direction of head movement. As the head moves in one direction, the VOR automatically compensates by producing a movement of the eyes in the opposite direction so that a stable image is viewed.

As one looks about a scene, the gaze alternates between periods of stability and periods when the gaze moves rapidly between objects and locations. Two types of gaze are found: a) those that are maintained on objects or locations for sufficient durations for information to be processed by the brain, and b) gaze that move so rapidly that information cannot be processed in a conscious way. Fixations and pursuit tracking are gaze that are stable enough to permit the processing of information. A fixation occurs when the gaze is held on an object or location within 3° of visual angle (or less) for 100 ms or longer (Carl and Gellman, 1987; Carpenter, 1988; Fischer, 1987; Optican, 1985). The 100 ms threshold is the minimum amount of time needed to recognize or become aware of external stimuli. Pursuit tracking occurs when the gaze follows a moving object, such as a ball or a person. The 100 ms threshold is used for pursuit tracking for the same reason it is used for fixations; it is only when the gaze is stabilized on the moving object or person that the individual is able to process the information provided by that object or person.

Saccades are rapid eye movements that bring the point of maximal visual acuity onto the fovea so that it can be seen with clarity. To see and comprehend a scene, we move our eyes rapidly from one fixated location or object to another using saccades. During saccades information is suppressed (Matin, 1974), but information is maintained across saccades using memory processes that produce a stable, coherent scene (Irwin, 1996; Irwin and Brockmole, 2004). We do not perceive the scene as blurred, nor are we able to see a new object that appears during a saccade; instead we perceive scenes that are cohesive and meaningful. Blinks occur when the eyelid covers the eyes and occludes visual information. Blinking is essential for refreshing the cornea and lens and for maintaining vision. During blinks, information is also suppressed (Volkmann, Riggs, and Moore, 1981).

SHIFTS OF GAZE AND SHIFTS OF ATTENTION

An important question is whether the locus of the gaze is also an indication of the focus of attention. Until recently it was difficult to make this association because of research showing it is very easy to dissociate the locus of the gaze from the locus of attention (eg. Posner, 1980). One often sees an athlete look in one direction while carrying out an action in another. But research now shows that when a performer saccades to a new location a shift in attention invariably occurs (Corbetta, 1998; Deubel and Schneider, 1996; Henderson, 2003; Kowler, Anderson, Dosher, and Blaser, 1995; Shepard, Findlay, and Hockey, 1986). Indeed, it is impossible to prevent this due to the close entrainment between the neural systems that control the gaze and those that shift attention. But it is important to stress that once the gaze has arrived at a new location, it does not mean that attention is always maintained at that location for the entire fixation duration. An athlete may covertly divert attention elsewhere even as they maintain a fixation at that location.

WHAT IS THE QUIET EYE?

Typically when a gaze study in sport is carried out all the gaze behaviours (fixations, pursuit tracking, saccades) to all the objects and locations in the visuo-motor workspace are analyzed in an effort to determine which affects performance. One gaze, called the quiet eye, has emerged as central to success in a wide range of sport tasks including golf (Vickers, 1992, 2004, 2007), basketball (Vickers, 1996; Oudejans et al., 2002, 2005), volleyball (Vickers and Adolphe, 1997; Adolphe, Vickers and LaPlante, 1997; McPherson and Vickers, 2004); darts (Vickers, Rodrigues and Edworthy, 2001); rifle shooting (Janelle et al., 2000; Vickers and Williams, 2007), billiards (Williams, Singer and Frehlich, 2002); table tennis (Rodrigues, Vickers and Williams 2002); ice hockey tactics (Martell and Vickers, 2004); tennis (Park, 2005); ice hockey goaltending (Panchuk and Vickers 2006); archery (Behan and Wilson, 2008). For a given motor task, the quiet eye is the final fixation or tracking gaze that is located on a specific location or object in the visuo-motor workspace within 3° of visual angle (or less) for a minimum of 100 ms. The onset of the quiet eye occurs prior to the final movement in the task. The offset of the quiet eye occurs when the gaze deviates off the object or location by more than 3° of visual angle (or less) for a minimum of 100 ms, therefore the quiet eye can carry through and beyond the final movement of the task. The quiet eye of elite performers is significantly longer than that of near-elite or lower skilled performers, meaning those who consistently achieve high levels have learned to fixate or track critical objects or locations for longer durations irrespective of the conditions encountered. The quiet eye onset of elite performers is invariably earlier; elite performers have found a way to see critical visual information earlier than near-elite and lower skilled performers and to process this information longer prior to making the final movement. Finally, the quiet eye of elite performers is of optimal duration being neither too long nor too short, but ideal given the constraints of the task being performed. A recent meta-analysis ($N = 42$ studies, 388 effect sizes) by Mann et al. (2007) has identified the quiet eye period as only one of three predictors of motor expertise. Effects were calculated for a variety of dependent measures (i.e., response accuracy, response time, number of visual fixations, visual fixation duration, and quiet eye period) using point-biserial correlation. The results showed that experts are better than non-experts in controlling the input of visual information with experts using fewer fixations of longer duration, including prolonged quiet eye periods, compared with non-experts.

In most studies elite or expert performers are compared to near-elites or lower skilled performers. Elite performers are defined as those who have attained the highest statistics in the task being investigated in competition as determined from external independent sources (such as league statistics), while near-elite performers compete in the same environment but have lower statistics, differences that are also echoed in the experimental setting. The overall goal of the elite–near-elite comparison is to hold constant as many of the biological (physiology, biomechanics) and environmental (training, coaching, type of competition) conditions as possible while exploring differences in the athletes' gaze, visual attention and decision making processes as the task is performed. The elite-near-elite comparison therefore includes individuals who have the prerequisite 10,000 hours of practice needed to attain expertise in a domain (Ericsson, Krampe, and Tesch-Römer, 1993; Helsen, Starkes, and Hodges, 1998). To replicate this amount of training within a laboratory context would be difficult if not impossible. Table 1 provides a summary of the quiet eye durations during selected targeting and interceptive timing tasks in which skill (elite, near-elite) and performance (hit, miss) differences were determined. In all cases the quiet eye duration was longer for elite than non-elite performers and also longer during successful trials, especially for the higher skilled performers.

Table 1. Quiet eye duration (ms or relative percent) of elite (E) and near-elite (NE) athletes during hits and misses in selected targeting and interceptive timing tasks (missing cells indicate the skill or performance group was not included)

Sport Tasks	Elite Hits	Elite Misses	Near-elite Hits	Near-elite Misses
Basketball free throw (Vickers, 1996)*	972	806	357	393
Basketball free throw (Vickers, 2007)**	448	304		
Basketball jump shot (Vickers, 2007)**	294	239		
Long distance rifle shooting (Janelle et al., 2000)	11500		5800	
Billiards hard shots (Williams et al., 2002)	1250	400	275	200
Archery (Behans et al., 2007) (relative %)			63%	50%
Biathlon rifle shooting (Vickers et al., 2007)	1762	600		
Ice hockey goaltending (Panchuk et al., 2006)	952	826		
Tennis return (Park, 2005)			13%	5%
Ice hockey defense (Martell et al., 2004) (relative %)	20%	17.5%		

* final movement defined as the first movement of the ball upward
** final movement defined as the final extension of the shooting arm at the elbow.

A GAZE CONTROL FRAMEWORK

Figure 1 presents a unique gaze control framework that has been derived from the current gaze research in sport (see Vickers, 2007 for an overview of studies). Rather than each motor task being viewed as having unique gaze characteristics, current research shows that the gaze is controlled in distinct ways within three large categories of motor tasks (targeting tasks, interceptive timing tasks, and tactical tasks). Within each of the categories (and sub-categories) shown in figure 1, four factors affect the control of the gaze: i) the number of visuomotor workspaces over which the gaze is controlled; ii) the number and type of objects and locations that exist in the visuomotor workspace; iii) the spotlight of attention; and 4) gaze and action coupling, or the optimal timing of the gaze with a specific phase of the motor behavior. At the bottom of figure 1 representative studies are presented with some including the quiet eye. As the number of gaze and quiet eye studies in each category and subcategory increases, there will most likely be changes in the framework. In the next section, each category and subcategory of gaze control is briefly explained.

GAZE CONTROL IN TARGETING TASKS

In targeting tasks the gaze fixates a target location in space prior to a precise aiming movement that propels an object away from the body toward the target. Within targeting tasks, there are three sub-categories of gaze control: to fixed targets (eg. basketball shooting; rifle shooting), to abstract targets (eg. golf putting, billiards), and to moving targets (e.g, passing to a receiver). Although the motor behaviors differ greatly in each case, the problem for the gaze and attention system is the same and that is to focus on the most critical part of the target and time the acquisition of external information so that there is an optimal coupling between the gaze and aiming movements leading to accurate performance.

When the target for the gaze and aiming is fixed in space, its location is stable and predictable in nature (e.g., basketball hoop, rifle target). Accuracy depends on fixating a specific location on the target before the aiming action is carried out. A high level of focus and concentration is required to perform well. When the target is abstract in nature there are often multiple targets for the gaze and attention and these are abstract in nature (e.g., golf putting on a sloped green, billiards). Precise sequences of fixations and saccades occur across distinct workspaces that must be accurately interpreted before aiming occurs. When the target is in motion (e.g., throwing to a receiver in football, passing to a teammate in soccer) multiple workspaces are involved and the gaze and attention systems are used to anticipate the movements of the receiver as well as a target location where the object is most easily and successfully caught.

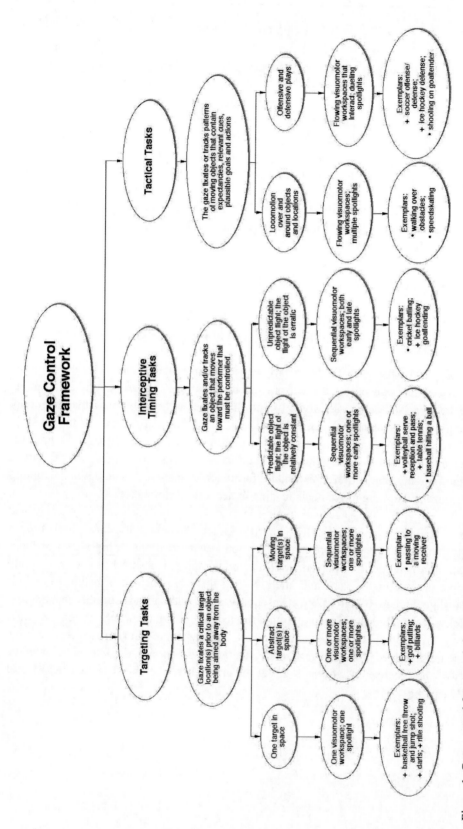

Figure 1. Gaze control framework for targeting, interceptive timing, and tactical tasks (used with permission Vickers, 2007, Human Kinetics Publishers).

GAZE CONTROL IN INTERCEPTIVE TIMING TASKS

In interceptive timing tasks, an object travels toward the performer usually at a very high speed (eg. hitting a ball, receiving a serve, goaltending) and the gaze and attention system functions within and across three sequential phases: object recognition, object tracking, and object control. During the object-recognition phase, fixation and pursuit tracking gaze are used to study the movements of the object and the individual propelling the object as it pitched, bowled, kicked, shot, or otherwise propelled toward the receiver. During the object-tracking phase, pursuit-tracking gaze are used to maintain the image of the object on the fovea in order to detect if it spins, accelerates or decreases in speed, changes direction; or is affected by wind, sun, or a host of other factors that can occur. During the object-control phase, the object is caught with the hand, kicked to a teammate, hit as in baseball or cricket, passed to a teammate as in volleyball, and so on. Many interceptive timing tasks in sport also require the object to be directed to a secondary target at contact. This target may be fixed in space, or it may be abstract or moving; therefore, the interceptive timing category may contains aspects of the gaze control found in the first category (targeting tasks).

There are two subcategories of gaze control in interceptive tasks and these depend on whether the flight of the object is predictable or unpredictable. Since objects can be propelled with either characteristic the performer has to develop two gaze control strategies—one that is used when the flight of the object is relatively constant, and the other when an object spins, slides, curves, or moves erratically as it approaches. When object flight is predictable, early fixation and/or tracking of the object (and person delivering the object) is usually sufficient to ensure accuracy, but when it is unpredictable, early fixation/tracking gaze is important, followed by a rapid saccade and late tracking of the object prior to reception.

GAZE CONTROL IN TACTICAL TASKS

Tactical tasks often subsume the gaze behaviors found in targeting and interceptive timing tasks but include a third category of gaze control, which requires reading complex patterns of moving objects. Think of reading the offense or defense in a team sport such as basketball or baseball, or reading a racecourse in skiing, kayaking, or speedskating. In each of these cases the motor behaviors differ greatly, but the problem for the gaze is always the same—to determine the overall relationship between moving objects and detect the most important cues present in an environment often under severe time constraints. Two subcategories are found: gaze control during locomotion (eg. walking, speedskating), and gaze control during set plays (eg. 1 vs 1, 3 vs 3, give and go; screen; zone, fast break).

FOUR GAZE CONTROL FACTORS

Within each of the categories (and sub-categories) shown in figure 1 there are four major factors that affect the control of the gaze and attention: the number of visuomotor workspaces over which the gaze is controlled; the number and type of locations and objects that exist in the perceptual-motor workspace; the location of critical cues and spotlight of attention; and gaze–action coupling, or optimally timing the gaze, spotlight of attention, and specific phases of the motor behavior. Each of these factors contains a level of decision-making that may be conscious or unconscious.

The first factor that affects the control of the gaze is the number of visuomotor workspaces over which the gaze must be controlled. The visuo-motor workspace is the spatial environment within which the performer's gaze and attention function. When the gaze of sport performers is recorded in real-world settings, it is soon apparent that they do not always look straight ahead and direct their gaze to one visuomotor workspace as is often the perspective found in visual-search studies where photo and videotape displays are used as stimuli; instead, they direct their gaze to multiple visual fields that can exist all about them depending on the task. Generally, the number of visuomotor workspaces increases from targeting tasks to interceptive tasks to tactical tasks. During targeting tasks with one fixed location (e.g., dart throwing or basketball), there is one visuomotor workspace (the board or basket). In abstract targeting tasks like golf or billiards there are often two or more visuomotor workspaces, and in interceptive timing tasks the number of visuomotor workspaces is sequential and dictated by the speed of the object, the size of the area over which the object travels, the relative position of the athlete and whether the flight of the object is predictable or not. Tactical tasks have the greatest number of visuomotor workspaces. In this case the gaze is controlled over both large and small spaces. For example, in ice hockey the athlete has to detect the movement of a puck that may be high or low, to the left or right, or in front of or behind the athlete, as well as moving quickly, slowly, or erratically (Martell and Vickers, 2004). As the number of visuomotor workspaces increases, decisions have to be made about how to control the gaze and attention given the goal of the athlete. A decision has to be made about which visuomotor workspace fields are most important and in which order information should be acquired prior to performing.

The second factor that affects gaze control is the number of locations and objects viewed when a task is performed. Objects are distinct from locations in that they are normally in motion, while locations are spatial and topographical in nature and do not have the capacity to move (Treisman, 1986b). Objects in sport include balls, pucks, shuttles, people (opponents, teammates, officials, coaches, judges, spectators, and all other persons), rackets, and mobile equipment. Locations range in complexity from a single target in space that is relatively easy for the gaze and attention system to locate and perceive (e.g., a fixed basketball hoop), to multiple target locations that provide more challenge for the gaze, attention, and motor systems (e.g., abstract targets), to whole fields of play, as found in tactical tasks.

The third factor that affects gaze control is the spotlight of attention. Within each visual field, one or more spotlights of attention are found. Optimal sport performance is defined not only by an ability to temporally control the gaze across visual fields, but also by an ability to define what is most important within and across each visuomotor workspace. Both bottom-up and top-down processes define the spotlight for the attention. During bottom-up processing, salient aspects of an object or location pop out and command the performer's gaze and attention. In top-down processing, the athlete applies previous expectancies and plans to how the environment is perceived. Elite performers function with both capacities, with novices being controlled more by bottom-up than top-down processes (Treisman, 1986a; Starkes and Ericsson, 2003).

The fourth and final factor that defines how the gaze is controlled is the timing of the gaze with the phases of the movement. Gaze research reveals that specific gaze locations are more important than others and that the ability to focus on the right object or location at the right time is a factor in both sport expertise and performance. The quiet eye is unique in identifying this moment within motor performance. Recall that for a given motor task the quiet eye is the final fixation or tracking gaze that is located on a specific location or object in the visuo-motor workspace, within 3° of visual angle (or less) for a minimum of 100 ms. The onset of the quiet eye occurs prior to the final movement in the task and the offset occurs when the gaze deviates moves off the object or location by more than 3° of visual angle (or less) for a minimum of 100 ms, therefore the quiet eye can carry through and beyond the final movement of the task. In effect, the quiet eye describes the optimal moment of attention and decision making in a motor task.

THE QUIET EYE AND DECISION MAKING

Part of being able to make good decisions in sport is to be spatially intelligent about accessing external information that is most useful. When we perform a motor skill we must decide the number of visuomotor workspaces over which we will control our gaze, the number and type of locations and objects that exist within the perceptual-motor workspace, the location of critical cues and the spotlight of attention or the area of the visual field that is most important (Newell and McDonald, 1994; Treisman, 1986a). Finally, we must control the timing of our movements to enable optimal perception-action coupling. To do this, fixations and tracking eye movements are directed to critical objects and locations that are of greatest use and this must occur at the most optimal moment within the movement. The quiet eye period represents the culmination of this process. When the location, onset, offset and duration of the quiet eye are all optimal then the resultant performance is superior; when any one of these dimensions is non-optimal then performance will be inferior.

QUIET EYE TRAINING

Since the quiet eye has been precisely defined in a number of sport tasks, then it has been trained in a number of studies (Adolphe and Vickers, 1997; Harle and Vickers, 2001; Oudejans et al., 2005; Vickers, 2007). Gopher (1993) states that in order for perceptual and attention training to be successful, a number of conditions must be met. First, it must be shown that control over the gaze and attention leads to better motor performance. Second, individuals must be identified who have difficulty controlling their gaze and attention in the task and grouped according to the depth and quality of training needed. Third, there must be evidence that these individuals have the ability to improve their gaze and attention with proper training. And fourth, it must be shown that the training of the gaze and attention contributes to improvements in motor performance in both the research and competitive setting. The first two conditions have been met by the many studies showing that elite sports performers possess unique gaze and quiet eye characteristics compared to those who are non-elite or near-elite. The third and fourth requirements have been met in sports studies where quiet eye training has led to improvements in gaze and motor performance in both experimental and field conditions.

Seven steps are involved in quiet eye training. i) It is first critical to carry out research in the task and identify the quiet eye characteristics of elite performers during successful trials. ii) Second, the athletes being trained are tested using a mobile eye tracker and motion analysis system while performing the task under conditions similar to step one. Their quiet eye location, onset, offset and duration is determined during successful and unsuccessful trials. iii) Third, using an expert model derived from step one, the athlete is taught how to control their gaze using a quiet eye location, onset, offset and duration similar to that found for expert performers on successful trials. Using a video model of an elite performer, the athlete is taught to reduce the frequency of fixation or tracking gaze to fewer locations with the final fixation, or quiet eye, being located on a critical location that is optimally timed with the final movement in the task. iv) Fourth, the athlete is then shown their own coupled gaze and motor data as recorded in step 2. An important part of this step is to ask the athlete questions about how their gaze and attention differs from or is similar to that of the elite prototype using frame-by-frame video comparison. Most athletes are adept at identifying the differences and many are surprised at how erratic their gaze and attention are compared to that of elite performers. v) The fifth step is to ask the athletes to make a decision about what aspect of their gaze they will change. During this decision-training phase it is important to encourage the athlete to concentrate only on adopting one or more of the quiet eye attributes *without* coaching any changes in their biomechanical technique. Studies have shown that this will change spontaneously later on as the athlete re-organizes the skill to accommodate the more effective control of the gaze and attention (Vickers and Adolphe, 1997; Vickers, 1996; Oudejans et al., 2005; Vickers, 2007). vi) The sixth step is to have the athlete practice in drills designed to promote the desired quiet eye focus. A variety of drills should be designed to train the quiet eye using a number of decision training tools that have strong support in the motor learning literature, including variable and random practice, bandwidth feedback, questioning and an external rather than an internal focus of attention (Vickers, Livingston, Umeris and Holden, 1999; Vickers, Reeves, Chambers and Martell, 2004; Vickers, 2006; Raab, Masters and Maxwell, 2005). vii) The seventh step is to measure the athletes' performance in competition over approximately six months and repeat as many of the steps above as is needed to improve the athlete's game performance.

Using the seven step quiet eye training process, Adolphe, Vickers and LaPlante (1997) found that elite Team Canada volleyball players receiving serves increased their quiet eye tracking on the ball from 640 ms to 1230 ms during pre and post quiet eye tests separated by 6 months. They also increased the accuracy in World Cup competitions from an average of 65% to 72% of successful receptions over a three-year period, which was significantly higher than for a 20 top World Cup receiver who did not receive quiet eye training. Similarly, Harle and Vickers (2001) found that elite basketball players significantly increased their quiet eye duration and accuracy by 12% in the experimental setting in season one, and in the second two, the team improved their games accuracy from 54% to 76%, an increase of 22%, which was significantly higher than two control teams who did not receive similar training. Oudejans et al., (2005) investigated the effects of visual control training on basketball jump shooting by expert male players who played in one of the top leagues in the Netherlands. All played either at the guard or forward position and were the best shooters on their teams. The goal of the training was to improve the athletes' pickup of information during the final period just before the ball release. Two methods were used over a training period of 8 weeks. The players wore the liquid-crystal goggles, which occluded the hoop so that players could see the hoop only during the final 350 ms before ball release. These goggles forced the players to attend maximally to the hoop during the short amount of time it was visible. In addition, the players were required to shoot from behind a screen set up at the free-throw line and placed at a height that blocked their view of the hoop. The players increased the duration of time the goggles were open from a mean of 353 ms before training to 386 ms following training. Shooting accuracy improved in games from a mean of 46 % before training to 61% following, for a mean increase of 15%. A matched control group, who did not receive similar training, did not improve their shooting but continued to shoot an average of 42%. The amount of improvement in these studies was considerable, and shows that athletes who are trained to improve control of their gaze, attention and decision making skills while physically training experience improvements in their performance that are much greater than when physical or psychological training are carried out alone.

INTERPRETATIONS OF THE QUIET EYE PERIOD

Although the quiet-eye period has been identified as a characteristic of skill and accuracy in a number of motor tasks interpreting what it means has provided a number of different perspectives. In the following section, four interpretations of the quiet-eye period are provided, first from cognitive neuroscience, second from ecological psychology and dynamic systems, third from sport psychology, and lastly from the Setchenov phenomenon.

COGNITIVE NEUROSCIENCE

The long quiet eye durations found in a wide range of motor tasks suggests that the complexity and precision of each task requires extended periods of neural organization. Posner and Raichle (1994) have identified three attention networks that may be central to this organization. The posterior orienting network is responsible for controlling the gaze and attention in space. This network, which is located in the parietal region, directs the gaze to specific locations of importance in a task. It is also responsible for preventing the disengagement of the gaze to other locations. Free-throw shooters, golfers, rifle shooters, and cricket players may use the posterior network to align their gaze to specific locations in space and maintain the gaze at a single location. The second network, the executive anterior executive network, is responsible for bringing into consciousness critical aspects of what is being fixated. The executive network interprets what is being viewed and imposes a higher-order understanding on the task based on past experience and knowledge. Skilled players possess a richer knowledge base and more refined rules than do lesser skilled performers, who are often unsure of what they need to see as they perform. The vigilance network is responsible for coordinating the posterior and anterior networks and preventing unwanted or distracting information from gaining access to the other networks during periods of sustained focus. The vigilance network is responsible for the sustained concentration seen in elite players, especially during pressure-filled games of long duration.

ECOLOGICAL PSYCHOLOGY AND DYNAMIC SYSTEMS

Researchers from an ecological or dynamic systems perspective argue that the quiet-eye period is not only a central aspect of the education of attention (Gibson, 1979; Oudejans, Koedijker, Bleijendaal, and Bakker, 2005; Oudejans, van de Langenberg, and Hutter, 2002) but also improves the biomechanics and self-organization of the skill. The quiet eye isolates information central to the intrinsic dynamics of skilled actions. Newell and McDonald (1994) and Williams, Janelle, and Davids (2004) describe the perceptual-motor workspace as the location where perception and action are specified; the quiet eye is a more specific location within this space. Quiet-eye analyses reveal the nature of the intrinsic dynamics between perception and action and the outcome of the skill. The quiet eye may also facilitate the orientation of the body and arm movements in space and allow for the execution of movements that are better attuned to the affordances and other constraints that are present. The quiet eye may also optimize optic flow and permit a better orientation of the performer relative to the target, object or tactical situation. Oudejans et al. (2002) explain that the quiet eye is a factor in basketball shooting because it permits the a continuous updating of the relation between shooter and rim, up until ball release, as this relation at ball release provides the best determination of force, direction and velocity needed to make a successful shot. This updating is not carried out by an internal feedback system but through the generation of dynamical relationships between the position of the athletes gaze in space and gaze relative to the target. The training study of Oudejans et al. (2005) also lends credence to this view. The shooting ability of basketball players increased significantly over that of a control group through the use of a screen that occluded the basket, enabling a longer quiet-eye period to be developed. Another equally plausible view within the ecological and dynamic systems perspective is that the quiet eye may act as a visual pivot (Ripoll, 1991; Williams, Davids, and Williams, 1999) that improves the egocentric orientation of the basketball player's body and arms to the target. In a recent attempt to replicate Oudejans et al's (2005) results, Vickers (2007) found that some players maintained a high level of accuracy when the hoop was screened completely so that only the top of the backboard could be seen. These players preserved their accuracy by selecting a unique quiet-eye location that was aligned with the hoop, such as the marks on the floor, letters in a sign above the hoop, or lines in the wall behind the hoop. As long as they refreshed this unusual but egocentric quiet-eye location, they were able to shoot accurately.

SPORT PSYCHOLOGY

Yet another perspective is offered from sport psychologists, who argue that the quiet-eye period is an index of focus and concentration. A recent biathlon study (Vickers and Williams, 2007) lends credence to this view in that only those shooters who increased their quiet-eye duration above that used in practice were able to overcome the normally debilitating effects of the high physiological workload, competitive pressure and anxiety. Using a long duration quiet eye also facilitates being in the zone, which many elite athletes report during optimal performance. It may be that when the same target location is fixated for a long duration, the stable quiet eye creates a feeling of emptiness because there is no change in external visual information. The gaze is stable and when the correct information is fixated processing can occur without as much change as when the gaze is constantly shifting to new locations.

COGNITIVE-PHYSIOLOGICAL FACILITATION: SETCHENOV PHENOMENON

A final perspective is related to the early work of Setchenov (1903/1935) who showed that individuals who were fatigued to exhaustion could do more physiological work when a diverting activity was used to direct attention to an external target or activity and away from internal processes. Subsequent studies have shown that directing attention externally to relevant task information improves performance in a wide variety of tasks, creates a greater effect with the eyes open compared to the eyes closed, and appears to be related to the reticular formations regulating physiological arousal and the perception of pain (Assmussen and Mazin, 1978a, 1978b; Valet, 2004). In combination, these studies suggest that maintaining a quiet eye focus that is optimal may insulate the athlete from the normally delimiting effects of extreme exercise, anxiety, and pain and allow them to maintain or even increase their level of performance. We (Vickers and Williams, 2007) found similar cognitive facilitation in a biathlon study where athletes who employed a longer duration quiet eye continued to perform well even after exercising at a *PO* level of 100% of their individual maximum, while athletes who had a lower duration choked under the combined weight of high pressure, high anxiety, and physiological arousal.

Regardless of the perspective taken, there is considerable research evidence showing that the quiet-eye period is a characteristic of higher levels of skill and accuracy in a wide range of motor tasks. Elite athletes find a way to get the visual information they need at just the right time during all playing conditions, and this is a factor why they perform so well. Gaze training studies also show that training the quiet eye improves attention and motor performance. Current evidence indicates that how the gaze functions in various motor tasks has a profound effect on the training of athletes and education of coaches. What is perhaps most exciting about the quiet eye and related gaze in action findings is that they allow the fields of perception, cognition and decision making in sport to move forward to more wide spread applied applications across multiple sports at all age and ability levels. Finally, although it is now possible to describe the location, onset, offset, and duration of the quiet eye in many sports tasks, there is still considerable research that needs to be done to provide a complete understanding of this intriguing phenomenon.

REFERENCES

Adolphe R., Vickers, J.N., and LaPlante, G. (1997). The effects of training visual attention on gaze behaviour and accuracy: A pilot study. *International Journal of Sports Vision. 4*(1), 28-33.

Assmussen, E., and Mazin, B. (1978a). Recuperation after muscular fatigue by "diverting activities." *European Journal of Applied Physiology, 38*, 1-8.

Assmussen, E., and Mazin, B. (1978b). A central nervous component in local muscular fatigue. *European Journal of Applied Physiology, 38*, 9-15.

Behan, M., and Wilson, M. (2008). State anxiety and visual attention: The role of the quiet eye period in aiming to a far target. *Journal of Sports Sciences, 26*(2), 207-215.

Carl, J., and Gellman, R. (1987). Human smooth pursuit: Stimulus-dependent responses. *Journal of Neurophysiology, 57*, 1446-1463.

Carpenter, R.H.S. (1988). *Movements of the eyes.* (2nd ed.). London: Pion.

Coren, S., Ward, L., and Enns, J.T. (2004). *Sensation and perception* (6th ed.). Hoboken, NJ: Wiley.

Corbetta, M. (1998). Frontoparietal cortical networks for directing attention and the eye to visual locations: Identical, independent, or overlapping. *Proceedings of the National Academy of Sciences, 95*, 831-838.

Deubel, H., and Schneider, W.X. (1996). Saccade target selection and object recognition: Evidence of a common attentional mechanism. *Vision Research, 36* (12), 1827-1837.

Ericsson, A., Krampe, R., and Tesch-Römer, C. (1993). The role of deliberate practice in the acquisition of expert performance. *Psychological Review. 100*(3), 363-306.

Fischer, B. (1987). The preparation of visually guided saccades. Review of Physiology, Biochemistry, *Pharmacology, 106*, 2-35.

Gibson, J.J. (1979). *The ecological approach to visual perception.* Boston: Houghton Mifflin.

Goldstein, E.B. (2007). *Sensation and Perception.* 7th Ed., Belmont, CA. Thompson Wadsworth.

Gopher, D. (1993). The skill of attention control: Acquisition and execution of attention strategies. In D. Meyer, and S. Kornblum (Eds.), *Attention and performance XIV* (pp. 299-322). Cambridge, MA: MIT Press.

Harle, S., and Vickers, J.N. (2001). Training quiet eye (QE) improves accuracy in the basketball free throw. *The Sport Psychologist, 15*, 289-305.

Helsen, W.F., Starkes, J.L., and Hodges, N.J. (1998). Team sports and the theory of deliberate practice. *Journal of Sport and Exercise Psychology, 20*, 12-34.

Henderson, J.M. (2003). Human gaze control during real-world scene perception. *Trends in cognitive science, 7*(11), 498-504.

Irwin, D. (1996). Integrating information across saccadic eye movements. Current Directions in Psychological Science. *Cambridge University Press, 5*, 94-100.

Irwin, D. and Brockmole, J.R. (2004). Suppressing where but not what. The effects of saccades on dorsal and ventral stream visual processing. *Psychological Science, 15*(7), 467-473.

Janelle, C.M., Hillman, C.H., Apparies, R.J., Murray, N.P., Meili, L., Fallon, E.A., and Hatfield, D.B. (2000). Expertise differences in cortical activation and gaze behavior during rifle shooting. *Journal of Sport and Exercise Psychology, 22*(2), 167-182.

Kowler, E., Anderson, E., Dosher, B., and Blaser, E. (1995). The role of attention in the programming of saccades. *Vision Research, 35*(13), 1897-1916.

McPherson S., and Vickers, J.N. (2004). Cognitive control in motor expertise [Special issue]. *International Journal of Sport and Exercise Psychology, 2*, 274–300.

Mann, D., Williams, A., and Ward P. (2007). Perceptual-Cognitive Expertise in Sport: A Meta-Analysis. *Journal of Sport and Exercise Psychology, 29*, 457-478.

Matin, E. (1974). Saccadic suppression: a review and an analysis. *Psychological Bulletin, 81*, 889 - 917.

Martell, S., and Vickers, J.N. (2004). Gaze characteristics of elite and near-elite ice hockey players. *Human Movement Science, 22*, 689-712.

Newell, K.M. and McDonald, P.V. (1994). Learning to coordinate redundant biomechanical degrees of freedom. In S. Swinnen, H. Heuer, J. Massion and P. Casaer (Eds.), *Interlimb coordination: Neural, dynamical, and cognitive constraints.* (pp. 517-531). New York: Academic Press.

Optican, L.M. (1985). Adaptive properties of the saccadic system. In A. Berthoz and M. Melvile-Jones (Eds.), *Adaptative mechanisms in gaze control: Facts and theories.* (pp. 71-79). New York: Elsevier Science.

Oudejans, R.R.D., van de Langenberg, R.W., and Hutter, R.I. (2002). Aiming at a far target under different viewing conditions: Visual control in basketball jump shooting. *Human Movement Science, 21*, 457-480.

Oudejans, R.R.D., Koedijker, J.M., Bleijendaal, I., and Bakker, F.C. (2005). The education of attention in aiming at a far target: Training visual control in basketball jump shooting. *International Journal of Sport and Exercise Psychology, 3*, 197-221.

Panchuk, D. and Vickers J.N. (2006). Gaze behaviours of goaltenders under spatial temporal constraints. *Human Movement Science. 25*(6), 733-752.

Park, S. (2005). The change of gaze behavior, eye-head coordination, and temporal characteristics of swing by task constraints in tennis volley strokes. International *Journal of Applied Sports Sciences, 17*(1), 51-70.

Posner, M.I. (1980). Orienting of attention. *Quarterly Journal of Experimental Psychology, 32*, 3-25.

Posner, M.I., and Raichle, M.E. (1994). *Images of mind.* New York, NY: Scientific American Library.

Raab, M., Masters, R. and Maxwell, J. (2005). Improving the 'how' and 'what' decisions of elite table tennis players. *Human Movement Science, 24*(3), 326-44.

Ripoll, H. (1991). The understanding-acting process in sport: The relationship between semantic and sensorimotor visual function. *International Journal of Sport Psychology, 22*, 221-243.

Rodrigues, S.T., Vickers, J.N. and Williams, A.M. (2002), Head, eye and arm co-ordination in table tennis: An exploratory study. *Journal of Sports Sciences, 20*(3), 171-186.

Schmid, R., and Zambarbieri, D. (1991). Strategies of eye–head coordination. In R. Schmid and D. Zambarbieri (Eds.), *Oculomotor control and cognitive processes.* (pp. 229-246). Amsterdam: Elsevier Science.

Setchenov, I.M. (1903/1935). Zur frage nach der Einwirkung sensitiver Reize auf die Muskelarbeit des Menchen. In *Selected works.* (pp. 246-240). Moscow.

Shepard, M., Findlay, J.M., and Hockey, R.J. (1986). The relationship between eye movements and spatial attention. *Quarterly Journal of Experimental Psychology, 38A*, 475-491.

Starkes, J.L., and Ericsson, K.A. (Eds.). (2003). *Expert performance in sports: Advances in research on sport expertise.* Champaign, IL: Human Kinetics.

Treisman, A. (1986a). Properties, parts and objects. In K.R. Boff, L. Kaufman, and J.P. Thomas (Eds.), *Handbook of perception and human performance.* (pp. 1-70). New York: Wiley.

Treisman, A. (1986b). Features and objects in visual processing. *Scientific American, 255*, 106-115.

Valet, M., Sprenger, T., Boecker, H., Willoch, F., Rummeny, E., Conttrad, B., Erhard, P. and Tolle, T.R. (2004). Distraction modulates connectivity of the cingulo-frontal cortex and the midbrain during pain – An fMRI analysis. *Pain, 109*, 399-498.

Vickers, J. N. (1992). Gaze control in putting. *Perception, 21*, 117-132.

Vickers, J.N. (1996). Visual control when aiming at a far target. *Journal of Experimental Psychology: Human Perception and Performance. 2*(22), 342-354.

Vickers, J.N. (2004). The quiet eye: it's the difference between a good putter and a poor one, here's proof. *Golf Digest, January*, 96-101.

Vickers, J.N. (2006). Gaze of Olympic speed skaters while skating at full speed on a regulation Oval. Perception-action coupling in a dynamic performance environment. *Cognitive Processing, 7*(1), 102-105.

Vickers, J.N. (2007). *Perception, cognition and decision training: The quiet eye in action.* Champaign, IL. Human Kinetics Publishers.

Vickers, J.N., and Adolphe, R.A. (1997). Gaze behaviour during a ball tracking and aiming skill. *International Journal of Sports Vision. 4*(1), 18-27.

Vickers, J.N., Livingston, L., Umeris S., and Holden, D. (1999). Decision Training: The effects of complex instruction, variable practice and reduced delayed feedback on the acquisition and transfer of a complex motor skill. *Journal of Sport Sciences. 17*, 357-367.

Vickers, J.N., Reeves, M.A., Chambers, K.L., and Martell, S.T. (2004). Decision training: cognitive strategies for enhancing performance. In A.M. Williams and N.J. Hodges (Eds), *Skill Acquisition in Sport: Research, Theory and Practice.* (p. 103-120). London: Routledge.

Vickers, J.N. and Williams. A.M. (2007). Performing under pressure: The interactive effects of physiological arousal, cognitive anxiety and gaze control in elite biathlon shooters. *Journal of Motor Behavior. 39*(5), 381-394.

Volkmann, F., Riggs, L., and Moore, R. (1981). Eyeblinks and visual suppression. *Science, 207*, 900-902.

Williams, A.M., Davids, K., and Williams, J.G. (1999). *Visual perception and action in sports.* London: E and FN Spon.

Williams, A.M., Janelle, C.M., and Davids, K. (2004). Constraints on the search for visual information in sport. *International Journal of Sport and Exercise Psychology, 2*(3), 301-318.

Williams, A.M., Singer, R.A., and Frehlich, S. (2002). Quiet eye duration, expertise, and task complexity in a near and far aiming task. *Journal of Motor Behavior, 34*, 197-207.

In: Perspectives on Cognition and Action in Sport
Editors: D. Araújo, H. Ripoll and M. Raab

ISBN: 978-1-60692-390-0
© 2009 Nova Science Publishers, Inc.

Chapter 17

THE ROLE OF ATTENTION AND MOVEMENT VARIABILITY IN THE PRODUCTION OF SKILLED PERFORMANCE

William M. Land and
Gershon Tenenbaum
Florida State University, USA

ABSTRACT

The production of skilled performance has been examined by a multitude of scientific disciplines and theoretical perspectives. To this extent, advances in the area of cognitive science have identified the role of attention as being vital to expert performance. Additionally, human movement sciences have recognized the important role that movement variability can play in securing optimal performance. However, thus far, findings from the various disciplines have gone largely unintegrated. In reviewing the literature connecting attention and movement variability to skilled performance, this chapter highlights recent findings supporting a link between the roles of attention and variability in the motor system. Specifically, findings presented in this chapter suggest that optimal attentional focus may facilitate functional and compensatory movement variability. In addition, examination of the effects of pressure on attention and movement variability offers further insights into this inter-relationship. Such investigations illuminate the need for further synthesis between various domains, which ultimately can help ensure a more unified theoretical framework for better elucidating skilled performance.

INTRODUCTION

As Tiger Woods swings a golf club, the multiple dimensions of human performance (i.e., emotional, physiological, cognitive, and biomechanical) are harmoniously integrated in the production of skilled movement. The study of expert performance has long been examined by multiple scientific disciplines, each with their own unique level of analysis. However, up to this point, there has been little research that has attempted to illuminate the interaction between cognitive and human movement systems in the production of skilled movement. As a result, an interdisciplinary approach to human performance may prove fruitful.

Specifically, cognitive science has identified the role of attention as being vital to expert performance (e.g., Wulf, 2007). Similarly, new research in the area of motor control and biomechanics has shed light on the functionality of movement variability (e.g., Davids, Bennett, and Newell, 2006). Although expert performance has been studied at various levels of analyses, there is a disconnect between the multiple scientific domains. A firm link between the role of attention and variability in the motor system has yet to be adequately established. Investigation of this relationship may provide insight into the mechanisms and conditions that support superior performance, while also providing new directions in the theoretical underpinnings of motor control. Therefore, the purpose of this chapter is to provide a synthesis of the research on attention and movement variability, and illuminate the need for more interdisciplinary research on skilled performance.

THE ROLE OF ATTENTION IN MOTOR PERFORMANCE

In recent years, information-processing theories have been at the forefront of expertise research (Hodges, Starkes, and MacMahon, 2006). As such, attention has played a fundamental role in the understanding of learning and human performance. The role of attention in regards to skilled performance is based on the assumption that successful task performance is dependent on attending to certain relevant information, while ignoring others (Beilock and Gray, 2007; Lewis and Linder, 1997). As a result, an individual's focus of attention can have a significant impact on task execution (Wulf, 2007). In recent years, a considerable amount of research has been conducted to delineate the effects of different types of attentional focus on performance. To this extent, a majority of the research on attention and performance has mirrored the dominant theories of skill acquisition (Anderson, 1982; Fitts and Posner, 1967).

Early in learning, novices must commit large resources of attention and working memory to the components of skill execution. At this point in learning, skill execution is dependent on unintegrated task control structures held in working memory and attended to in step-by-step fashion. This controlled step-by-step processing results in slow, attention demanding, serial, and error prone movements that are typical of novice performance (Beilock, Bertenthal, McCoy, and Carr, 2004; Beilock, Carr, MacMahon, and Starkes, 2002; Gray, 2004; Lidor, Reeves, and Tenenbaum, submitted; Schmidt and Lee, 1999; Schneider and Shiffrin, 1977). However, as ability increases, less demands are placed on attentional resources resulting in tasks that are performed quicker, smoother, and with less effort. At this point, the task becomes 'automatised' to some degree freeing up attentional resources, which can be devoted to other processes. Once a task has become highly automated, skill execution becomes governed by fast, procedural knowledge that runs largely outside of attention (Fitts and Posner, 1967). In fact, research has shown that asking experts to refocus attention on the details and control of movement can negatively impact performance (Beilock and Carr, 2001; Beilock et al., 2002; Beilock et al., 2004; Beilock and Gray, 2007; Jackson, Ashford, and Norsworthy, 2006; Kimble and Perlmuter, 1970).

In order to delineate the relationship between attention and performance, numerous studies have attempted to manipulate attentional focus in order to study its impact on performance. One such study that attempted to define the proper attentional focus for optimal learning and performance was conducted by Wulf, Höß, and Prinz (1998). Wulf et al. examined learning and performance on a ski simulator using different instructional sets designed to draw attention to or away from skill execution. One set of instructions used to induce an "internal" focus (i.e., the movement of the body) required participants to pay attention to the movements of their outer foot as it exerted force on a ski simulator. A second instructional set was used to induce an "external" focus (i.e., the effects of one's movement on the environment), which required participants to pay attention to the movement of the ski simulator itself. A third group of participants were given no attentional focus instructions. Results revealed that the external focus group showed greater improvements in learning and performance on the ski simulator task compared to both the internal and control conditions. Follow-up retention tests also revealed that the immediate advantages of performing under external focus appeared to be relatively robust over time. These results highlight the importance attentional focus can have on performance.

While attention and performance have been explicitly linked, the nature of this relationship appears to be dependent upon levels of skill. To this end, Beilock et al. (2004) differentiated the attentional control structures governing performance on a golf-putting task across differing skill levels. In the study, attentional focus was manipulated through the use of secondary tasks (i.e., an additional cognitive task performed simultaneously with the primary task), which were designed to draw attention to or away from task execution. Novice and expert golfers performed a putting task under both a skill-focused and a distracting secondary task condition. The skill-focused condition was designed to draw attention towards the step-by-step components of skill execution (e.g., monitoring the motion of the putting stroke), while the distracting secondary task condition was designed to draw attention away from skill execution (e.g., tone monitoring). The results suggested that performance of novices and experts are governed by different cognitive control structures, and that task performance is dependent upon proper attentional focus. Novice performance was harmed by the demands placed on attentional resources by the distracting task. Novices, who require dedicated attention to controlling skill execution, do not have adequate working memory capacity to attend to both the skill execution and the extraneous secondary task, thus performance is impaired. Experts, however, who do not require constant online attention, have adequate attentional resources to meet the demands of the extraneous secondary task without compromises to performance. Under skill-focused attention, however, the opposite performance results were seen. Novices who require attention to the processes of skill execution were benefited by the addition of the skill-focused task, which acted to increase inward attentional focus. The experts, however, showed performance decrements due to attention being forced on the components of task execution. The shift in attention to the processes of skill execution harmed performance through a disruption in the automatic control processes underlying expert performance. Thus, expert performance appears to be supported by an external focus of attention, whereas, novice performance appears to benefit from internal foci of attention.

In a similar experiment, Gray (2004) examined the effects of attending to extraneous information on a baseball-batting task across levels of expertise. Similar to previous studies, Gray assessed the impact of an extraneous secondary task (i.e., tone monitoring) and a skill-focused secondary task (i.e., identifying direction of the bat at ball contact) on baseball swing kinematics. Consistent with previous findings, the results suggested significant difference in the attentional mechanisms governing expert and novice performance. Expert performance was unharmed during the extraneous secondary task condition designed to draw attention away from performance, but was impaired under skill-focused conditions. Conversely, novice performance was unimpaired by performance during the skill-focused condition, but suffered performance decrements under extraneous secondary task performance. These findings are in accordance with skill acquisition theories stating that expert performance runs off control structures largely outside of working memory, freeing up attentional resources to attend to other environmental stimuli (Fischman and Oxendine, 2001). Novice performance, however, requires constant online attention to skill execution, thus skill-focused attention appears to aid performance.

More recently, Castaneda and Gray (2007) examined the proper attentional focus for baseball players during baseball batting. Similar to the previous studies, secondary tasks were used to manipulate direction of attention. Results revealed that experts benefited most from attention directed externally to the effects of their movements (in this case, the baseball leaving the bat). In accordance with common-coding theory of perception and action (see Prinz, 1990), actions are believed to be coded in terms of their desired outcome or perceivable effects. In this regard, focus on the external effects of movement is believed to benefit skilled performance through strengthening the connection between the perceivable effects and the action. In contrast, when experts direct attention to the skill execution itself, the attempts to consciously control movement interferes with automatic motor control processes that coordinate and organize movements (McNevin, Shea, and Wulf, 2003; Poolton, Maxwell, Masters, and Raab, 2006). In addition, for novice performance, Castaneda and Gray (2007) found that attention directed to the components of skill execution aided performance, whereas attention directed externally to the environment was detrimental to performance. Again, these findings are in accordance with skill acquisition theories, which state that early in learning, skill execution is held in working memory and attended to in step-by-step fashion. Thus, skill-focused attention appears to facilitate optimal performance in novices.

The role of attention is believed to be in part responsible for the expert advantage (Hodges, Starkes, and MacMahon, 2006). Recent research on attention has highlighted that proper allocation of attentional resources are explicitly linked to optimal outcomes. To this extent, traditionally, the cognitive sciences have primarily focused on outcome measures of performance in regards to examining the impact of attention. Alone, outcome performance is inadequate to describe the numerous processes that are integrated in the production of skilled performance (Pijpers, Oudejans, and Bakker, 2005). Performance outcomes can indicate what happens, but not necessarily how and why. Thus, skilled performance must be studied at various behavioral and theoretical levels (Collins, Jones, Fairweather, Doolan, and Priestley, 2001).

THE ROLE OF MOVEMENT VARIABILITY

The role of variability is a central issue in motor control. Traditionally, movement variability has been seen as a problem for the control and coordination of motor movements

(Newell and Corcos, 1993b). With skilled performance often characterized by low variability in outcomes, it naturally followed that movement patterns underlying performance were assumed to be equally as consistent (Glazier, Wheat, Pease, and Bartlett, 2006). As a result, many teachers and coaches considered consistency essential for skilled performance, and thus overemphasized consistent, stereotyped, and repeatable movements (Handford, 2006). To this extent, movement variability, or differences in instances of the same basic movement, has become viewed as dysfunctional resulting from error and random fluctuations (i.e., noise) in the motor system (Glazier et al., 2006; Newell and Corcos, 1993b).

Early research in the area of movement variability tended to focus on the end result of performance rather than the quality of the movement itself (Newell and Corcos, 1993b; Weinberg and Hunt, 1976). Initially, variability was studied only in terms of result outcomes (Müller and Sternard, 2004; Newell and Corcos, 1993b). This research was dominated by studies employing movements defined by a single degree of freedom. From these movements, variability in outcomes was assumed to reflect underlying variability in the motor system (Glazier et al., 2006; Newell and Corcos, 1993b). However, new advances in technology has allowed for a reconsideration of the role of variability. Specifically, advances in computer-driven motion analysis systems have allowed for movement dynamics to become a primary focus of study rather than inferred through outcome measures (Newell and Corcos, 1993b).

More recent research examining the movement dynamics of skilled performance has indicated that variability can be functional and can play a clear role in attaining consistent outcomes (Handford, 2006). Research has revealed that a central ability of the motor system is to achieve consistency without zero variability. In fact, variability of results can reach almost zero, while variability in execution can remain high (Müller and Sternard, 2004). As such, there does not appear to be a linear relationship between execution variability and variability of results. Thus, movement variability is not a single determinant of result variability (Glazier et al., 2006; Müller and Sternard, 2004). Rather, it is the qualitative nature of movement variability relative to the task goal that is essential rather than the amount of variability itself (Hodges, Starkes, and MacMahon, 2006). Therefore, movement variability must be interpreted in relation to performance outcome.

Aiding in the interpretation of movement variability, new theoretical approaches (i.e., dynamic systems and ecological psychology) have emerged that provide an alternative framework for understanding variability in motor movements. From these perspectives, motor variability is often viewed as functional and compensatory, whereas, previous more cognitive theories of motor control (i.e., motor programs, mental schemas) tended to view movement variability as dysfunctional (i.e., motor error). Under a dynamical systems framework, movement patterns emerge through neuromuscular synergies and self-organizational processes, rather than emanating from some higher-order cognitive agent (Glazier et al., 2006; Kelso, 1995; Vickers, 2007). As such, movement variability affords the sensorimotor system the adaptability and flexibility needed for the stability of coordinated movements. Similarly, ecological psychology (see Gibson, 1979) stresses the compensatory role of variability through ongoing interaction between sensory systems and the environment. The central idea being that perception guides action, which in turn produces additional perceptual information that can be used to further attune motion (Buekers, Montagne, and Laurent, 1999; Savelsbergh, van der Kamp, and Rosengren, 2006). In turn, this "perception-action cycle" results in functional variability (i.e., variability that is beneficial to outcome performance) through the ongoing modulation of movements. Thus, variability of the motor system is regarded as movement fluctuations rather than movement error (Newell and Corcos, 1993a).

Numerous studies have illuminated the functional nature of variability for skilled performance. While investigating skilled marksmen on a pistol shooting task, Arutyunyan, Gurfinkel, and Mirskii, (1968) observed that increased joint movements accompanied reductions in the spatial variability of the pistol barrel. In contrast, these compensatory arm movements were not evident in novice marksmen, and resulted in increased aiming error. Thus, variability can be compensatory and functional, when movement fluctuations in one parameter are compensated for by fluctuations in another. Compensatory variability is one of the distinguishing features of goal-directed behavior in that a tight fit between the current state of the action and the outcome goal can be created through ongoing modulation and compensation of movements (Dupuy, Mottet, and Ripoll, 2000; Stretch, Bartlett, and Davids, 2000). Therefore, skilled performance may exhibit increased functional variability resulting from compensatory mechanisms in the production of skilled performance.

Compensatory variability has been observed in a number of different skilled actions. Bootsma and van Wieringen (1990) found that during execution of a table tennis forehand, experts modulated and fine-tuned a forehand drive up until the point of contact. Reductions in variability over the course of the movement suggested that the initial increased variability was functional, and represented compensatory movements resulting in reduced variability at the point of contact. More recently, Katsumata (2007) observed functional modulation in the skill of baseball hitting. Specifically, Katsumata found that the temporal variability of successive motion phases was functionally flexible, and that movement error in one phase can be compensated for during subsequent motion phases. The resulting compensatory modulation produced reductions in temporal variability of the baseball swing up until bat-ball contact. These findings suggest that the baseball swing is not a fixed monotonous movement, but flexible so as to compensate and adapt to the task constraints (i.e., fast or slow pitch) in order to ensure optimal performance.

RELATIONSHIP BETWEEN ATTENTION AND MOVEMENT VARIABILITY

Although extensive research has examined attention and movement variability in relation to outcomes, less is known about the inter-relationship between the two in the production of skilled performance. New theoretical perspectives on motor control and functional/compensatory variability point to movements relying on information from the environment in the coordination of movements (i.e., perception-action cycle). To this extent, proper allocation of attentional focus would appear to be vital in aiding perception-action coupling. Establishing a firm link between attention and functional variability may help identify situations and conditions that facilitate optimal motor system functioning.

Providing insight into this relationship, Gray (2004) identified changes in the kinematics of a baseball swing under varying attentional foci. Similar to previous studies examining the affects of attentional focus, Gray directed attentional focus in novice and skilled baseball players through the use of a dual task paradigm. As established by prior research, experts perform optimally under external focus, whereas novice performance requires focus directed towards skill execution. Findings by Gray support this contention while also establishing a relationship between attention and kinematics. Under non-optimal (i.e., skill-focused) attentional focus, expert performance was degraded accompanied by increased dysfunctional variability (i.e., variability in movement dynamics that leads to increased variability in outcome) in the relative timing of multiple phases in a baseball swing. Similarly, novice performance was impaired under extraneous dual-task constraints, and exhibited increased variability in swing kinematics. The authors suggested that the degradation in performance under non-optimal attentional focus was partially due to increased dysfunctional variability. More specifically, a return to conscious processing under skill-focused attention resulted in expert performers relying heavily on working memory, subjecting performance to increased amounts of noise from delays in reaction times and memory retrieval. While not forwarded by the authors of the study, an alternative explanation for the relationship between attention and movement variability could be that the non-optimal attentional focus did not provide access to the appropriate environmental information, which could be used in aiding action perception-coupling. As a result, performance was degraded and increases in dysfunctional variability were seen. Regardless, the findings of Gray provide a glimpse of the interconnectedness of variability and attentional focus.

More recently, the work of Land and Tenenbaum (submitted) suggests that proper allocation of attentional resources under pressure may aid compensatory mechanisms in skilled performers. During a putting task, skilled and novice golfers performed a series of putts under control and secondary task conditions designed to aid external focus. The externally focused secondary tasks were employed to facilitate optimal attentional focus in experts, and prevent a return to conscious processing of motor actions under pressure. Specifically, the two secondary tasks consisted of a discrete sport-relevant secondary task (i.e., monitoring clubhead-ball contact) and a continuous non-relevant secondary task (i.e., random letter generation task). In order to measure performance, both a product-oriented and a process-oriented approach were adopted, which provided a more comprehensive account of skilled performance under optimal focus. Outcome performance was measured in terms of final ball locations, while movement variability was measured using a computer-driven motion analysis system designed specifically to analyze key parameters of the putting stroke deemed essential for performance. Data generated from the motion analyses were used to derive standard deviations (SDs) in movement patterns from trial-to-trial. Subsequently, the SD in the movement parameters of the putting stroke were examined across the control and secondary task conditions. Variability was thus determined by the average squared distances from the mean in each parameter within each subject's trials.

Interestingly, findings revealed that under both external focus manipulations, skilled performance under pressure improved accompanied by increased variability in key kinematic parameters associated with the putting stroke. The increased movement variability in the relevant aspects of the putting stroke along with improved outcome performance suggested that the optimal attentional focus brought about by the secondary tasks facilitated functional (i.e., beneficial to outcome performance) and compensatory mechanisms that aided performance. Although, increased variability was seen in select parameters, not all parameters exhibited this same rise in variability. Instead, temporal ordering of the kinematic parameters revealed the largest variability to be associated with initial movements in the putting stroke, but decreasing up until the point of clubhead-ball contact (see figure 1). We suggest that the change in kinematic variability over the course of the movement indicates functional modulation of the putting stroke, which occurred to ensure superior performance. Under optimal conditions, skilled participants may make minute adjustments during the putting stroke to account for inconsistencies in the initial setup condition or any unexpected perturbations. Thus, the increased movement variability seen under both secondary tasks may have been functional in nature. Furthermore, the continuous nature of the non-relevant secondary task appeared to further facilitate compensatory mechanisms compared to the discrete sport-relevant secondary task. The continuous nature of the non-relevant secondary task was believed to further eliminate any residual skill-focused attention through an ongoing cognitive demand.

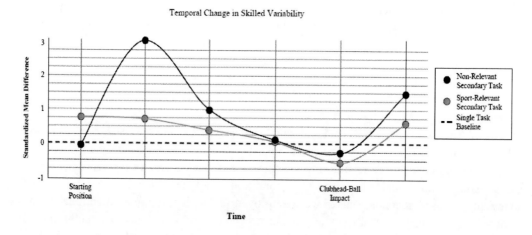

Figure 1. Temporal change in variability for skilled participants under sport-relevant and non-relevant secondary task conditions using single task variability as a baseline.

As for novice participants, performance under external focus manipulations, which is non-optimal for beginners, did not impact outcome performance, but resulted in less kinematic variability (see figure 2).

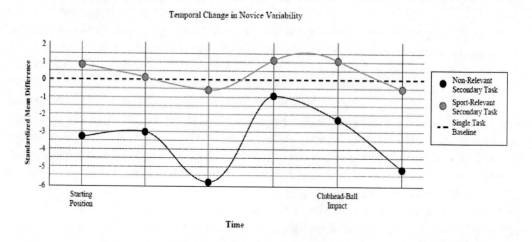

Figure 2. Temporal change in variability for novice participants under sport-relevant and non-relevant secondary task conditions using single task variability as a baseline.

We suggest that the increased task demands brought about by the secondary tasks may have resulted in an attempt to freeze additional degrees of freedom in order to reduce task complexity. Such a strategy would result in rigidly locking and coupling of the joints (e.g., the wrist, elbow, shoulder, etc.), which could potentially decrease movement variability. Overall, these findings highlight the relationship between attention and compensatory variability, and suggest that attentional focus may be vital to facilitating compensatory mechanisms in the motor system.

Studies examining the effects of attention on postural sway also illuminate the potential relationship between attention and movement variability. Examining the effects of external-focus instructions and feedback on a balance task (i.e., stabilometer), Shea and Wulf (1999) observed that participants in an externally focused group outlearned participants in an internally focused group. In addition, under external focus, participants produced smoother movements while balancing compared to the internal focus group. The authors suggested that the movement of the stabliometer platform might reveal characteristics of movement production. Under external focus, participants were believed to be dynamically incorporating more degrees of freedom resulting in smoother motion, whereas, under internal focus, participants may shift attention to skill execution resulting in a reduction in the number of degrees of freedom producing less fluid movements.

Similarly, Vuillerme and Nafati (2007) directly assessed the impact of attention on postural sway. Specifically, participants were instructed to stand as immobile as possible on a flat solid surface under one of two attentional focus conditions. Under the control condition, participants were given no further instructions regarding attentional focus. However, under the attention condition, participants were told to deliberately focus attention on their body sways and consciously attempt to intervene in postural control. Findings revealed increased neuromuscular activity in the leg muscles controlling posture under deliberate attempts to reduce sway. Furthermore, the increased neuromuscular activity associated with the "attention condition" represented less efficiency in controlling posture. The adverse effects of attention directed towards controlling movement were suggested to have disrupted automatic control processes reducing overall efficiency in postural control.

Findings from the previous studies illuminate the relationship between attention and movement variability. However, the exact nature of the variability observed appears to be in large part dependent on the kinematic variables examined. Whether optimal attentional focus results in increased or decreased variability will depend on what aspect of the movement is observed (Beilock and Gray, 2007; Gray 2004). To this extent, it is the qualitative nature of the variability in regards to the movement goal that will determine whether optimal attentional foci result in functional or dysfunctional variability (Hodges, Starkes, and MacMahon, 2006).

Pressure, Emotions, and Attention/Movement Variability

To further clarify the inter-relationship between these mediating components, additional insight may be derived from research examining the impact of anxiety and the associated changes in attentional focus and movement variability. Under pressure and anxiety, research has demonstrated that alterations occur in both attentional resources and motor functioning. These parallel alterations may highlight a link between the two subsystems.

Research on the mechanisms underlying *choking under pressure* have emphasized the impact performance pressure can have on the allocation of attentional resources. *Explicit monitoring theories* argue that performance pressure can impact performance through heightening self-consciousness, which leads to an increased focus on the step-by-step processes of skill execution (Gray, 2004). This shift in attention to the details of movement disrupts the automaticity of well-learned skills resulting in performance breakdown (i.e., choking; Baumeister, 1984; Beilock and Gray, 2007; Kimble and Perlmuter, 1970; Masters, 1992). In other words, under pressure, task importance becomes more salient, thus more attention is given to ensuring the correctness of skill execution.

Supporting this contention, Gray (2004) demonstrated that performance pressure facilitated performance on a skill-focused secondary task. If the assertions made by explicit monitoring theories are correct, performance pressure should increase internal skill-focused attention. Thus, performance on a secondary task requiring internal focus should be facilitated. Indeed, findings revealed that performance of a skill-focused secondary task was facilitated under pressure compared to an extraneous secondary task. These results support explicit monitoring accounts of choking, suggesting that pressure alters the deployment of attentional resources leading to non-optimal internal focus and a return to more conscious attempts to control skill execution.

Likewise, research has identified various biomechanical changes associated with stress and anxiety (e.g., Beuter and Duda, 1985; Collins et al., 2001; Pijpers, Oudejans, Holsheimer, Bakker, 2003; Weinberg and Hunt, 1976). Specifically, anxiety has been linked to movements that are less smooth, less efficient in terms of time and energy, and less variable (e.g., Beuter and Duda, 1985; Pijpers et al., 2003; Weinberg and Hunt, 1976). In a study examining British soldiers on a stepping task, Collins et al. (2001) found alterations in movement patterns across high- and low-anxiety conditions. Under high-anxiety, reductions in movement variability were seen in the rigid coupling of the hip, knee, and ankle joints. Alternatively, performance under low-anxiety revealed movements less limited and reflecting greater degrees of variability. Pijpers et al. (2003) found similar findings while investigating novice rock climbers. While climbing high on the wall, participants experienced increased levels of anxiety accompanied by changes in movement behavior. Specifically, movements were longer and less fluent resulting in less overall efficiency. Finally, Beuter and Duda (1985) reported anxiety related changes in the coordination patterns of children on a stepping task. Under high-anxiety conditions, children produced movements that were less efficient and smooth when compared to performance under low-anxiety. Findings such as these provide a glimpse of the impact performance pressure can have on human movement processes.

Perhaps the most prominent theory used to account for anxiety's impact on performance is centered on the idea of "freezing degrees of freedom" (Beilock and Gray, 2007). First proposed by Bernstein (1967), the degrees of freedom (dof) problem is concerned with how the body controls the numerous separate and independent elements (e.g., wrist, elbow, joints, etc.) in the production of coordinated motion. According to Bernstein (1967), and later Vereijken, van Emmerick, Whiting, and Newell (1992), early learning is typified by attempts to "freeze" extraneous dof in order to reduce task complexity. As such, novice motor movements appear rigid, uncoordinated, and stiff (Vickers, 2007). However, as skill develops through practice, novices begin to "thaw" or release previously frozen dof, ultimately learning to exploit the built-in mechanical-inertial properties of the limbs (Schmidt and Lee, 1999). As a result, motor performance becomes smoother, faster, and more fluent. Under pressure, however, Bernstein postulated that skilled performers might attempt to "re-freeze" dof in an attempt to reduce task complexity. As a result, movement execution regresses and parallels earlier stages of skill acquisition (Pijpers et al., 2003). The return to novice "freezing" strategies produces motor movements typified by motions that are rigid and jerky.

Examination of the kinematic changes associated with anxiety and pressure mirror to a great extent the alterations in the cognitive processes associated with pressure induced performance failure. In each case, pressure and anxiety appear to regress individuals to a previous lower level of skill functioning (Beilock and Carr, 2001). Cognitive theories of choking under pressure state that performance pressure disrupts automaticity through a return to earlier levels of conscious processing. Human movement theories, similarly, propose that pressure and anxiety revert experts back to previous novice "freezing" strategies (Bernstein, 1967). These similarities bear witness to the parallels and interactions that each subsystem has with one another.

CONCLUSION

Skilled performance has been examined at length from various theoretical and behavioral levels. Thus far, the various analyses have mainly been considered independently. However, understanding the inter-relationships between the various dimensions of human performance will help afford a unified theoretical framework for better elucidating skilled performance. To this end, the relationship between the role of attention and movement variability has gone largely unexplored.

Cognitive science has identified the role of attention as being fundamental to skilled performance. Specifically, the proper allocation of attention towards the external effects of movements has been shown to facilitate superior performance in experts. Likewise, more human movement perspectives have noted the functional and beneficial role that variability can play in producing optimal outcomes. According to ecological psychology and dynamical systems perspective, motor variability plays an adaptive role in which movement patterns can adapt and become more attuned to alterations in the environment and task demands (Katsumata, 2007). As a result, skilled movement is realized through coordination and ongoing modulation of movement patterns to achieve a given motor task. Recent interdisciplinary research has highlighted the potential relationship attention shares with variability in the motor system. Early findings suggest that proper allocation of attentional resources may facilitate functional and compensatory variability. Additionally, improper attentional focus may be accompanied by dysfunctional alterations in the movement dynamics underlying performance. These initial findings provide a glimpse to the interactions and the need for further integration of interdisciplinary research.

Although attention and movement variability have both been explicitly linked to the production of skilled performance, the underlying theoretical accounts governing the role of attention and variability in the motor system are largely contradictory. Traditional cognitive science, from which the role of attention is derived, is based on information-processing accounts of performance. From this perspective, internal representations (i.e., motor programs, mental representations) are thought to contain sets of instructions for coordinating movements prior to their execution (Schmidt, 1975, Rosenbaum, 2005). Proper allocation of attentional resources is therefore thought to facilitate automaticity resulting in optimal motor program execution. However, a dynamical systems approach, which accounts for the functional role of variability, emphasizes movements that are self-organized and aided by perceptual guidance as opposed to movements generated by internal motor programs/mental representations. Original formulations of dynamical systems theory have largely ignored the influences of cognitive processes in the coordination and control of movements (Wulf, McNevin, Shea, and Wright, 1999). However, Wulf et al. (1999) clearly note a number of cognitive mediations (e.g., mental imagery, observational practice, goal setting, attentional focus, and variability of practice) that have been shown to influence behaviors that have yet to be accounted for by dynamical systems research. To this extent, certain factors such as attention have not been adequately addressed by a dynamical systems perspective (Wulf et al., 1999).

At the present moment, a unified theoretical framework does not exist which can account for the various findings surrounding the production of skilled performance. The apparent link between attention and movement variability remains incompatible under the dominant theories of motor control (Wulf et al., 1999). Future research must seek integration of the various levels of analyses in the explanation of the expert advantage. Specifically, further research is needed to clarify the exact nature of the relationship between attention and movement variability. Such research must address the mechanisms in which alterations in attention aids or disrupts functional variability. Towards this end, the influence of attention on perception-action coupling may be fruitful in delineating this relationship. Ultimately, investigating performance on a more holistic account across multiple dimensions of human performance will provide valuable insight into the mechanisms and conditions that promote superior performance.

REFERENCES

Anderson, J.R. (1982). Acquisition of a cognitive skill. *Psychological Review, 89*, 369-406.

Arutyunyan, G.H., Gurfinkel, V.S., and Mirskii, M.L. (1968). Investigation of aiming at a target. *Biophysics, 13*, 536-538.

Baumeister, R.F. (1984). Choking under pressure: Self-consciousness and paradoxical effects of incentives on skillful performance. *Journal of Personality and Social Psychology, 46*, 610-620.

Beilock, S.L., Bertenthal, B.I., McCoy, A.M., and Carr, T.H. (2004). Haste does not always make waste: Expertise, direction of attention, and speed versus accuracy in performing sensorimotor skills. *Psychonomic Bulletin and Review, 11*, 373-379.

Beilock, S.L. and Carr, T.H. (2001). On the fragility of skilled performance: What governs choking under pressure? *Journal of Experimental Psychology: General, 130*, 701-725.

Beilock, S.L., Carr, T.H., MacMahon, C., and Starkes, J.L. (2002). When paying attention becomes counterproductive: Impact of divided versus skill-focused attention on novice and experienced performance of sensorimotor skills. *Journal of Experimental Psychology: Applied, 8*, 6-16.

Beilock, S.L., and Gray R. (2007). Why do athletes choke under pressure? In G. Tenenbaum and R.C. Eklund (Eds.), *Handbook of sport psychology (3rd ed.)* (pp. 425 – 444). New Jersey: Wiley.

Bernstein, N.A. (1967). *The coordination and regulation of movements.* Oxford: Permagon Press.

Beuter, A., and Duda, J.L. (1985). Analysis of the arousal/motor performance relationship in children using movement kinematics. *Journal of Sport Psychology, 7,* 229-243.

Bootsma, R.J., and van Wieringen, P.W.C. (1990). Timing an attacking forehand drive in table tennis. *Journal of Experimental Psychology: Human Perception and Performance, 16,* 21-29.

Buekers, M.J., Montagne, G., and Laurent, M. (1999). Is the player in control, or is the control somewhere out of the player? *International Journal of Sport Psychology, 30,* 490-506.

Castaneda, B., and Gray, R. (2007). Effects of focus of attention on baseball batting performance in players of differing skill levels. *Journal of Sport and Exercise Psychology, 29,* 60-77.

Collins, D., Jones, B., Fairweather, M., Doolan, S., and Priestley, N. (2001). Examining anxiety associated changes in movement patterns. *International Journal of Sport Psychology, 31,* 223-242.

Davids, K., Bennett, S., and Newell, K. (2006). *Movement System Variability.* Champaign, Illinois: Human Kinetics Publishers.

Dupuy, M.A., Mottet, D., and Ripoll, H. (2000). The regulation of release parameters in underarm precision throwing. *Journal of Sports Sciences, 18,* 375-382.

Fischman, M.G. and Oxendine, J.B. (2001). Motor skill learning for effective coaching and performance. In J.M. Williams (Ed.), *Applied sport psychology: Personal growth to peak performance* (pp. 13-28). United States: Mayfield.

Fitts, P.M., and Posner, M.I. (1967). *Human performance.* Belmont, CA: Brooks/Cole.

Gibson, J.J. (1979). *The ecological approach to visual perception.* Boston: Houghton Mifflin.

Glazier, P.S., Wheat, J.S., Pease, D.L., and Bartlett, R.M. (2006). The interface of biomechanics and motor control: Dynamic systems theory and the functional role of movement variability. In K. Davids, S. Bennett and K. Newell (Eds.), *Movement system variability* (pp. 49-69). Champaign, Illinois: Human Kinetics Publishers.

Gray, R. (2004). Attending to the execution of a complex sensorimotor skill: Expertise differences, choking and slumps. *Journal of Experimental Psychology: Applied, 10,* 42-54.

Handford, C. (2006). Serving up variability and stability. In K. Davids, S. Bennett and K. Newell (Eds.), *Movement system variability.* (pp. 73-83). Champaign, Illinois: Human Kinetics Publishers.

Hodges, N.J., Starkes, J.L., and MacMahon, C. (2006). Expert performance in sport: A cognitive perspective. In K.A. Ericsson, N. Charness, R.R. Hoffman and P.J. Feltovich (Eds.), *The Cambridge handbook of expertise and expert performance.* (pp. 471- 488). New York: Cambridge UP.

Jackson, R.C., Ashford, K.J., and Norsworthy, G. (2006). Attentional focus, dispositional reinvestment, and skilled motor performance under pressure. *Journal of Sport and Exercise Psychology, 28,* 49-68.

Katsumata, H. (2007). A functional modulation for timing a movement: A coordinative structure in baseball hitting. *Human Movement Science, 26*, 27-47.

Kelso, J.A.S. (1995). *Dynamic patterns: The self-organization of brain and behavior.* Cambridge, MA: MIT Press.

Kimble, G.A., and Perlmuter, L.C. (1970). The problem of volition. *Psychological Review, 77*, 361-384.

Land, W.M., and Tenenbaum, G. *Facilitation of automaticity: Sport-relevant vs. non-relevant secondary tasks.* Paper submitted for publication.

Lewis, B., and Linder, D. (1997). Thinking about choking? Attentional processes and paradoxical performance. *Personality and Social Psychology Bulletin, 23*, 937-944.

Lidor, R., Reeves, J.L., and Tenenbaum, G. *Attention and Performance: When is Paying Attention Detrimental to Performance?* A manuscript submitted for publication.

Masters, R.S.W. (1992). Knowledge, knerves and know-how: The role of explicit versus implicit knowledge in the breakdown of a complex motor skill under pressure. *British Journal of Psychology, 83*, 343-358.

McNevin, N.H., Shea, C.H., and Wulf, G. (2003). Increasing the distance of an external focus of attention enhances learning. *Psychological Research, 67*, 22-29.

Müller, H. and Sternard, D. (2004). Decomposition of variability in the execution of goal oriented tasks: Three components of skill improvement. *Journal of Experimental Psychology: Human Perception and Performance, 30*, 212-233.

Newell, K.M., and Corcos, D.M. (1993a). *Variability and motor control.* Champaign, Illinois: Human Kinetics.

Newell, K.M., and Corcos, D.M. (1993b). Issues in variability and motor control. In K.M. Newell and D.M. Corcos (Eds.), *Variability and motor control* (pp. 1-12). Champaign, Illinois: Human Kinetics.

Pijpers, J.R., Oudejans, R.D.D., and Bakker, F.C. (2005). Anxiety-induced changes in movement behaviour during the execution of a complex whole-body task. *The Quarterly Journal of Experimental Psychology, 58A*, 421-445.

Pijpers, J.R., Oudejans, R.R.., Holsheimer, F., and Bakker, F.C. (2003). Anxiety-performance relationships in climbing: A process-oriented approach. *Psychology of Sport and Exercise, 4*, 283-304.

Poolton, J.M., Maxwell, J.P., Masters, R.S.W., and Raab, M. (2006). Benefits of an external focus of attention: Common coding or conscious processing? *Journal of Sports Sciences, 24*, 89-99.

Prinz, W. (1990). A common coding approach to perception and action. In O. Neumann and W. Prinz (Eds.), *Relationship between perception and action* (pp. 167 – 201). Berlin: Springer-Verlag.

Rosenbaum, D.A. (2005). The Cinderella of psychology. The neglect of motor control in the science of mental life and behavior. *American Psychologist, 60*, 308-317.

Savelsbergh, G.J.P., van der Kamp, J., and Rosengren, K.S. (2006). Functional variability in perceptual motor development. In K. Davids, S. Bennett and K. Newell (Eds.), *Movement system variability* (pp. 185-198). Champaign, Illinois: Human Kinetics Publishers.

Schmidt, R.A. (1975). A schema theory of discrete motor skill learning. *Psychological Review, 82*, 225-260.

Schmidt, R.A., and Lee, T.D. (1999). Attention and performance. In R. Schmidt and T. Lee (Eds.), *Motor control and learning: A behavioral emphasis* (pp. 61 – 91). Champaign, IL: Human Kinetics.

Schneider, W. and Shiffrin, R.M. (1977). Controlled and automated human information processing: I: Detection, search and attention. *Psychological Review, 44*, 627-644.

Shea, C.H., and Wulf, G. (1999). Enhancing motor learning through external-focus instructions and feedback. *Human Movement Science, 18*, 553-571.

Stretch, R.A., Bartlett, R., and Davids, K. (2000). A review of batting in men's cricket. *Journal of Sports Sciences, 18*, 931-949.

Vereijken, B., Van Emmerik, R.E.A., Whiting, H.T.A., and Newell, K.M. (1992). Free(Z)ing degrees of freedom in skill acquisition. *Journal of Motor Behavior, 24*, 133-142.

Vickers, J.N. (2007). *Perception, cognition, and decision training: The quiet eye in action.* Champaign, Illinois: Human Kinetics.

Vuillerme, N., and Nafati, G. (2007). How attentional focus on body sway affects postural control during quiet standing. *Psychological Research, 71*, 192-200.

Weinberg, R.S., and Hunt, V.V. (1976). The interrelationships between anxiety, motor performance and electromyography. *Journal of Motor Behavior, 8*, 219-224.

Wulf, G. (2007). *Attention and motor skill learning.* Champaign, Illinois: Human Kinetics.

Wulf, G., Höβ, M., and Prinz, W. (1998). Instructions for motor learning: Differential effects of internal versus external focus of attention. *Journal of Motor Behavior, 30*, 169-179.

Wulf, G., McNevin, N., Shea, C.H., and Wright, D.L. (1999). Learning phenomena: Future challenges for the dynamical systems approach to understanding the learning of complex motor skills. *International Journal of Sport Psychology, 30*, 531-557.

INDEX

J

K

L

Q

R

T